'Pray as you have seen me praying.'

THE PROPHET MUHAMMAD

Presented to ....

....

From ....

Date ....

Also by Ruqaiyyah Waris Maqsood

Teach Yourself Islam

Living with Teenagers

For Heaven Sake

The Challenge of Islam (for boys)

The Love of Islam (for girls)

The Muslim Marriage Guide

The Beautiful Commands of Allah

The Beautiful Promises of Allah

Basic Dictionary of Islam

THE MUSLIM
PRAYER
ENCYCLOPAEDIA

A COMPLETE GUIDE TO PRAYERS
AS TAUGHT BY THE PROPHET MUHAMMAD

Ruqaiyyah Waris Maqsood

Goodword
B·O·O·K·S

Dedicated, with great respect and admiration, to
Maulana Wahiduddin Khan

⚜

First published 1998
© Goodword Press 1998

Distributed by
Al-Risala Books
The Islamic Centre
1, Nizamuddin West Market, New Delhi 110 013
Tel. 4611128, 4611131
Fax: 91-11-4697333
E-mail: risala.islamic@axcess.net.in
Website: http://www.alrisala.org

Printed and bound in India

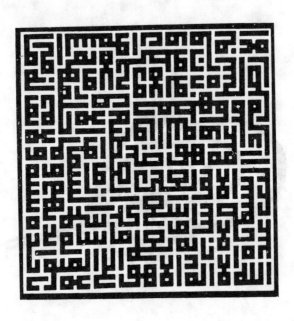

Contents

....................✿....................

The Call to Prayer

Ablution—The *Wudu'*

Preparation for Prayer

The Good Manners of Prayer
(Concerning the performance of public prayers)

Sunnah Prayers

Healing Prayer

Preface

The aim of this work has been to present before the reader a comprehensive overview of the teachings about prayer, and the particular practice and recommendations of the Blessed Messenger of Allah ( ), as recorded in the authentic   hadith collections of al-Bukhari, Muslim and Abu Dawud. It is beyond the scope of the average Muslim to buy and own the full text of these hadiths, and it is hoped, therefore, that this book will provide a useful tool for the Muslim student eager to understand Islamic prayer in its spirit and practice.

Every quotation from the *hadiths* is given with its full reference, so that the scholar can refer back to the source if desired.

It covers every topic, including the basic outline to guide the beginner's performance of the *rak'ah*, a selection of prayers and blessings for particular occasions, a guide to the correct behaviour in the mosque and the performance of congregational prayer, thoughts on the importance of the realisation of the Compassion and Mercy of Allah, the ministry of healing, and prayer for the deceased.

True to the spirit of the *hadith* collections themselves, it also includes interesting details of the Blessed Prophet's   private prayers and what it was like for a child to spend a night in his company (recorded by his nephew Anas); it highlights the intimate love of the Blessed Mother of the Faithful, Aishah, the Prophet's   beloved (may peace be upon both of them), and reveals her authority as a faithful witness to the Prophet's thoughts and practice. From the sublime to the mundane, it also picks out such fascinating matters as correct toilet procedure and the medical use of camel's urine!

May Allah be pleased with my humble efforts to work in His service:

'To Him we belong, and to Him is our return.'

Ruqaiyyah Waris Maqsood
Hull (U.K.)

The Way of Devotion

INTRODUCING MUSLIM PRAYER

When Muhammad, the Blessed Prophet of Islam ﷺ taught his people to bow down in prayer five times during the day to the One True God, Allah the Almighty, it set a great standard and pattern for millions of human beings. They were to follow his practice not only in his own time but in all the times to come.

Muslim prayer is of two sorts—*salah* and *du'a*. The *salah* prayers are the five compulsory prayers offered at specific times during the day by every devout Muslim, male or female; they follow set patterns and have various words and phrases which are also standard.

Du'a prayers are private and personal supplications, the normal practice of any believer in God who feels the need to address God in a personal way about a personal matter at any time. True believers, to whom God is both Master and Closest Friend, tend to think of Allah whenever they are overflowing with joy and happiness, or alternatively at the times when they are unhappy, oppressed, worried, under stress, and so on.

Awareness of the Presence of God, an experience known as *taqwa*, is the hallmark of the true Muslim and also the creative religious urge. Once the presence of God has dawned upon a person's life—the moment known as *ihsan* or 'realisation'—then every aspect of that life is touched and changed. The human mind opens like a flower to the knowledge that a Great and Benevolent

Power of infinite love and justice is aware of us, knows all our actions seen and unseen, our thoughts, our motivation.

This awareness is not something that can come and go, but for the true believer it is constant, no matter what the Muslim happens to be doing. Many attempts have been made to define what is meant by prayer—but basically it is any thought, word or action done with God in mind, and the true Muslim—who is aware of God constantly—really spends every waking moment of his or her life in a state of prayer.

As far as the Blessed Prophet Muhammad ﷺ was concerned, his life could be described as a 'living prayer'. Virtually the whole of his time and teaching was involved in bringing people into the awareness of God by his example and specific suggestions. Ever since, devout Muslims have centred their *niyyah* or 'intention' on the desire to live in a way pleasing to Allah, by learning as much as they can from the Holy Qur'an and the Blessed Prophet's ﷺ *sunnah* (way of life, or example).

There are five compulsory duties in Islam—declaration of belief (the *Shahadah*), ritual prayer five times per day (*salah*), fasting during the month of Ramadan (*sawm*), making a portion of one's income and belongings over to the service of others (*zakah*), and making the pilgrimage to the holy city of Makkah in Arabia once in a lifetime, if at all possible (*Hajj*). These five duties are often known as the *Pillars of Islam,* for they are the outward practices upon which the *Ummah* or Family of the Faith depends.

Of these, the ritual prayer is the one that affects the Muslim every day, from a moment before dawn until the Muslim lays down to sleep. Therefore Muslims concentrate hard not only on the right and most fitting way to live, but also on the correct performance of this ritual prayer, the basic demonstration of which is the uniform pattern of movements followed by every

Muslim when they stand, bow and prostrate themselves.

The ability to follow the movements by copying the rows of men, or by being taught by one's family, is one of the earliest experiences of Islam taken up by new converts or infant Muslims.

Once the movements, or routine, is mastered, the second step is to find out what it is that has to be said—what are the words that go with the prayer? Can you just pray as you like, or are there set words to go with the set movements? At this stage, it is not so easy to be precise. The newcomer observes that certain words or phrases are pronounced out loud, most by the Imam (or leader), and some by the entire congregation. From the periods of silence during the prayers, it is obvious that other words are being said, although they cannot be heard by anyone there except Allah.

At some prayers the Blessed Prophet used to recite the Qur'an out loud, but at other times he did it silently. One *hadith* records Abu Ma'mar asking Khabbab:

'Did the Messenger of Allah recite (the Qur'an) during the noon and afternoon prayers? He replied: 'Yes.' We then asked: 'How do you know?' He said: 'By the shaking of his beard, may peace be upon him!' (Abu Dawud 800, Bukhari 12.10.713 etc.)

In other words, the Prophet ﷺ at these times did not recite the Qur'an aloud for the congregation—but they could tell he was praying or reciting because they could see his beard moving as he whispered the words to himself.

It was the greatest wish of the Blessed Prophet ﷺ to bring people to awareness of Allah, and love of Him Who is perfect Compassion. He was surrounded by people who not only loved God, but who wished to copy his own slightest detail of *sunnah* or practice. Sometimes this exasperated the Prophet. He was well aware that because of their very eagerness, there was also amongst his followers a tendency towards over-zealous pietism, a tendency to pronounce that 'this is the way a thing *must* be done', which might suit that disciple concerned, but might actually become rather oppressive and divisive for other people.

For example, 'A'ishah, the beloved wife of the Blessed Prophet ﷺ recorded that: 'Allah's Messenger ﷺ used to pray in his room at night. As the wall of his room was low the people could see him, and some of them stood up to follow him in the prayer. In the morning they told other people. The following night the Prophet ﷺ stood for prayer and (more) people copied him. This went on for two or three nights. Thereupon Allah's Messenger ﷺ did not stand for the prayer the following night, and did not come out. In the morning the people asked him about it. He replied that he was afraid that the night prayer might become compulsory.' (Bukhari 11.79.696)

Muslims, although they should be one unified *Ummah*, are not all alike. There are all sorts and types of people within the Faith, and prayer means different things to different people. Some Muslims concentrate on one aspect of it while others have an entirely different 'worship'.

One sort of Muslim will make it their enormous concern to perform the prayers punctiliously and correctly with strict emphasis on exact details; another will study and reflect in order to try to capture the correct spirit of devotion, and perhaps not be so insistent on details. One person might feel that true devotion was shown by the number of *rak'ahs* (units of prayer movements) prayed, whereas another might argue that what mattered most was not how many *rak'ahs* were performed in devotion, but in the content and *understanding* of the words recited (whether aloud or in the head).

Abu Hurayrah recorded: 'Faith has over seventy branches, the most excellent of which is the declaration that there is no God but Allah, and the humblest of which is the removal of a bone from the road. And modesty is a branch of faith.' (Abu Dawud 4659, Muslim 55-56).

No Muslim ever has the right to assume that his or her form of worship, or discipline of worship, or words spoken in worship, is better than that of anyone else, or more pleasing to Allah. This is something that only Allah Alone can possibly know.

Abu Hurayrah recorded the Blessed Prophet ﷺ as saying: 'Many a person with dishevelled hair and covered in dust is turned away from the doors, (whereas he is held in such high esteem by Allah) that if he were to beseech (anything) in the name of Allah, Allah would fulfil it.' (Muslim 6351)

There is a very human temptation for people who take the point of view that certain things are 'correct' while other things are 'incorrect' or 'less correct' to fall into that old temptation of believing themselves to be superior. It is only a short step from that to believing that all those that differ are actually wrong. Allah the Almighty, the Compassionate, on the other hand: 'is pleased with a shepherd of goats who calls to prayer on the mountain peak, and bows down. Allah the Exalted says: Look at this servant of Mine; he calls to prayer and offers it, and he respects Me. Therefore I forgive him, and admit him to Paradise.' (Abu Dawud 1199, recorded by Uqbah ibn Amir)

Abu Hurayrah recorded: 'The Prophet ﷺ said: Religion is very easy, and whoever overburdens himself in it will not be able to continue in that way. So you should try not to be extremists, but try to be near to perfection and accept these good tidings that you may be rewarded; gain strength by worshipping in the mornings, afternoons, and during the last hours of the nights.' (Bukhari 1.30.38)

The tendency of extremism cropped up in all sorts of spheres of life; the Blessed Prophet ﷺ referred to it generally as the urge to make *haram* (forbidden) things which were perfectly *halal* (allowed). It also occured in the desire to bring in *bid'a* or 'innovations' — so-called compulsory practices which had not in fact been made compulsory at all, either by Allah or by His prophet.

Urwah, quoting 'A'ishah, recorded: 'What is the matter with people who make conditions which are not in Allah's Book? If anyone makes a condition which is not in Allah's Book, he has no right to it, even he stipulates it hundreds of times. Allah's condition is more valid and binding.' (Abu Dawud 3918)

The duty of the truly devout Muslim was and is to adhere as closely as possible to the *actual* commands of Allah, as laid down in the Qur'an and the reliable *hadith*, and to absorb as fully as possible the spirit of love, moderation and compassion that went with them.

The whole object of Islam is love of Allah, and not the servitude of an unhappy and flustered slave. It is a joyful release of the soul, an awareness of blessedness and grace; it should not be the terrible guilt-ridden burden of trying to get this detail or that detail in one particular way that will not cause criticism from one's peers in congregation.

The Blessed Muhammad was well aware of misguided pietism, which is so difficult to reason with. The people concerned are totally convinced that what they are doing really is the will of Allah, and if anyone does anything to deviate from this, that person is in the wrong.

However, the real worship of Allah is not a matter of reciting formulas or keeping rigid time-tables (although these have their place), but in directing the heart towards God and having one's *niyyah* (or intention) towards Him.

'Umar ibn al-Khattab recorded: 'The reward of deeds depends upon the intention, and every person will get the reward according what he has *intended*.' (Bukhari 2.42.51)

To have one's heart truly directed towards Him does not leave any room for directing it towards agonising over whether or not you are making mistakes, or whether or not you should try to overrule anyone else.

There is certainly a right way of performing *salah* which has to be learned, whether for prayer said in congregation or in the privacy of one's own home; but many people coming into Islam may have had their faith and goodwill daunted by those who are already Muslim invalidating their genuine worship by telling them that they have done this or that wrong.

The innocent beginner might inquire what it is one has to do, and will be told when and how to stand, raise the hands, bow, kneel and prostrate, and so forth. They will be told that the series of movements is known as a *rak'ah*, and that there are a certain number of *rak'ahs* which should be done at the different prayer times.

They will be told the times of day between which the *salah* should be said: after the first light of dawn but before sunrise (*fajr*); just after the high point of noon (*zuhr*); in mid–afternoon when the shadows have lengthened (*'asr*); just after sunset (*maghrib*) and at some time during the night (*isha'*). They will be told that the number of *rak'ahs* laid down as compulsory are two for *fajr*, four for *zuhr* and *'asr*, three for *maghrib* and four for *isha'*. The noon and afternoon prayers are known as *sirri* prayers, and the others are *jahri* prayers.

They will be told that a person should be clean before prayer, and will learn the routine of *wudu'* or ritual washing, in readiness for prayer. They will possibly provide themselves with a prayer mat, and even perhaps a compass, a hat, a little chain of 99 beads for reciting (known as a *tasbih* or *sibha*). They will know that they should find the direction of Makkah if at all possible, and face in that direction (known as *qiblah*).

They might then be furnished with a print-off of the words of the *salah* in Arabic (hopefully with a translation as well).

Armed with all this, they might then begin to practise prayer, hesitantly at first, but with growing confidence as it is gone through five times per day, until it becomes almost second nature.

And then, they might suddenly find that even with all this learned and loved in their hearts, that their prayers will still considered to be invalid or at fault by certain zealots; they might discover that all this knowledge learned so far is just beginners stuff—they have now to become aquainted with concepts of *fard* and *nafl*, *witr*, *sunnah*, *tashahhud*, *tahajjud* and so forth. They will discover straight away that many Muslims at prayer do not just do the compulsory number of *rak'ahs*, but add others before the congretation starts to do them together, and will continue to do many others afterwards. They may well wonder how many they are *really* expected to do, in order not to fall short—and they might wonder whether there was any particular merit for one Muslim to pray a whole lot more than another Muslim, and if so, how many?

Swamped by the plethora of all these details and recommendations, there is a danger that believers might actually come to think of prayer as some kind of test of correctness, and that Allah was not really the 'Most Compassionate, the Most Merciful and Gracious One' but a stern Judge meticulously watching to catch people out and invalidate any prayer that was not done or said correctly.

However, Islamic prayer does not just consist of reciting and bowing and kneeling and prostrating together (although this performance is important, and the Blessed Prophet ﷺ in his *sunnah* recommended certain things and disapproved of others). What is 'unseen' by the casual observer is that along with the physical routines and set words there is also an attitude of mind and all sorts of prayerful thoughts that accompany these movements, and that these are, in fact, the real Islam as opposed to the 'formal worship' of Islam.

The Blessed Prophet ﷺ did far more praying than just the 'set routine' of the five compulsory *salah*s, as we shall see. He never 'lost contact' with Allah, or ceased to lay before him the problems and distresses of the believers.

Hudhayfah recorded: 'When anything distressed the Prophet ﷺ, he prayed.' (Abu Dawud 1314).

So let us study not just the manner and performances of today's congregations, wherever we may happen to be, or however we come into the faith. Let us look closely at the best example of all, that of the Prophet ﷺ himself as he taught his followers in Madinah.

GOING THROUGH THE RAK'AH

It is taken as accepted practice that in each *rak'ah*, the person praying will recite *al-Fatihah*, (the opening *surah* of the Qur'an) and other *surah*s or passages, of shorter or greater length. It is regarded as an act of merit for those who do not actually speak Arabic as their natural language, to be able to recite these in Arabic, the actual language of the Qur'an, for any translation of the holy words does not carry the same validity as the original.

However, it is not particularly an act of merit to be able to chant away foreign words without understanding at all. The *meaning* of the *surah* should be learned alongside the Arabic, if the

person praying is not an Arabic speaker.

QIBLAH

Before the prayer starts, he or she should try to find out the direction of Makkah, the direction known as *qiblah*. Before revelation was given, believers used to pray facing Jerusalem, but Allah revealed:

> 'Indeed, We see the turning of the face to heaven, wherefore We shall assuredly cause you to turn towards *qiblah*, which shall please you. So turn your faces towards the holy mosque' (Sūrah 2:144)

The effect was instantaneous:

> Anas recorded: A person from the Banu Salamah (found the people) in *ruku'* praying the dawn prayer, and they had said one *rak'ah*. He said in a loud voice: Listen! The *qiblah* has been changed! And they turned towards (the new) *qiblah* in that very state.' (Muslim 1075; see also Bukhari 2.31.39 for other details.)

NIYYAH

Next, the believer should make *niyyah* (declare intention) in his or her mind, for the number of compulsory and optional *rak'ahs* they intend to make. This intention is not declared aloud, but should be a conscious decision, and then the believer is ready to begin.

TAKBIR

There are eight separate acts of devotion. First comes *takbir tahrima*, in which the world and all its distractions, both delights and miseries, are shut out. Muslims stand to attention, with their hands raised to the level of their shoulders, and acknowledge the majesty of God, and say:

> '*Allahu akbar!*'—'Allah is the Most High!'

Secondly, they place their hands by their sides, or more preferably the right hand over the left just above the navel as the Blessed Prophet ﷺ used to do, and say the *ta'auwudh*:

Subḥānak Allahumma wa biḥamdika wa tabārak asmuka wa ta'āla jadduka wa lā ilāha ghayruka. 'A'uzu billahi minash shaitan ir-rajim.'

'Glory and praise to You, O Allah; blessed is Your Name and exalted is Your Majesty. There is no God other than You. I come, seeking shelter from Satan, the rejected one.'

Women at prayer usually cross their hands at the level of their chest.

These prayers before starting the *rak'ah* are also known as the *Du'a al-Istiftah* (*Du'a* of Starting) and are only said at the commencement of the first *rak'ah*. Another frequently used *du'a* is the prayer of the Blessed Muhammad:

'Allah humma baeed baynee wa bayna khatayaya kama ba'adta baynal mashriqi wal maghribi, Allah humma naqinee min khatayaya kama yunaqqath-thawbul abyadu minad-danasi, Allah hum maghsilnee min khatayaya bil maee wa'ath-thalji wa'al bardi.'

'O Allah, set me as far away from my sins as the East is from the West; O Allah, cleanse me of my sins as a white garment is rid of its dirt by washing; O Allah, wash my sins away with water, snow and hail.'

TASMIYA

Then follows the tasmiya (recommendation):
Bismillah ar-Rahman ir-Rahim—In the name of the Compassionate, the Merciful.

AL-FĀTIḤAH

Now comes the first part of the recitation of the Qur'an. The prayer always begins with *al-Fatihah*, the first *sūrah* (or chapter of the Qur'an), which the Imam or leader always says aloud:

'Al-hamdu lillahi rabbil aalamin, ar-rahman ir-rahim, Maliki yawmiddin. Iyyaka na'budu wa iyyakana stai'in. Ihdinas siratal mustaqeem, siratal ladeena ana'amta alayhim, ghayril maghdoobi alayhim wa lad daalleen.'

'Praise be to Allah, Lord of the Worlds, Most Gracious Most Merciful, Master of the Day of Judgement. You alone do we worship, and from You alone do we seek help. Show us the straight path, the way of those on whom You have bestowed Your grace, those whose portion is not wrath and who have not gone astray.' (*Sūrah* 1)

This recitation of *al-Fatihah* is so important that the Blessed Prophet 🕮 stated that no prayer was valid without it!

At the end of this *sūrah*, it was the Blessed Messenger's practice to say '*Amin*' aloud, and encourage the congregation to do so too. This practice is known as *tamin*, and means 'O Allah, grant our prayer.' Since *al-Fatihah* is a fervent supplication for our Lord to show us what to do next, and lead us on the path of righteousness, the believer makes humble appeal to be granted this by Allah's grace and mercy; it is not regarded as a matter of right.

Abu Hurayrah recorded: 'When the Imam recites the verse 'not of those with whom You are angry, nor of those who go astray' all of you should say 'Amin;' for whoever says 'Amin' and his voice blends with that of the angels, he (or she) will be forgiven past sins.' (Bukhari 13.32.749, Abu Dawud 935, Muslim 816, Ahmad, Nisai). Bilal added that the congregation should not say Amin before the Imam.

RECITATION

Al-Fatihah is then followed by another passage from the Qur'an of the Imam or leader's choice. This choice of *sūrah*, is the

section of the prayer which differs every time, the moments where the audience has the opportunity to learn something about the will of Allah by meditating upon His holy words.

Sometimes it will be a long recitation, or at other times only a few verses, at the leader's discretion. It is the only part of the prayer that varies on each and every occasion, and it is obvious that this recitation is of little worth if the congregation does not understand the meaning of the passage, even if they find chanted Arabic beautiful to listen to. Many Muslims who cannot speak Arabic as their natural language make every attempt to learn it, or at least to learn some *surahs* in Arabic with their meanings. Any person who has memorised the whole of the Qur'an is known as a *hafiz* (plural huffaz). Some people know the words of some of the *surahs* by heart—but they should not distract the prayer-leader by trying to accompany his recitation, by whispering them out loud. It is better manners to keep quiet, and allow the leader to lead.

RUKU'

After the recitation comes *ruku'*, the bowing. The believer says *takbir* and raises the hands to the level of the shoulders and then bends over, hands placed on knees with fingers spread out, a straight back, and the arms not touching the body, and says three times:

'Subhana Rabbi al-Azeem wa bihamdihi'

'Glory be to my Great Lord, and praise be to Him.'

Abu Qatadah recorded: 'The worst thief is one who steals in his prayer.' The Companions asked: 'How can someone steal from his (or her) prayer?' The Prophet ﷺ answered: 'He does not make his back straight in *ruku'* and Sajdah.' (Ahmad, Tabrani, Ibn Khuzaimah, Hakim)

Women do not bend down as far as the men, but they incline their bodies and bow their heads. It is usually a moment of deep silence in the mosque.

'A'ishah recorded that the Blessed Prophet ﷺ frequently said: *'Subhanak Allah humma rabbana wabihamdika; Allah hum maghfirlee'* — 'Glory be to You, O our Lord, and all praise be to You. O Allah, forgive me.' (Bukhari, Muslim)

QIYAM

Next comes *qiyam* or *qawmah*, when the back is straightened again, and the hands raised again, and the presence of Allah is acknowledged with the words known as the tasmee and tahmid:

The tasmee — (said by the Imam): *'Sami Allahu liman hamidah.'*

The Tahmid—(response from the people)— *'Rabbana wa lak al-hamd!'*

'Allah always hears those who praise Him.'

'O God, all praise be to You, O God greater than all else.'

Some people, incidentally, disapprove of this raising of the hands, but there are *hadith* that the Blessed Prophet ﷺ did this at the beginning of prayer, before and after *ruku'*, and when standing up for the third *rak'ah*. However, although it is *sunnah*, it is not compulsory, and no Muslim has the right to think their brother or sister wrong if they either do or do not do it.

Abu Hurayrah recorded that when these words are said, 'if what anyone says blends in with what the angels say, all past sins will be forgiven.' (Muslim 809)

SUJUD

Now comes the humblest position, the *sujud* or *sajdah*. This is when Muslims prostrate themselves upon the ground, demonstrating that they love God more than they love themselves.

Abu Hurayrah recorded: 'The nearest a servant comes to his Lord is when he (or she) is prostrating, so make supplication (in this way).' (Muslim 979)

They kneel, touching the ground with their forehead, nose, palms of both hands, knees and toes, (what the Blessed Prophet ﷺ called the 'seven bones'—Abu Dawud 888, Muslim 991, etc.), and repeat three times:

'*Subhana Rabbi a'ala wa bihamdihi.*'

'Glory be to my Lord, the Most High.'

As in *ruku'*, the bowing, it is a moment of deep silence.

Abu Hurayrah recorded one prayer of the Blessed Prophet ﷺ: 'O Lord, forgive me all my sins small and great, former and latter, open and secret.' (Muslim 980)

Sa'd al-Khudri commented that 'the mark of earth was seen on the forehead and nose of the Messenger ﷺ due to the prayer.' (Abu Dawud 893)

JALSA

After this comes *jalsa* when the worshipper raises the head saying *takbir*, and kneels—bending the left foot and sitting on it while keeping the right foot upright with toes pointing towards the *qiblah*, palms resting on the knees—a moment's rest before the next prostration. A *du'a* for this position is:

'*Allah humma ghfirlee warhamnee wahdinee wa 'afinee warzuqnee wajburnee warfa'nee.*'

'O Allah, forgive me and have mercy upon me, and keep me on the right path, and keep me in good health, and provide me with *halal* sources of living, and make up for my shortcomings, and make my rank high.'

Then comes *takbir*, and the sujud is repeated again, with another deep silence.

TASLIM

After this, Muslims either repeat the *rakah* or finish it, if it is the final one of the 'set'. At the end of the whole sequence, believers pray for the Prophet ﷺ, for the faithful and the congregation, and make a plea for forgiveness of sins. The last action is to turn their heads to the right and the left shoulders, to acknowledge the other worshippers and the guardian angels, with the words:

'*As-Salam alaykum wa rahmatullah*'—'Peace be with you, and the mercy of Allah'.

This final prayer is called the *salaam* or *taslim*.

So here we have the basic outline of the *rak'ah*, the routine and performance of prayer which has to be learned by every Muslim.

Before leaving the prayer, two final du'as remain, known as *tashahhud* and *darud*. For *tashahhud*, the believer sits up and rests his or her hands on the knees. Then the fist of the right hand is closed except for the index finger, which points to *qiblah*. The *tashahhud* prayer is:

'*At-tahiyyatu lillahi, wassalawatu wa tayyibatu assalamu alayka ayyu-hannabiyyu wa-rahmat ullahi wa barakatuhu assalamu alayna wa 'ala 'ibadillah is-saliheen. Ash-hadu an la ilaha illallahu wa ashadu anna Muhammadan 'abduhu wa rasuluhu.*'

'All the worship of my tongue, my body and my material possessions belong to Allah. O Prophet, may peace be upon you and the mercy and blessings of Allah. May peace be upon us, and upon all His pious servants. I bear witness that there is no God but Allah, and I bear witness that Muhammad is His Prophet and servant.'

While saying this last phrase, the believer raises the index finger slightly, and places it back when he (or she) has finished.

The final prayer is *darud* or salat an-Nabi:

'Allahumma salli 'ala Muhammadin wa 'ala ali Muhammadin kama sallayta ala Ibrahima wa 'ala ali Ibrahima innaka hamidun majid. Allahumma barik 'ala Muhammadin wa 'ala ali Muhammadin kama barakta 'ala Ibrahima wa 'ala ali Ibrahima innaka hamidun majid.'

'O Allah, send Your blessings on Muhammad and on his descendants as You sent Your blessings on Ibrahim and his descendants. Truly, You are the Praiseworthy and Exalted One. O Allah, bless Muhammad and his descendants as You blessed Ibrahim and his descendants. Indeed You are Praiseworthy and Exalted One.'

THE PERIODS OF SILENCE

The Blessed Prophet ﷺ stood silently at two points during his prayer—once when he had pronounced the *takbir*, and again after he had finished reciting *al-Fatihah*. The Blessed Prophet's ﷺ friend Abu Hurayrah reported: 'I asked him, for whom I would give my father and my mother as ransom: 'What do you say during your period of silence between the *takbir* and the recitation?' The Blessed Prophet ﷺ replied:

'O Allah remove my sins as far from me as You have removed the east from the west. O Allah purify me from sins as a white garment is purified from filth. O Allah, wash away my sins with snow, water and hail.' (Abu Dawud 780, M. 1245)

The fact that the Blessed Prophet ﷺ said these silent prayers was verified by several recorders of *hadith*. For example, Samurah ibn Jundub and Imran ibn Husayn had a discussion about it, and Imran rejected Samurah's opinion that the Blessed Prophet had kept silence the second time, after reciting *al-Fatihah*.

Samurah claimed: 'I remember from the Messenger of Allah ﷺ two periods of silence... one when he began his prayer and one when he finished the recitation... of 'Not of those with whom Thou art angry, nor of those who go astray.' (Abu Dawud 779)

They wrote for confirmation to Ubayy ibn Ka'b, who replied that it was Samurah who had remembered correctly.

The schools of Malik and Abu Hanifah still keep only one period of silence, after the *takbir* ('Awn al-Mabad, 1,283). Other scholars recommend three periods, the two outlined here and another after the recitation of the *sūrah*.

THE SILENT PRAYERS OF THE BLESSED PROPHET

Thanks to the Blessed Prophet's nephew and son-in-law, 'Ali ibn Abi Talib, we have one record of some of the inner thoughts of the Blessed Messenger from his most intimate prayer moments. One of the long *hadiths* recorded by 'Ali took the believer through all the thoughts flowing in that great but humble mind from the moment he stood up to pray.

'Ali recorded that after he had stood up and uttered the *takbir* ('Allah is Most Great') the Blessed Prophet ﷺ stood in silence for a few moments. His private prayer consisted of these words:

'I have turned my face, breaking with all others, towards Him Who created the heavens and the earth, and I am not a believer in any other god. My prayer and my devotion, my life and my death belong to Allah, the Lord of the Universe, Who has no partner. This is what I have been commanded, and I am the first of submitted people. O Allah, You are the King. There is no god but only You. You are my Lord, and I am Your servant. I have wronged myself, but I acknowledge my sin, so forgive me all my sins, You Who alone can forgive sins, and guide me to the best qualities, You Who alone can guide to the best of them, and turn me from evil ones, You Who alone can turn from evil qualities. I come to serve and please You. All good is in Your hands, and nothing evil has anything to do with You. With You I seek refuge, and I turn to you, Who are the blessed and exalted One. I ask Your forgiveness and turn to You in contrite heart.'

When he bowed, he said:

'O Allah, to You I bow down, in You I trust, and to You I submit myself. My hearing, my sight, my brain, my bones, and my sinews humble themselves before You.'

When he raised his head, he said:

'Allah listens to the one who praises Him. O our Lord, all praise be to You in the whole of the heavens and the earth, and what is between them, and the whatever You created afterwards.'

When he prostrated himself, he said:

'O Allah, to You I bow myself down, in You I trust, and to You I submit myself. My face prostrates before Him Who created it, fashioned it, and fashioned it in the best shape, and brought forth its hearing and seeing. Blessed is Allah, the best of Creators.'

When he saluted at the end of the prayer, he said:

'O Allah, forgive me my former and my latter sins, my open and my secret sins, my sins in exceeding the limits, and what You know better than I. You are He Who puts forward and puts back. There is no God but You.'

(All from Abu Dawud 759, Muslim 1695)

Ibn Abbas recorded that the Blessed Prophet ﷺ used to say 'O Allah, forgive me, show mercy to me, guide me, heal me and provide for me' in between the two prostrations. (Abu Dawud 849). Ibn Abbas, incidentally, was a child at the time of the Blessed Prophet ﷺ and used to pray in the last row. (Abu Dawud 807 n.367)

Perhaps the most famous private prayer of the Blessed Prophet ﷺ was his Prayer for Light:

'O Allah, place light in my heart, light in my sight, light in

my hearing, light on my right hand, light on my left hand, light
above me, light below me, light before me, and light behind me,
increase the light.' (Muslim 1671, etc.)

SHOULD ONE OFFER *DU'A* DURING THE *SALAH?*

Although some scholars maintain that one of the disciplines
of *salah* is to keep the mind clear of personal worries and needs for
those few moments dedicated to praise and communion with
God Alone, nevertheless, it is in these most intimate moments,
when one is so crucially aware of one's own shortcomings in the
light of God's presence, the urge to seek God's forgiveness is very
natural and strong. Also, at these times when God's presence
seems particularly close, it is natural to present before Him any
deep agony of mind, for example, the strong desire for the well-
being of a loved one who is suffering in some way.

Abu Hurayrah reported the Messenger of Allah ﷺ as saying:
'The nearest a servant comes to his Lord is when he is
prostrating himself, so make supplication often.' (Abu Dawud
874)

He also recorded that the Blessed Prophet ﷺ used to say
while prostrating:

'O Allah, forgive me all my sins, small and great, first and last.'
And Ibn al-Sarh added: 'Open and secret.' (Abu Dawud 877)

It was commended that as part of the supplication, a Muslim
should pray for forgiveness of his or her sins, and never give up
or regard themselves as beyond hope.

Abu Bakr reported the Messenger of Allah ﷺ as saying: 'The
one who asks for pardon is not a confirmed sinner, even if he
returns to his sin seventy times a day!' (Abu Dawud 1509)

Al-Agharr al-Muzani recorded the Prophet's ﷺ words: 'My
heart is invaded by unmindfulness, and I ask Allah's pardon a

hundred times in the day.' (Abu Dawud 1510)

Nobody need fear that Allah will not deign to hear them.

Abu Hurayrah recorded the Messenger ﷺ stating that Allah said: 'I live in the thought of My servant as he thinks about Me, and I am with him when he remembers Me. And if he remembers Me, and I am in his heart, then I shall also remember him in My heart, and if he remembers Me in congregation, then I remember him in congregation, more than he does; and if he draws near Me by the span of a palm, I draw near him by the reach of an arm... and if he comes towards Me walking, I go towards him running.' (Muslim 6498 etc.)

Abu Musa recorded: 'Truly, you are not praying to One Who is deaf or far away!' (Muslim 6258 etc.)

Private prayers are recommended too, especially those that are unselfish requests for others:

Abu al-Darda said: 'I heard the Messenger of Allah ﷺ say: 'When a Muslim supplicates for his absent brother, the angels say 'Amin', and may you receive likewise.' (Abu Dawud 1529)

The blessed Muhammad ﷺ particularly stressed that Allah the merciful hears the pleas of three especial types of people—the father, the refugee, and one who has been wronged (Abu Dawud 1531—on the authority of Abu Hurayrah)

Sometimes a Muslim knows the words and routine of the *salah* so intimately that while he or she is saying them, the mind has wandered away to whatever matter it is that he or she wishes to make supplication for before Allah. Such a Muslim need not fear that they have 'failed' or invalidated their prayer, or that there is a need to repeat it again with undistracted mind. Allah understands everything.

Malik recorded: 'There is no harm in uttering supplication in prayer, in its beginning, in its middle, and in the end; in obligatory prayer or any other.' (Abu Dawud 768)

'A'ishah recorded that the Messenger of Allah used to make supplication during his prayers, saying:

'O Allah, I seek refuge in You from the punishment of the grave; I seek refuge in You from the trial of the Antichrist; I seek refuge in You from the trial of life and the trial of death; O Allah, I seek refuge in You from sin and debt.' Someone said to him: 'How often you seek refuge from debt!' He replied: 'When a person is in debt, he talks and tells lies, makes promises and breaks them.' (Abu Dawud 879)

Sometimes the Blessed Prophet's ﷺ supplications were intensely personal. Abu Hurayrah, for example, recorded that for one month the Messenger ﷺ prayed: 'O Allah, rescue al-Walid ibn Walid; rescue Salamah ibn Hisham, rescue the weak believers!' One morning Abu Hurayrah noticed that the Prophet ﷺ did not pray for them and commented upon it. He said: 'Did you not see that they have come back?' (Abu Dawud 1437)

This shows that it is not considered wrong to make direct personal petitions to Allah for individuals who are in need, even if we do not know the will of Allah for them, and even if we do not doubt that Allah knows best.

These prayers are known as *qunut* prayers, the word meaning to be obedient or humble, but in the context of prayer implying a special supplication made at such times as when Muslims are overtaken with calamity.

DON'T JUST PRAY FOR YOURSELF

When one is concentrating on private prayers, obviously the subject matter of these prayers will be what is uppermost in the believer's mind. It might be something they are worried about, or something they need help in, or a prayer for healing or release from suffering. Inevitably, many private and personal prayers are concerned with one's self, and there is no harm in this, so long as the person praying is not doing it in the attitude of selfishness but of genuine desire to be near to Allah and find out His will and supplicate His help.

However, if someone is leading public prayer, it is not correct at all to concentrate on a private matter. The needs and concerns of the whole congregation have to be taken into account.

Thawr ibn Yazid recorded: 'It is not permissible for a person who believes in Allah and the Last Day that they should lead people in prayer but with their permission; and that they should not supplicate to Allah exclusively for themselves, leaving out all others. If they do so, they violate the trust.' (Abu Dawud 91)

In other words, if they direct the public prayer towards nothing but their own concerns, no matter how worthy those might be, they are not acting correctly in their capacity as an Imam. Imams have a responsibility towards others, and should never make their position an opportunity for self-gratification.

On the other hand, there is obviously nothing wrong in everyone in the congregation praying for the particular needs of the person leading them if there is a specific need; the point is that the leader should not be taking inconsiderate advantage of the authority placed upon him as leader by ignoring the needs of others.

Thawban recorded: 'The Messenger of Allah ﷺ said: 'One is not allowed to do three things—supplicate to Allah specifically for oneself and ignore others while leading people in prayer; if one does so, one is deceiving them; looking inside a house without permission—if one does so, it is the same as going into the house; and saying prayer while one is feeling the call of nature, until one has relieved oneself.' (Abu Dawud 90)

TASHAHHUD AND DARUD—INVOKING BLESSINGS ON THE PROPHET

'Allah and His angels send blessings on the Prophet. O you that believe! You send blessings on him (also), and salute him with all respect.' (*Sūrah* 33:56)

Our blessing on the Holy Prophet is a token of our love and devotion, and human gratitude to him for guiding us to the path of Allah.

Abdallah ibn Mas'ud said: 'While observing prayer behind the Messenger of Allah ﷺ we used to recite: 'Peace be upon Allah, peace be upon (so-and-so).' One day, the Messenger ﷺ said to us: 'Truly, Allah Himself is Peace. When any one of you sits during the prayer, he should say: 'All service rendered by words, by acts of worship, and by all good things are due to Allah. Peace be upon you, O Prophet, and Allah's mercy and blessings. Peace be upon us and upon Allah's righteous servant in heaven and earth; (and say further): 'I bear witness that there is no God but Allah, and Muhammad is His servant and messenger.' Then he may choose any supplication that pleases him and offer it.' (Muslim 793)

He added: 'The Messenger of Allah ﷺ taught me *tashahhud* taking my hand within his palms, in the same way as he taught me a *sūrah* of the Qur'an.' (Muslim 797, 780 etc.)

At the end of the *rak'ahs*, the Blessed Prophet ﷺ used to pray: 'O Allah, join our hearts (in comradeship) and mend our social relationship, and guide us to the path of peace; bring us from darkness into light, and save us from obscenities, outward or inward; and bless our ears, our eyes, our hearts, our wives, our children; and relent towards us—for You are the Relenting, the

Merciful. And make us grateful for Your blessing, and make us more full of praise of it while accepting it, and give it to us in full.' (Abu Dawud 964—recorded by Abdallah ibn Mas'ud)

Ka'b ibn Urjah asked how to make blessing on the Messenger himself ﷺ, as he had requested it. He said:

'Say: O Allah, bless Muhammad and Muhammad's family as You did bless Ibrahim and Ibrahim's family. O Allah, grant favours to Muhammad and Muhammad's family as You did grant favours to Ibrahim; You are indeed glorious and worthy of praise.' (Abu Dawud 971)

The Blessed Prophet Muhammad ﷺ was in fact the direct descendant of Ibrahim, and the Qur'an recorded how both Ibrahim and his son Isma'il made supplication for Muhammad ﷺ while raising the foundations of the Ka'bah.

'Our Lord! Make us both submissive to You, and raise from our offspring a nation submissive to You, and show us our ways of devotion and turn to us in mercy. Surely You are the Oft-Returning, the Merciful, Our Lord. And raise up in them a messenger from among them.' (2:128-129)

Many scholars regard this blessing on the Prophet ﷺ as an obligatory part of the *salah*, although others hold it as recommended but not obligatory. Abu Mas'ud al-Ansari added the details that it was while the Prophet ﷺ was at a meeting with Sa'd ibn Ubadah that Bashir ibn Sa'd said to him: 'Allah has commanded us to invoke blessing on you, Messenger of Allah. How should we invoke it?' The Messenger kept silent so long that we wished we had not asked him. Then he recited the above prayer (Muslim 803)

Another version of the prayer, recorded through Abu Humaid al-Sa'idi included specific mention of the Prophet's ﷺ wives:

'Say: O Allah, bless Muhammad, his wives and his offspring,

as You did bless Ibrahim's family, and grant favours to Muhammad's family, his wives and offspring as You did grant favours to Ibrahim's family; You are indeed praiseworthy and glorious.' (Abu Dawud 974, Muslim 807)

Abu Hurayrah's version goes:

'O Allah, bless Muhammad the unlettered Prophet, his wives who are the mothers of the faithful, his offspring, and the people of his house as You did bless the family of Ibrahim. You are indeed glorious and worthy of praise.' (Abu Dawud 977)

THE SITTING POSITION FOR TASHAHHUD

While he sat for the *tashahhud* prayer, the Prophet ﷺ used to place his left foot under his right thigh and shin, and spread his right foot; and he placed his left hand on his left knee and his right hand on his right thigh, and he pointed with his finger (Muslim 1201)

This position is known as *tawarruh*. The right foot is usually kept in a standing position as in *sajdah*, with only the tips of the toes touching the ground. However, here the stretching of the right foot is mentioned to show that if a person finds it too difficult to adopt this position, he or she may adopt the easier sitting posture.

Tawus recorded: 'We asked Ibn Abbas about sitting on one's buttocks (in prayer). He said: 'It is *sunnah*.' We said to him: 'We find it a sort of cruelty to the foot.' Ibn Abbas said: 'It is the *sunnah* of your Prophet ﷺ.' (Muslim 1093)

Abdallah ibn Abdallah said: 'I saw Abdallah ibn 'Umar crossing his legs while sitting in the prayer, and I, a mere youngster in those days, did the same. Ibn 'Umar forbade me to do so, and said: 'The proper way is to keep the right foot propped up and bend the left in prayer.' I said questioningly: 'But you are doing so!' He said: 'My feet cannot bear my weight!' (Bukhari 12.63.790)

Some people can be seen moving their fingers up and down or round and round during the prayer, but Abdallah ibn al-Zubayr added that he did not move his finger, and that he kept his gaze fixed upon the finger he was pointing. (Abu Dawud 984-5)

Malik ibn Numayr al-Khuzai reported that he used to raise his finger and curve it a little (Abu Dawud 986). Other traditions suggest various other ways that the Prophet used to point and count with his fingers, and al-Safi'i is of the opinion that one should point at the moment one recites 'There is no god but Allah', the pointing referring to Allah's unity (Abu Dawud 983 n. 475)

THE BASIC MINIMUM OF THE FAITH

Talhah ibn Ubaydallah recorded that a man with unkempt hair who came from Najd asked the Blessed Prophet ﷺ about Islam. The Messenger ﷺ said:

'You have to offer prayers perfectly five times in the twenty-four hours.' The man asked: 'Is there any more (praying)?' The Messenger ﷺ replied: 'No, but if you want to offer voluntary prayers, (you may).' He then said to him: 'You have to observe fasts during the month of Ramadan.' The man asked: 'Is there any more fasting?' The Messenger ﷺ replied: 'No, but if you wish to observe voluntary extra fasts, you may,' Then he said to him: 'You have to pay zakah.' The man asked: 'Is there anything other than the zakah to pay?' He replied: 'No, unless you wish to give charity of your own free will.' The man left him saying, 'By Allah! I will do neither less nor more than this.' Allah's Messenger ﷺ said: 'If he keeps his word, then he will find success.' (Bukhari 2.36.44)

THE BASIC MINIMUM FOR THE PERSON WHO CANNOT LEARN QUR'AN

Some Muslims, who are blessed with good memories and perhaps an academic turn of mind, are able to make a virtue out of being able to recite long and impressive passages. Most ordinary people, however, have not been blessed with the memory or intellectual equipment to be able to do this, especially if it is a case of learning long passages in a language they do not understand. The Blessed Prophet 🕮 did not regard them as in any way inferior to those who had great knowledge and memorisation of verses.

'A'ishah recorded: 'One who is skilled in the Qur'an is associated with the noble, upright, recording angels: but the one who falters when reciting the Qur'an and finds it difficult will have a double reward!' (Abu Dawud 1449, Muslim 1745)

A man once came to the Blessed Prophet 🕮 and said that he could not memorise anything from the Qur'an. He wanted the Prophet 🕮 to teach him in a simple way as much of Qur'an and prayers as would make his devotions reasonable and acceptable. The Blessed Prophet 🕮 said:

'Say: Glory be to Allah, and praise be to Allah, and there is no God but Allah, and Allah is Most Great, and there is no might and no strength but in Allah.' The man said 'Messenger of Allah—this is for Allah, but what is for me?' He said: 'Say: O Allah have mercy upon me, and sustain me, and keep me well, and guide me.' When he stood up, he made a sign with his hand. The Messenger of Allah 🕮 said: 'He filled up his hand with virtues.' (Abu Dawud 831)

However, all Muslims should do their best to memorise as much as they can of the Qur'an, and the Blessed Prophet 🕮 pointed out that regular practice was what was needed to stop the verses 'slipping away' out of the mind.

Abdallah ibn 'Umar recorded: 'When one who has committed the Qur'an to memory gets up and recites it night and day, it remains fresh in his (or her) mind: but if he does not get up (for prayer) he forgets it.' (Muslim 1723)

A similar *hadith* of Abdallah's records:

'What a wretched person is he amongst them who says: 'I have forgotten such-and-such a verse.' (He should say): 'I have been made to forget it.' Try to remember the Qur'an, for it is more apt to escape from the mind than a hobbled camel!' (Muslim 1724)

ALLAH HEARS ALL PRAYERS WITH GENUINE NIYYAH

Occasionally we all come across people who suffer from a kind of snobbery: they are all too ready to judge by appearances, and anybody whose doesn't quite fit is regarded as 'second class'. However, Allah always looks to the heart, and not to the external appearance. On the same principle, it is the *niyyah* or intention of a person that always counts, even more than what the person actually says or does.

Abu Hurayrah recorded: 'Many a person with dishevelled hair and covered with dust is turned away from the doors (whereas he is held in such high esteem by Allah) that if he were to adjure in the name of Allah (about anything), Allah would fulfil it." (Muslim 6351)

Uqbah ibn Amir recorded that he heard the Messenger of Allah ﷺ say: 'Allah is pleased with a shepherd of goats, who calls to prayer at the peak of a mountain and offers prayer. Allah the Exalted says: Look at this servant of Mine; he calls to prayer and offers it, and he fears Me. So I forgive him and admit him to Paradise.' (Abu Dawud 1199)

Allah always listens, and always hurries towards us. It is not Allah who is reluctant, but ourselves!

Abu Hurayrah recorded: 'I am near to the thought of My servant when he thinks about Me, and I am with him as he remembers Me... If he draws near me a hand's span, I draw near him an arm's length... and if he walks towards me,,, I come rushing towards him.' (Muslim 6471, etc.)

SOME OF THE BLESSED PROPHET'S PRIVATE PRAYERS

Many people used to ask the Blessed Prophet's ﷺ beloved wife 'A'ishah about the prayers the Prophet used during his private moments with her, during the hours of darkness. It was well known that the Blessed Prophet ﷺ did not limit himself to the five compulsory prayers, but when he was alone he spent a very great deal more of his time in prayer in contemplation, much of it with 'A'ishah either praying with him, or present in the room.

There is no doubt that as regards the private prayer practice of the Blessed Messenger of Allah ﷺ he was a most remarkable man. Even before he received the first revelations of the Qur'an, it is known that he frequently went off to the hills surrounding Makkah, to pray by himself throughout the watches of the night.

As Guide and Leader of the Muslims, this practice of his continued unabated until his death; he prayed long hours during every night, and frequently prayed all night long. This marked him out as being a most remarkable person, a man of powerful health and determination as well as extreme piety and devotion.

Yet, as one reads the *hadith* about his life and teaching, there is no hint anywhere that his practice was the result of great sacrifice on his part, or that he found it in any way burdensome. It was as if it all came naturally to him; and indeed, his Lord Allah was his dearest Friend and Companion, and Guide to his life.

The Presence of God was more real to him than the presence of any human being. It is impossible to study the *hadiths* of the Prophet's 鬱 life and separate any moment of his day from his awareness of God's guiding Presence.

Those who become Muslim also try to live devout and God-conscious lives; but for most people the opportunity to pass long hours of the night in prayer is hardly practicable, because of what must follow in the daytime—the normal routine of earning a living, and providing for a family. Yet the Blessed Prophet 鬱 gave a great deal of guidance to those who wished to attempt devotions over and above the compulsory prayers, particularly those that took place when the world slept; and many people were highly interested in what he did or said while he prayed.

(These extra prayers are known as *tahajjud* prayers—Allah requested 'And in some parts of the night offer the prayer with it (Qur'an) as an additional prayer, (O Muhammad).' (17:79)

For example, Asim ibn Humaid said:

'I asked 'A'ishah with what words the Messenger of Allah 鬱 would begin his prayers at night.' She replied: 'You ask me about a thing nobody asked about before! When he stood up he uttered *takbir* (Allah is most great) ten times, then uttered 'Praise to Allah' ten times, and 'Glory be to Allah' ten times, and 'There is no god but Allah' ten times, and sought forgiveness ten times, and said: O Allah, forgive me and guide me, and give me sustenance, and keep me well; and he sought refuge in Allah from the hardship of standing before Allah on the Day of Judgement.' (Abu Dawud 765—who reported that this tradition was also narrated by Khalid ibn Ma'dan from Rabi'ah al-Jarashi on the authority of 'A'ishah).

Abu Salamah ibn Abd al-Rahman ibn Awf also asked 'A'ishah a similar question. She said:

'When he stood up at night, he began his prayer by saying: 'O Allah, Lord of Jibril, Lord of Mika'il, Lord of Israfil, Creator of the heavens and the earth, the Knower of what is seen and of what is unseen; You decide between Your servants in which they used to differ. Guide me to the Truth where there is a difference of opinion by Your permission. You guide anyone You wish to the right path.' (Abu Dawud 766—a saying which was also reported by 'Ikramah with a different chain of narrators).

Abu Hurayrah recorded that he said to him, 'Messenger of Allah, for whom I would give my father and my mother in ransom, what do you recite during your silence between the *takbir* and the recitation?' He said: 'I say—O Allah, remove my sins from me as far as You have removed the East from the West. O Allah, purify me from sins as a white garment is purified from filth. O Allah, wash away my sins with water, snow and hail.' (Muslim 1245)

Ibn Abbas recorded another of the Blessed Prophet's ﷺ beautiful private prayers, one which he said during an extra prayer after the *isha'* or night prayer. After the *takbir*, the Blessed Prophet ﷺ prayed:

'O Allah, praise be to You: You are the light of the heavens and the earth, and to You be praise. You are the maintainer of the heavens and the earth, and to You be praise. You are the maintainer of the heavens and the earth and what is between them; You are the Truth, and Your statement is Truth; and Your promise is Truth, and the visitation with You is true, and the Paradise is true, and the Hell-fire is true, and the Hour is true. O Allah, to You I have submitted, and in You I have believed, and in You I trusted, and to You I turned my attention, and by You I reasoned, and to You I brought forth my case; so forgive me my former and latter sins, and my secret and open sins. You are my God, there is no god but You. (Abu Dawud 770—on the authority of Ibn Abbas)

If anyone wanted guidance as to a course of action, the Blessed Prophet ﷺ recommended praying in this way:

'O Allah, I ask guidance from Your knowledge, and power from Your might, and I ask for Your great blessings. You are capable and I am not. You know, and I do not know the unseen. O Allah, if You know that this (matter) is good for my religion, my life and my Hereafter, then ordain it for me and make it come easy for me and bless me in it; but if You know that this (matter) is harmful to me in my religion or my life or my Hereafter, then keep it away from me and let me be far from it. And ordain for me whatever is good for me, and let me be satisfied with it.' (Bukhari 21.27.263)

Mughirah ibn Shubah recorded: When the Messenger ﷺ finished the prayer and pronounced the salutation he said: 'There is no God but Allah. He is Alone, He has no partner. To Him belongs the sovereignty and to Him all praise is due, and He has the power over everything. O Allah, no-one can hold back what You choose to give, or give what You withhold; and riches cannot avail a wealthy person with You. (Muslim 1230)

Prayer was his great joy, because he was in constant communion with the Presence of God that gave him strength and filled him with peace and serenity.

ALLAH PREFERS REGULAR ROUTINES

The Blessed Prophet ﷺ was very much a creature of habit, and approved believers establishing any routines that they could maintain as a regular practice.

'A'ishah recorded that when the Blessed Prophet ﷺ was asked about the act most pleasing to Allah, he replied: 'That which is done regularly (continuously), even if it is (only) small.' (Muslim 1711)

The Blessed Prophet ﷺ wanted people to establish routines that would become a normal part of their everyday lives. He pointed out that Allah never intended their religion to become a burden to them, or to be so excessive that it made them rebellious and resentful, if not exhausted and ill.

Abu Hurayrah recorded: 'Religion is very easy, and whoever overburdens himself in his (or her) religion will not be able to continue in that way. So you should not be extremists, but try to be (as good as possible), and accept (and believe) the good news that you will be rewarded (for it); and gain strength by worshipping in the mornings, afternoons, and during the last hours of the nights.' (Bukhari 2.30.38. See also 2.33.41)

The fact that religion is not supposed to be a burden seems to be missed by those who imagine that the more they torture themselves the more Allah will approve and reward them. This is not the case, and actually reveals a kind of perverse religious pride—which is the wrong attitude in Islam.

Anas recorded that the Blessed Messenger ﷺ said: 'Allah is not in need of this man torturing himself' when he saw a man (who had vowed that the would perform the *hajj* on foot, even though he was old and sick) being supported by his two sons.' (Bukhari 78.32.692)

The religious routines of Muslim believers should include any practices they can manage without making themselves ill, or making themselves a burden to other people, or making other people feel uncomfortable.

The blessed Prophet ﷺ particularly did not appreciate the privacy of his night prayers being invaded by those striving over-zealously to emulate him.

'A'ishah recorded that the Messenger of Allah ﷺ had a mat, and he used it for making a separated area during the night and observed prayer in it, and the people used to pray with him... They crowded round him one night. He then said: 'O people, perform such acts as are within your capability; Allah never grows weary, but you will become exhausted. The acts most pleasing to Allah are those which are done regularly, even if they are small.' And it was the habit of the members of Muhammad's ﷺ household that whenever they did an act they did it regularly.' (Muslim 1710).

Sometimes he deliberately broke his routines, because he did not wish his followers to start regarding all the things he did as being compulsory for them too.

'A'ishah recorded: 'Allah's Messenger ﷺ used to pray in his room at night. As the wall of the room was low, the people saw him and some of them stood up to follow him in the prayer. In the morning they told others. The following night the Prophet ﷺ stood for the prayer and the people copied him; this went on for two or three nights. Thereupon the Messenger ﷺ did not stand for prayer the following night, and did not come out in the morning. When the people asked about it, he replied that he was afraid they would start to regard the night prayer as compulsory.' (Bukhari 11.79.696)

Times And Places

....................❦....................

THE TIMES OF THE PRAYERS

It is the practice of many mosques these days to issue an information sheet giving the times of the various prayers. These information sheets give the exact times, down to the minute, for each prayer, each day of the year.

Whereas it is obviously very important that worshippers know the times of the prayers said together in the mosque, it is not particularly required for worshippers who are not praying together to pray at any of the exact times stated. Many earnest Muslims misunderstand this, and some even regard the prayers of people said at the 'wrong' times as not being valid.

The Blessed Prophet ﷺ made it very clear that there were certain times *between which* the prayers had to be said, and not that they were to be said at any exact moment. There were a few exact moments when prayers were *not* to be said—and these were the moments of sunrise, sunset and high noon, because these times were especially revered by many pagans.

Hisham's father recorded that Ibn 'Umar said: 'Allah's Messenger ﷺ said: 'If the edge of the sun appears (above the horizon) delay the prayer till it becomes high, and if the edge of the sun disappears, delay the prayer till it sets (i.e. disappears completely.' (Bukhari 10.30.557)

Abu Sa'id al-Khudri recorded: 'There is no prayer after the morning prayer till the sun rises, and there is no prayer after the 'asr prayer till the sun sets.' (Bukhari 10.31.560)

The five compulsory prayers had to be said *between* certain times.

Abu Musa recorded: (One day) he offered (the dawn prayer) when a man could not recognise the face of his companion (due to darkness), or know who was standing by his side; he then announced the noon prayer when the sun had only just passed the meridian, so that people asked 'Has the noon come?'... He then commanded Bilal who announced the beginning of the time of the afternoon prayer when the sun was white and high. When the sun set he commanded Bilal who announced the beginning of time of the sunset prayer. When the twilight (just) disappeared he commanded Bilal who announced the beginning of the night prayer. The next day he offered the dawn prayer and left it so late that we said 'hasn't the sun risen?' He observed the noon prayer at the time he had previously observed the afternoon prayer. He offered the afternoon prayer at the time when the sun had become golden, or the evening had come. He offered the sunset prayer (just) before the twilight ended. He observed the night prayer when a third of the night had passed. He then asked: 'Where is the man who was asking me about the time of prayer? (Then replying to him, he said:) The time (of your prayer) lies within these two limits.' (Abu Dawud 395, see also Muslim 1278-81)

Abd Allah ibn 'Amr recorded: 'The time of the noon prayer is as long as the time of the afternoon prayer has not come; the time of the afternoon prayer is as long as the sun has not turned to gold; the time of the sunset prayer is as long as the twilight has not ended; the time of night prayer is up to midnight; and the time of the morning prayer is as long as the sun has not risen.' (Abu Dawud 396, Muslim 1273)

The Blessed Prophet ﷺ always considered the comfort and

welfare of the worshippers to be far more important than exact times. Muhammad ibn 'Amr commented that the Blessed Prophet ﷺ used to offer the night prayer early when many people were present, but late if they were few (Abu Dawud 397). In the former case, since many had turned up and it was convenient to them, it was considered better manners and kinder to get on with the prayer. In the latter case, the Prophet gave more time for others to arrive. If only a few were present, they would very likely consult and agree on the time together. As for the Prophet (ﷺ), he disliked leaving it so late that people were taking sleep before the night prayer, or staying at the mosque talking to anyone after it.

As regards the noon prayer, sometimes it was so hot that it became uncomfortable. People in cooler countries may not realise that in some places the ground becomes so hot that you cannot tread on it without shoes. Jabir ibn Abdallah was one who used to pray in the open, no matter what the heat. He mentioned that he used to pick up a handful of gravel and let it cool down in his hand so that he could put his forehead on it when he prostrated (Abu Dawud 399). However, the Prophet ﷺ did not think this necessary. He usually delayed the noon prayer until later when the extreme heat had faded away. (Abu Dawud 401, Muslim 1282)

Abu Dharr recorded: The Muadhdhin called for the noon prayer. Upon this, the Messenger of Allah ﷺ said: 'Let it cool down!' Or he said: 'Wait, wait, for this intensity of heat is (as if it comes) from Hell breathing out! When the heat is intense, delay the prayer until it becomes cooler.' Abu Dharr commented: (We waited) until we saw the shadow of the mounds.' (Muslim 1289, Bukhari 10.9.511) This may even that they waited until the praying place was in the shade when the sun had moved on.

Abu Hurayrah and Abdallah ibn 'Umar recorded that he said: 'If it is very hot, then pray the *zuhr* prayer when it becomes cooler, as the severity of the heat is from the raging of the Hell-fire.'

However, the fact that they sometimes did pray when it was indeed very hot was revealed by Anas ibn Malik:

'When we offered the *zuhr* prayers behind Allah's Messenger ﷺ we used to prostrate on our clothes to protect ourselves from the heat!' (Bukhari 10.11.517) In other words, the ground was still too hot to kneel on.

'A'ishah commented that when the Prophet ﷺ prayed the afternoon prayer with her in their house, he did it while the sunlight was (still) present in her apartment, before it climbed up the walls' (Abu Dawud 407, Muslim 1271, Bukhari 10.12.519)

As regards *asr* prayer, the Blessed Prophet ﷺ disapproved of people who did not bother to think about God until the last possible moment they were reminded by the gold of the setting sun and then prayed quickly—he regarded that as hypocrisy and gave a crushing description of it.

Ala ibn Abdal Rahman recorded that they came to the house of Anas ibn Malik in Basra after saying the noon prayer. His house was situated beside the mosque. As we visited him, he said: 'Have you said the afternoon prayer?' We said to him: 'It is only a few moments since we finished the noon prayer.' He said: 'Offer the afternoon prayer.' So we stood up and said our prayer, and when we completed it, he said: 'I heard the Messenger of Allah ﷺ say: 'This is how the hypocrite prays—he sits watching the sun, and when it is between the horns of the devil he rises and strikes the ground (with his head—i.e. prostrations) four times, mentioning Allah a little in it!' (Muslim 1301, Abu Dawud 413)

Rafi ibn Khadij recorded an occasion in which *asr* was offered a long time before *maghrib*: 'We used to say the afternoon prayer with the Messenger of Allah ﷺ and then the camel was slaughtered and ten parts of it were distributed, then it was cooked, and then we ate this cooked meat—(all) before the setting of the sun!' (Muslim 1304)

Anas ibn Malik recorded: 'We used to pray the 'asr, and after that if any of us went to Quba he could arrive there while the sun was still high!' (Bukhari 10.13.526)

Anas ibn Malik commented that when he prayed with the Prophet ﷺ they used to shoot arrows after the sunset prayer, and still be able to see where the arrows had fallen. (Abu Dawud 416)

The Blessed Prophet ﷺ regarded the 'asr as most precious, and not to be missed if at all possible.

Ibn 'Umar recorded: 'Whoever misses the 'asr prayer, it is as if he lost his family and property.' (Bukhari 10.14.527)

Abu al-Malih recorded: 'Whoever leaves the 'asr prayer, all his good deeds will be annulled!' (Bukhari 10.15.528)

On the other hand, he preferred to pray the night prayer late rather than early.

Mu'adh ibn Jabal recorded: 'We waited for the Prophet ﷺ to offer the night prayer. He delayed until people began to think that he would not come out, and some of us thought he (must have already) offered the prayer. At the very moment when we had decided this, the Prophet ﷺ came out (to pray).' (Abu Dawud 421)

Abdallah ibn 'Umar's version added that he said: 'Are you waiting for this prayer? Were it not that it would impose a burden on my people, I would pray with them at this time as my normal practice.' (Abu Dawud 420)

Abu Sa'id al-Khudri's version added: He did not come out until half the night had passed. He then said: 'Take your places.' We then took our places. Then he said: 'The people have prayed and gone to bed, but you are still engaged in prayer so long as you wait for the prayer. Were it not for the weakness of the weak and for the sickness of the sick, I would (always) delay this prayer till half the night had gone.' (Abu Dawud 422, Muslim 1333)

Ibn Abbas recorded: Once Allah's Messenger ﷺ delayed the *isha'* prayer to such an extent that the people slept and got up and slept again and got up again. Then 'Umar ibn al-Khattab stood up and reminded the Prophet ﷺ of the prayer. The Prophet came out as if I am seeing him now, with water trickling from his head, and he was putting his hand on his head, and he then said: 'If I hadn't thought it hard for my followers, I would have ordered them (always) to pray (*isha'*) at this time.' (Bukhari 10.24.545)

After the night prayer, the Blessed Prophet ﷺ was not one of those who liked to linger with friends holding conversations. Having made thoughts of God his last thoughts at night, he liked to go straight home to bed.

Abu Barza recorded: 'Allah's Messenger ﷺ disliked to sleep before the *isha'* prayer, or to talk after it.' (Bukhari 10.23.543)

PRAYING WHILE SLEEPY

While appreciating the discipline and self-sacrifice of devoted followers who put their worship before their own comfort or laziness, the Blessed Prophet ﷺ never considered it a good thing to try to pray while exhausted—if struggling to fight off the strong urge to sleep. 'A'ishah recorded that he said:

'When one of you is dozing at his prayer, he should (go and) sleep till his sleepiness is gone.' (Abu Dawud 1305)

And Abu Hurayrah recorded: 'When one of you gets up by night (to pray) and falters in reciting the Qur'an (due to sleep), and he does not know what he is saying, he should sleep.' (Abu Dawud 1306).

'A'ishah recorded: Allah's Messenger ﷺ said: 'If any of you feels drowsy while praying, he should go to bed till his slumber is over, because in praying while drowsy one does not know whether one is asking forgiveness or for a bad thing for oneself!' (Bukhari 4.55.211, Muslim 1718)

Moreover, the Blessed Prophet ﷺ taught that nobody should feel upset or guilty if they missed a prayer when it was their regular habit.

'A'ishah recorded: 'Any person who offers prayer at night regularly but (on a certain night) is overcome by sleep, will be given the reward as if he (or she) did pray.' (Abu Dawud 1309)

IF ONE MISSES THE DAWN PRAYER

If anyone actually oversleeps and misses the compulsory *fajr* prayer, the way to put it right is to pray whenever one awakes. It is not a disastrous sin. Human nature being what it is, it frequently happens that people oversleep and miss the prayer. It even happened to the Blessed Prophet ﷺ himself.

Abu Hurayrah recorded: When the Messenger ﷺ returned from the battle of Khaybar, he travelled during the night. When we felt sleep, we stopped to rest. He asked Bilal to keep vigil for them. But Bilal, who was leaning against the saddle of his mount, was (also) overcome by sleep. Neither the Prophet ﷺ nor Bilal nor any of the companions woke up until the sunshine struck them. The Messenger ﷺ awoke first of all, and was embarrassed, and said: 'O Bilal!' He replied: 'He Who detained your soul detained my soul also, Messenger of Allah, may my parents be sacrificed for you!' The Prophet ﷺ performed ablution and commanded Bilal to call to prayer. When he finished the prayer, he said: 'If anyone forgets prayer, he should observe it as soon as he remembers it, for Allah has said: 'Establish prayer for My remembrance'.' (Abu Dawud 435)

A variant version was recorded by Abu Qatadah:

Abdallah ibn Abu Qatadah recorded: My father said: One night we were travelling with the Prophet ﷺ and some people said, 'We wish that Allah's Messenger ﷺ would take a rest along with us during the last hours of the night.' He said: 'I am afraid that you will sleep and miss the *fajr* prayer.' Bilal said: 'I will make you get up.' So all slept, and Bilal rested his back against his rahila, and he too was overwhelmed by sleep. The Prophet ﷺ woke up when the edge of the sun had risen and said: 'O Bilal! What about your promise?' He replied: 'I have never slept such a sleep!' The Prophet ﷺ said: 'Allah captured your souls when He wished, and released them when He wished. O Bilal! Get up and pronounce the *adhan* for the prayer.' The Prophet ﷺ performed the ablution, and although the sun had come up and was bright, he stood up and prayed.' (Bukhari 10.35.569, see also Muslim 1448, 1450, Abu Dawud 439)

Anas ibn Malik reported the Prophet ﷺ as saying: 'If anyone forgets a prayer or oversleeps, he should observe it when he remembers it; there is no expiation except for that.' (Abu Dawud 442)

THE RIGHT PLACE FOR PRAYER

Any place or building which is specifically set aside for worship is called a masjid or place of prostration. In Muslim countries one can find little areas set aside all over the place, under trees in quiet corners, near stations, and so on. Muslim houses will have a special area kept clean, where one can pray.

A building kept specially for Muslim prayer is called a mosque. Originally these were very simple—the mosques in the time of the Blessed Prophet ﷺ were little more than enclosures of mud-brick with a *qiblah* and a water-supply. Soon they developed to become comfortable and hospitable places, and nowadays one can see numerous very grand buildings on a huge scale. The size and scale of the building makes no difference to the quality of the prayer offered by the worshippers. It is the hearts of the believers that Allah sees, and not the fine buildings—although we should not assume that Allah is not also pleased with the intention (*niyyah*) of those who built lovely buildings in which to worship Him.

Since Allah sees people in whatever place they happen to be, it should be emphasised that *any* clean place can be used as a prayer to Allah, whether it be in the home, in the field, in the city or in the jungle.

Whereas the building of a mosque is highly recommended— 'For the one who builds a mosque for Allah, the Exalted, Allah will build a house in Paradise' (Muslim 1084)—at the same time, Allah has declared the whole earth clean and pure, and a place where prayer should be offered.

Jabir ibn Abdallah al-Ansari recorded: The Prophet ﷺ said: I have been granted five things which were not granted to anyone before me; every prophet was sent in particular to his own people, but I have been sent to all the red and the black—(see *surah* 34:28—'And We have not sent you but as a bringer of good tidings and as a warner unto all humanity, but most of humanity does not realise it); the spoils of war have been made lawful for me, and these were never lawful to anyone before me; and the earth has been made sacred and pure and a mosque for me—so whenever the time of prayer comes for any one of you, he (or she) should pray wherever he (or she) is, and I can overawe my enemies from a distance, and I have been granted the right to intercede.' (Muslim 1058)

Hudhayfah recorded: The Messenger of Allah ﷺ said: 'We have been made to excel other people in three (things); our rows have been made like the rows of the angels—(see *Sūrah* 37:166—Truly, we are arranged in ranks (for service), and truly we are those who declare God's glory'); and the whole earth has been made a mosque for us, and its dust has been made a purifier for us when water is not available.' (Muslim 1060)

The making clean of the earth is a significant matter, especially since before the coming of Islam it was frequently thought that the material world was profane and had nothing to do with the spiritual life of humanity, and that a spiritual person should look down on this world as being something impure. The Prophet ﷺ made it clear that the material world was neither profane nor impure, and that a special prayer-house was not necessary in any way except as a focus and convenience.

Abu Dharr recorded: 'And whenever the time comes for prayer, pray there, for that is a mosque.' (Muslim 1056)

Ibrahim ibn Yazid al-Taymi recorded that he used to read the Qur'an with his father in the vestibule (i.e. before the door of the mosque). When he recited the verses concerning prostration, he prostrated himself. I said to him: 'Father, do you prostrate yourself in the roadway?' He said: 'I heard Abu Dharr ask the Messenger of Allah ﷺ about the first mosques to be built on earth... (see the next *hadith* quoted) and he further said: 'The earth is a mosque for you, so wherever you are at the time of prayer, pray there!' (Muslim 1057)

Therefore Muslims can offer prayer in any place and any situation, except places which are dirty, dangerous, inconvenient for other people, or associated with non-Muslim worship.

Many Muslims were interested in the history of the very first mosques:

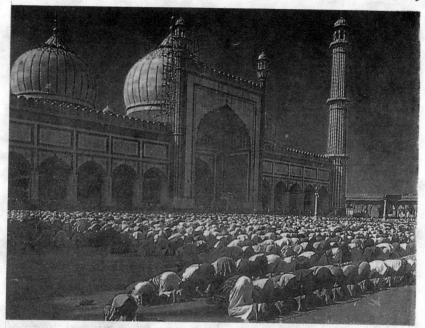

Abu Dharr recorded that he said: 'Messenger of Allah, which mosque was set up first on earth?' He said: 'Al-Masjid al-*Haram* (the sacred mosque, the Ka'bah).' I said: 'Then which next?' He said: 'It was the Masjid al-Aqsa (i.e. the great mosque at Jerusalem).' I said: 'How long was there between the building of the two?' He said: 'It was forty years. But whenever the time comes for prayer, pray there, for that is a mosque for you.' (Muslim 1056)

Some people have thought the Prophet ﷺ made a mistake in only allowing forty years between the building of these two mosques, thinking that the Ka'bah was built by Ibrahim and the Aqsa over a thousand years later by Solomon. Muslim scholars conclude that he was either referring to an ancient tradition that both places were built originally by Adam, or that Jacob the son of Isaac, son of Ibrahim laid the foundations of the Aqsa forty years after rebuilding of the Ka'bah by Ibrahim (See Fath al-Mulhim

Vol. 11, p114, Muslim 1056, n. 723)

'The Messenger came to Madinah and stayed in the upper part of the city for fourteen nights with a tribe called Banu 'Amr ibn Auf. He then sent for the chiefs of Banu al-Najjar, and they came with swords around their necks. I perceive it as if I am seeing the Messenger of Allah ﷺ now, riding with Abu Bakr behind him and the chiefs of Banu al-Najjar around him, until he halted in the courtyard of Abu Ayyub. The Messenger ﷺ said prayer when the time came for prayer, and he prayed in the fold of goats and sheep. He then ordered mosques to be built, and sent for the chiefs of Banu al-Najjar, and they came (to him). He said: 'O Banu al-Najjar—sell these lands of yours to me.' They said: 'No, by Allah, we do not ask any money for them, but (reward) from the Lord.' Anas commented that there were trees and graves of the idol-worshippers and ruins (in these lands). The Messenger ﷺ ordered that the trees should be cut and the graves dug out and the ruins be levelled. The trees were placed in rows facing the qiblah and the stones were set on both sides of the door, and they sang rajaz verses along with the Messenger ﷺ: 'O Allah! There is no good but the good of the next world, so help the Ansar and the Muhajirun.' (Muslim 1066)

Returning to the idea of prayers said anywhere, or in the home—how does one guarantee a clean space? If one is praying at home, or somewhere out in the open, it is useful to keep a special board or a prayer-mat for this purpose. Prayer-mats are small fine carpets which are kept folded and clean, and can be placed down anywhere to make a 'clean space' for the worshipper. These little mats are purchased in any Muslim country or Islamic shop for a few pounds, and can be very beautiful. They usually include the shape of a mihrab or arch, to point the direction of the qiblah, and sometimes come equipped with a compass. The designs include pictures of the Ka'bah and other mosques, but not pictures of people or animals, or anything that would distract the mind of the worshipper from his or her prayer.

PLACES WHERE PRAYERS SHOULD NOT BE SAID

The Blessed Prophet 嶽 declared that any place was suitable for prayers except graveyards, bathrooms and toilets, rubbish tips, slaughter-houses, or camel-pens, although the Blessed Prophet 嶽 did not object to the pens of sheep.

Abu Dharr recorded: 'The (whole) earth is made pure for me as a place of prayer.' (Abu Dawud 489, see also Bukhari 8.56.429, Muslim 1058)

Sayd recorded: 'The whole earth is a place of prayer except public baths and graveyards.' (Abu Dawud 492)

Bara ibn Azib recorded: 'Do not say prayers at places where the camels kneel down because they are the places of devils.' And he was asked about praying in the folds of sheep. He replied: 'Pray there, because they are places of blessing.' (Abu Dawud 493)

Anas recorded: The Messenger of Allah 嶽 used to pray in the folds of sheep and goats before the mosque built.' (Muslim 1069, Bukhari 8.49.421; 2.49.241)

The commentator noted that camels are quite dangerous beasts to have in the proximity when praying, because they are large, unpredictable and lurch about, and could hurt unsuspecting worshippers—even though the Blessed Prophet frequently used his camel as his sutrah, whereas one is generally quite safe from harm from sheep whilst at prayer!

It is forbidden to pray salah (namaz) on the top of or facing a grave. This last point is important, for it has always been the habit of respectful people to honour the last resting-places of dead persons of importance, or members of their own families.

'A'ishah recorded: Umm Habibah and Umm Salamah (two other wives of the Blessed Prophet ﷺ) made mention of a church which they had seen in Abyssinia which had pictures in it. The Messenger ﷺ said: 'When a pious person among them dies, they build a place of worship on his grave and then decorate it with such pictures. They will be the worst of creatures on the Day of Judgement in the sight of God.' (Muslim 1076, Bukhari 8.48.419)

The Blessed Prophet ﷺ was very well aware of the danger that when he died his own followers might resort to this kind of veneration, and on his deathbed he tried to make sure that they never did so by issuing a specific curse upon those who turned graves of eminent people into places of worship:

'A'ishah and Abdallah recorded: 'As the Messenger ﷺ was about to breathe his last, he drew his sheet upon his face, and when he felt uneasy, he uncovered his face and said in this very state: 'Let there be a curse upon the Jews and the Christians because they took the graves of their prophets as places of worship.' (Muslim 1082). 'A'ishah added: 'Had it not been so, his (i.e. the Prophet's) grave would have been in an open place, but it could not due to the fear that it might have been taken as a mosque.' (Muslim 1079)

In fact, the Blessed Prophet ﷺ was buried under the earth of his beloved wife 'A'ishah's chamber, and later on her father Abu Bakr, the first caliph, was buried alongside him. 'A'ishah had hoped that she too would be buried next to him, but when the next caliph, 'Umar, died, he also asked to buried there, and she granted his request. Up to that time she had shared the small room with her two dead loved ones, but when 'Umar was buried she had the area sectioned off by a wall. The room is now part of the complex in the mosque at Madinah.

Sadly, out of excessive veneration, what the Prophet ﷺ feared has indeed come true all over the Muslim world. One can find numerous shrines of the saints, or descendants of the

Prophet's 🕋 own family, that have become special places of prayer, particularly for those who wish to have a particular request fulfilled, such as the prayer for a barren couple to have a child, or for a person incurably ill to be made better.

It is perfectly acceptable to vist the last resting-places of the honourable dead and pray du'a for their souls—the Blessed Prophet 🕋 frequently did that.

Rabiah ibn al-Hudair recorded that he did not hear Talhah ibn Ubaydallah narrating any tradition from the Messenger of Allah 🕋 except one: 'We went out along with the Messenger of Allah 🕋 who was going to visit the graves of the martyrs. When we went to Harrah Waqim and then came down from it, we found some graves at turning the valley. We asked: 'Messenger of Allah, are these the graves of our brothers?' He replied: 'Graves of our companions.' When we came to the graves of martyrs, he said: 'These are the graves of our brothers.' (Abu Dawud 2038).

What is wrong is if a Muslim should ever offer prayers *to* them—as if the will of that particular saint could be more powerful or more compassionate than the will of Allah Himself! To believe such a thing is a form of shirk.

THE AGE TO START PRAYER

Abd al-Malik al-Rabi ibn al-Saburah reported that his grandfather reported the Blessed Prophet saying:

'Command a boy to pray when he reaches the age of seven years. When he becomes ten years old,

then beat him to prayer.' (Abu Dawud 494)

Others suggest that prayer for a child should begin when it reaches the age of reason. Hisham ibn Sa'd recorded: 'When a boy distinguishes his right hand from his left hand.' (Abu Dawud 497)

THE IMPORTANCE OF PRAYING TOGETHER

The prayer in congregation was not compulsory, but the Blessed Messenger ﷺ always desired his followers to come together in the mosque for prayer, even if it was a very humble praying-place and the numbers of worshippers were very few.

Abu Musa recorded: 'The Prophet ﷺ said: 'A faithful believer to another faithful believer are like bricks in a wall, supporting each other.' While (saying this) he clasped his hands and interlaced his fingers.' (Bukhari 8.88.468)

Abu Sa'id al-Khudri recorded: 'The prayer in congregation is twenty-five times superior to the prayer offered by the person alone.' (Bukhari 11.30.618, Muslim 1360)

However, the Blessed Prophet ﷺ did not mean by this that the prayer offered in the home or elsewhere was not as valid as that made in congregation together, but simply that he recommended believers to gather together for the compulsory prayers whenever possible, and by this means to support each other in their faith and fellowship.

The being in congregation was never compulsory—the Blessed Prophet ﷺ himself excused people from attendance at the mosque on the grounds of illness, and adverse weather conditions such as very heavy rain or extreme cold. However, it was preferred, if possible.

Abu Darda recorded that he heard the Messenger ﷺ say: 'If there are three men in a village or in the desert among whom prayer is not offered, the devil has got mastery over them.

Observe prayer (together) in congregation, for the wolf eats the straggler!' (Abu Dawud 547)

Abdallah ibn Mas'ud recorded: I have seen the time when no-one stayed away from prayer except a known hypocrite. I witnessed the time when a man would be brought swaying between two others until he was set up in the row. Every one of you has a mosque of his own, in his house. If you were to pray (always) in your houses and stay from your mosques, you would abandon the *sunnah* of your Prophet; and if you were to abandon that, you would become an unbeliever!' (Abu Dawud 550)

Ubayy ibn Ka'b recorded one occasion when the Messenger ﷺ led the dawn prayer one day and noticed the absence of one or two people he expected to be there. He said:

'Is so-and-so present?' They said: 'No.' He said: 'These two prayers are the ones which are the most burdensome to hypocrites. If you knew what (blessings) they contain, you would come to them, even though you had to crawl on your knees. The first row is like that of angels, and if you knew of the nature of its excellence you would race to join it. A man's prayer said along with another is purer than his prayer said alone, and his prayer with two men is purer than his prayer with one; and if there are more it is more pleasing to Allah the Almighty, the Majestic.' (Abu Dawud 554)

'Uthman ibn Affan recorded: 'If anyone says the night prayer in congregation, it is as if he kept the vigil until midnight; and he who says both the night and dawn prayers in congregation, it is as if he kept vigil the whole night.' (Abu Dawud 555)

However, the Blessed Messenger ﷺ stressed that the amount of effort a person put in towards performing the prayer counted to their credit, whether they were in congregation or alone. For example, the further one had to come, the more merit in it; and if one had to walk it would earn more merit than someone who managed to get an easy ride.

Abu Musa recorded: 'The most eminent among human beings (as a recipient of) reward (is one) who lives farthest away, and who has to walk the farthest distance, and he who waits for the prayer to observe it along with the Imam, his reward is greater than one who prays (alone) and then goes to sleep.' (Muslim 1401)

One had to be careful, however, not to exercise one's piety for the wrong motives:

Ubayy ibn Ka'b recorded: There was a man among the Ansar whose house was situated at the farthest end of Madinah, but he never missed any prayer along with the Messenger of Allah ﷺ. We felt pity for him, and said to him: 'If you bought a donkey, it would save you from the burning sand and the reptiles of the earth.' He said: 'Listen! By Allah, I do not want my house to be any nearer to the side of Muhammad ﷺ.' I took these words badly, and went and told the Blessed Messenger ﷺ about what he had said. He called him, and he repeated exactly what he had said to Ubayy ibn Ka'b, but made mention of the fact that he desired a reward for his steps. Upon this, the Messenger of Allah ﷺ said: 'In fact, you will receive the reward you expect.' (Muslim 1404, Abu Dawud 556-559)

The Blessed Prophet ﷺ did not mean that the person who prayed alone should be looked down on. It depended on the circumstances. Congregational prayer was never declared compulsory for a Muslim; it was simply the case that the Prophet ﷺ preferred the spirit of community that could be gained when people made the effort to come together in like spirit. The person who prayed alone, perhaps in difficult circumstances, may have put in just as much effort as the person who came to the mosque.

Abu Sa'id al-Khudri recorded: 'Prayer in congregation is

worth twenty-five prayers (prayed alone). But if he prays in a jungle (alone) and performs the bowings and prostrations perfectly, it is equivalent to fifty prayers!' (Abu Dawud 560, see also Bukhari 11.30,618f)

Abd al-Wahid ibn Ziyad's version was:

'Prayer said by a solitary person in a jungle is more excellent by many degrees than prayer said in congregation.' (Abu Dawud 560)

The point is, the prayer has not been said for any reason other than pure worship of Allah, since it has been witnessed by no one but Allah alone. Worshippers who carry out their daily practice totally unseen, without any encouragement or support from others, are highly recommended. This is particularly relevant to women worshippers, who frequently pray alone in the home with no communal support, and whose discipline and routine nobody sees but Allah.

There is no reason why a woman should not go to the mosque to pray, but those who maintain their regular routine without any encouragement from others are earning good reward and blessing.

IF ONE HAS ALREADY PRAYED, BUT THEN JOINS A CONGREGATION PRAYER

The Blessed Prophet ﷺ always recommended joining in with a communal prayer if one was being offered, even if one had already prayed the set prayer alone elsewhere.

Yazid ibn Al-Aswad, who prayed along with the Messenger ﷺ when he was a young boy, once saw two people sitting in the corner of the mosque. The Prophet ﷺ called them over and asked why they did not pray along with them. They said they had already prayed in their houses. The Prophet ﷺ said: 'If any of you prays in his house and then finds that the Imam has not prayed, he should pray along with him, and it will count as a voluntary extra prayer.' (Abu Dawud 575-578)

ON WOMEN GOING TO THE MOSQUE

A casual visitor to many of today's mosques might be forgiven for thinking that Islam was mainly a religion for men, since there would probably be only a few ladies present if any, and they would be saying their prayers either in a separate area from the men, or well away from them, in rows behind them. This is not because the faith of women believers is in any way inferior to that of men, but because female Muslims are encouraged to be modest, and not to let their presence be in any way a distraction to other worshippers. The Blessed Prophet ﷺ disapproved in principle of anything that distracted any person, man or woman, from their worship. For this reason, male and female worshippers do not pray together side by side in the mosque, but the women pray in rows behind the men.

In fact, over fifty percent of the world's Muslims are women. It was the custom of many women to go to the mosque during the Prophet's lifetime, none more so than the ladies of his own family. The sunnah of his wives was to attend regularly. The commendation for the prayers of women who prayed in private was indicated by only one or two *hadith*, that suggested that their prayers were more meritorious if they were done just between the women and Allah, and not in a public place.

Abdallah ibn Mas'ud recorded: 'It is more excellent for a woman to pray in her house than in her courtyard, and more excellent for her to pray in her private chamber than in her house.' (Abu Dawud 570)

This *hadith* seems to have originated with the Prophet's words to Umm Humaid, to console her for not being able to

come to the mosque. He was pointing out that to come there was not a necessity, and her prayers elsewhere were perfectly valid — even the most private and solitary of them.

Umm Humaid once said to the Holy Prophet ﷺ: 'Messenger of Allah, I long to pray with you.' Upon this, the Messenger of Allah ﷺ consoled her, and stopped her worrying by observing: 'I know that you love to say prayer with me; but the prayer you offer in your chamber is more excellent than that you offer in your apartment, and the prayer you say in your apartment is better than that you observe in your courtyard; and the prayer you say in your courtyard is better than that you observe in the mosque of your tribe (which is near your house), and the prayer which you say in the mosque of your tribe is better than that which you say in my mosque.' (Ahmad)

It is strange how so many male Muslims have concentrated on this *hadith* and even made use of it to exclude women from *salah*—perhaps thinking how overcrowded their mosques would be if all the Muslim women attended. They use it to suggest that the Prophet disapproved of women going to the mosques, whereas on the contrary a vast number of *hadiths* prove beyond any shadow of doubt that prayer in the mosque was quite normal for Muslim women. Chauvinistic men did not like it then, and many still do not like it now—but this is an example of how Islam struggled to bring acceptance of the equality of women to a society that found the notion hard to accept.

'A'ishah recorded: 'The women believers observed the morning prayers along with the Messenger of Allah ﷺ, wrapped in their mantles. They would then return to their homes and nobody could recognise them because of the Messenger's ﷺ praying in the darkness before dawn.' (Muslim 1346, 1347; Bukhari 10.27.552, 12.83.831)

Ibn Abbas recorded that Umm Fadl, daughter of al-Harith heard him reciting 'By those sent forth to spread goodness (*surah* 77), and remarked: 'O my son, your recitation of this *surah* reminded me that it was the last *surah* that I heard from the Messenger of Allah ﷺ; he recited it during one evening prayer.' (Muslim 929).

The Blessed Prophet ﷺ was always well aware of mothers with their children in the rows behind him, and far from discouraging them, he simply used to adjust the length of his recitations when he heard restless babies.

'Abdallah ibn Abu Qatadah recorded that he said: 'Whenever I stand for prayer, I would prefer to make it long, but whenever I hear the cries of a child I shorten it, as I dislike putting mothers to inconvenience.' (Bukhari 12.80.827)

The Blessed Prophet ﷺ pointed out that the prayers of women who prayed in their homes were just as valid as those said in congregation. However, it is not correct Islam to *prevent* any woman from joining the men in communal prayer.

Abu Hurayrah recorded that the Prophet commanded: 'Do not prevent the female servants of Allah from visiting the mosques of Allah; they may go out, if they have not perfumed themselves.' (Abu Dawud 565)

The restriction on perfume was necessary, for the sweet scent of women might have distracted the men from their worship.

Ibn 'Umar recorded the same saying, but added: 'Do not prevent your women from going to the mosques; but their houses are better for them (for praying).' (Abu Dawud 567)

Salim ibn Abdallah recorded the Prophet ﷺ as saying: '(You must) Allow women to visit the mosques (even) at night.' A son of his (Bilal) said: 'I swear by Allah, we shall never allow them, because they will cheat on us. I swear by Allah we shall not allow them.' He ('Umar) then became angry and shouted at him, and said: 'I tell you that the Messenger of Allah ﷺ said 'Allow them', (so how dare) you say 'We shall not allow them!' (Abu Dawud 568, Muslim 885 etc.)

The commentator made the point in Bilal's defence that he was thinking of the Prophet's ﷺ opinion that it was better for women to pray in their houses, and that since the Prophet's ﷺ time things had undergone a change for the worse and it was a time of unrest —it might not have been safe for the women. Another suggestion made here was that some Muslim men were not permitting their women to join them in prayer on account of tribal pride and vanity which still had traces left in their minds, and this still needed correcting. (Muslim 885 n.666)

A variant *hadith* recorded: 'Ibn 'Umar reported: You must grant permission to women for going to the mosque in the night. His son who was called Waqid said: 'Then they would make mischief.' He thumped his (son's) chest and said: 'I am narrating to you the *hadith* of the Messenger of Allah ﷺ, and you say: No!' (Muslim 890)

Ibn 'Umar recorded that one of the wives of 'Umar ibn al-Khattab used to offer the *fajr* and the *isha'* prayer in congregation in the mosque. She was asked why she had come out for the prayer, as she knew that 'Umar disliked it, and he had great self-esteem. She replied: 'What prevents him from stopping me doing this?' The other replied: 'The statement of Allah's Messenger ﷺ 'Do not stop Allah's maidservants from going to Allah's mosque' prevents him.' (Bukhari 13.11.23)

Umm Salamah, one of the Prophet's ﷺ wives, recorded that it was their practice to get up and leave before the men, so that there was no question of social mixing in the mosque.

Umm Salamah recorded: 'In the lifetime of Allah's Messenger ﷺ the women used to get up when they finished their compulsory prayers with *taslim*. The Prophet ﷺ and the men would stay in their places as long as long as Allah willed. When the Prophet ﷺ got up, the men would then get up. (Bukhari 12.80.825)

The Blessed Prophet's ﷺ wife 'A'ishah certainly went to the mosque to pray as her regular practice, but she did not approve of some of the things she observed about the women, after the Prophet's death. If women expected the same privileges of Islam as the men, then they had to behave like equal Muslims. She said:

'If the Messenger of Allah ﷺ had seen what the women have invented, he would have prevented them from visiting the mosque as the women of the children of Israel were prevented.'

(Abu Dawud 569, Bukhari 12.81.828)

The Prophet frequently prayed together with his beloved wives and other women of his family in the privacy of their own homes. For example, Thabit recorded on the authority of Anas (his nephew):

'The Messenger ﷺ came to us and there was none in our house but I, my mother and my aunt Umm Haram. He said: 'Stand up, so that I may lead you in prayer'; and he led us in prayer. Someone asked Thabit: 'Where did Anas stand with him?' He replied: 'He was on the right side. He then blessed us, the members of the household with every good of this world and the Hereafter. My mother said: 'Messenger of Allah—here is your little servant, invoke the blessings of Allah on him too.' He then blessed me with every good, and he concluded his blessings for me (with these words)—'Allah! Increase his wealth, and his children and make (them a source of) blessing for him.' (Muslim 1389— The Prophet's nephew Anas, incidentally, died in 91 AH at the age of over a hundred!)

One important *hadith* is that recorded by the Prophet's wife Maymunah:

Maymunah recorded: 'The Messenger of Allah ﷺ said prayer while I was by his side, and (we were so close that) at times when he prostrated, his cloth touched me.' (Muslim 1392)

This is very significant as an indicator of the true status of women in Islam.

The Call to Prayer

......❧......

MUADHDHIN AND IQAMAH

The traditional Muslim call to prayer came about as the result of special revelations during dreams. Before the muadhdhin method was revealed, the Blessed Prophet ﷺ had been considering various methods that might have been used to call the people together.

Abu Umayr ibn Anas recorded: The people suggested to him: 'Hoist a flag at the time of prayer; when they see it, they will tell each other.' But the Prophet did not like it. Then someone mentioned to him the horn. Ziyad said: 'A horn of the Jews.' The Prophet did not like it. He said: 'This is a matter for the Jews.' Then they mentioned to him the bell of Christians (and he again did not like it). Abdallah ibn Zayd became anxious because of the anxiety of the Messenger ﷺ, and he was then taught the call to prayer in his dream. Next day, he came to the Messenger ﷺ and told him about it. He said: 'Messenger of Allah, I was between sleep and wakefulness; all of a sudden a stranger came to me and taught me the call to prayer.' 'Umar ibn Khattab had also previously seen it in a dream, but he (had) kept it hidden for twenty days. The Prophet ﷺ said to me ('Umar): 'What stopped you from telling me?' He said: 'Abdallah ibn Zayd had already told you about it before me; hence I was shy.' Then the Messenger ﷺ said: 'Bilal, stand up and see what Abdallah ibn Zayd tells you to do, then do it.' Bilal then called to prayer.' (Abu Dawud 498).

Abu Bishr added on the authority of Abu Umayr that if Abdallah ibn Zayr had not been ill on that day, he would have been made the muadhdhin himself, and not Bilal.

The full account of his dream is recorded in Abu Dawud 499, followed by various traditions of teaching it to others, including the pious Abu Mahdhurah who refused to cut his hair after the Prophet ﷺ rested his hands on his head before teaching him. (Abu Dawud 501)

The public call to prayer is known as the *adhan*, and the 'private' call to begin the prayer usually said within the mosque is called the *iqamah*. There is a difference of opinion amongst the jurists as to the number of phrases in *adhan* and *iqamah*.

The phrases of the *adhan* are as follows:

'Allahu Akbar!'—'Allah is Most Great'—four times; *'Ash-hadu an la ilaha illal lah'*—'I bear witness that there is no god but Allah'—twice; *'Ash hadu anna Muhammad ar-rasullul lah'*—'I bear witness that Muhammad is the Messenger of Allah' (twice) *'Hayyah 'alas salah'*—'Come to prayer'—twice; *'Hayyah 'alal falah'*—'Come to salvation'—twice; *'Allahu Akbar'*—'Allah is Most Great'—twice; *'La ilaha illal lah'*—'There is no god but Allah'—once at the end.

In the *iqamah* the same phrases are pronounced with the addition of 'The time for prayer has come' twice after giving testimony. (*qad qamatis salah*).

Some scholars have slightly differently variations upon this call—for example, Ahmad ibn Hanbal Malik called 'Allah is Most Great' twice at the beginning, and then 'There is no God but Allah' four times in both places.

The practice of repeating the call in a low voice and then out loud is called tarji or 'repetition of testimony'. It is not compulsory (see Abu Dawud 514)

Abu Mahdhruah recorded that the phrase 'Assalatu khayrum minan nawm'—'Prayer is better than sleep, prayer is better than sleep' was to be pronounced in the first adhan of the morning prayer. (Abu Dawud 501)

The believer listening to the adhan makes a response:

'A'ishah recorded that when the Blessed Messenger ﷺ heard the muadhdhin uttering the testimony, he would say: 'And I too, and I too.' (Abu Dawud 526)

Whenever believers hear the call, they should listen in silence and repeat the phrases in their minds; and when the muadhdhin says 'Come to prayer' and 'Come to your salvation' they should say in reply:

'La hawla wala quwwata illa billah'—'There is no power nor ability to avoid harm or do good except by the help of Allah!'

At the end of the adhan, believers usually recite blessings on Muhammad ﷺ and other prayers. A favourite prayer is:

'Allahhumma rabba hazi hid d'wa tittammati wassalatil Qa imati ati Muhammadanil waseelata wal fadeelata wab'ath-hu maqamam mahmudan illadhee wa at-tahu.'

'O Allah! Lord of this complete prayer of ours, by the blessing of it grant Muhammad ﷺ his eternal rights of intercession, distinction and highest class (in Paradise), and raise him to the promised rank You have promised him.'

Bilal originally used to make the call to prayer from the highest roof in Madinah, the house of a woman of Banu al-Najjar. (Abu Dawud 519)

It is considered good practice for the caller to turn to the right and to the left while calling. (Abu Dawud 520)

There is always a certain space of time left between the adhan and iqamah in the mosque, to give people time to assemble.

'A'ishah recorded: 'The Prophet ﷺ used to offer two light

rakahs between the *adhan* and the *iqamah* of the *fajr* prayer.'

Another version records; "A'ishah said: 'The Prophet ﷺ used to pray two light *rakahs* before the morning prayer after the day dawned and the *muadhdhin* had finished his *adhan*. He would then lie down on his right side until the *Muadhdhin* came to pronounce the *iqamah*.' (Bukhari 22.15.599)

It was pointed out that the *adhan* for the *fajr* prayer was made while it was still during the hours of darkness, so a person still had time to eat quickly before the prayer.

Abdallah ibn Mas'ud recorded: 'The *adhan* pronounced by Bilal should not stop you from taking suhur (light breakfast), for he pronounces the *adhan* at night, so that the one offering the late night prayer (*tahajjud*) might hurry up and the sleeper might wake up. It does not mean that the dawn or morning has started. (Bukhari 11.13.595)

At other times of the day, the Blessed Prophet ﷺ allowed people to take their meals before prayer, if they were ready and had been served.

Ibn 'Umar recorded: 'If the supper is served and the *iqamah* is pronounced, start with the supper and don't be in haste till you finish it.' (Bukhari 11.42.642, Abu Dawud 3748)

However, it should be born in mind that the meals of the Prophet ﷺ were extremely simple; he did not intend that Muslims should sit down and tuck into feasts instead of going to prayer.

Jabir ibn Abdallah recorded: 'Prayer should not be postponed for taking meals nor for any other thing.' (Abu Dawud 3749)

Abdallah ibn Ubayd ibn Umayr recorded: 'I was with my father in the time of Ibn al-Zubayr, sitting beside Abdallah ibn 'Umar. Then Abbad ibn Abdallah ibn al-Zubayr said—'We have heard that the evening meal is taken just before the night prayer.'

Thereupon Abdallah ibn 'Umar said: 'Woe to you! What was their evening meal? Do you think it was like the meal of your father?' (Abu Dawud 3750)

Sometimes the call to prayer came while Muslims were involved in helping their wives and families in the house.

Al-Aswad recorded that he asked 'A'ishah: 'What did the Prophet ﷺ used to do in the house?' She replied: 'He used to busy himself serving his family, and when it was the time for the prayer, he would go for it.' (Bukhari 11.44.644)

The character of the *muadhdhin* has to be trustworthy. If they call too early, or make some other mistake, they have to announce it publicly (Abu Dawud 532—534). It is not considered to be a matter for which a person should be paid (Abu Dawud 531), but should be done for love of Allah.

Once the call has been given, it is considered wrong for a person to continue *nafl* prayers, or to leave the mosque until after the prayer (Abu Dawud 536), except to answer the call of nature or to perform ablution. Of course, there is no prohibition in any case of need—such as an urgent summons, or an accident, or a sudden attack of illness. (Abu Dawud 536 n.228)

Ablution—The Wudu'

.... ❦ ....

ABLUTION BEFORE PRAYER

Muslims have been asked by Allah to pray in a state of ritual purity. This involves cleansing oneself in a particular way known as wudu', according to the command of Allah laid down in the Qur'an:

> 'O ye who believe! When you prepare for prayer wash your faces, and your hands to the elbows; rub your heads; and your feet to the ankles. If you are in a state of ritual impurity bathe your whole body. But if you are ill or on a journey, or you have answered the call of nature or have been in contact with a woman, and there is no water available, then take for yourselves clean sand or earth and rub your faces and hands with it. God does not wish to place you in a difficulty, but to make you clean, and to complete His favour to you that you may be grateful.' (4:43; 5:7)

The object of *wudu'* is to make a person clean, and to prepare him or her for prayer by a symbolic washing away of sins.

Abu Hurayrah recorded: 'When a believer washes his face (in ablution), every sin he contemplated with his eyes will be washed away from his face along with the water (or—with the last drop of water); when he washes his hands, every sin they carried out will be washed off with the water; and when he washes his feet, every sin towards which he walked will be washed away with the water, with the result that one comes out pure from all sins.' (Muslim 475)

'Uthman ibn Affan recorded: 'He who performs ablution well, his sins will seep out of his body, even from under his nails!'

(Muslim 476)

Wudu' is an integral part of Muslim prayer, so much so that prayer is not considered valid without it.

Some *hadiths* concentrate on the moral aspect of purification:

Abu al-Malih reported: 'Just as Allah does not accept charity from goods acquired by embezzlement, so He does not accept prayer without purification.' (Abu Dawud 59)

Musab ibn Sa'd recorded: 'Prayer is not acceptable without purification, neither are gifts accepted from ill-gotten gains, even if you are the Governor of Basra!' (Muslim 433)

Others mention the physical aspect of it. Ritual purification is particularly necessary to restore purity after defilement, and this was caused by any loss of consciousness, or emission of substance from the body, as well as the touching of unclean things:

Abu Hurayrah recorded: 'Allah the Exalted does not accept the prayer of any of you when you are defiled until you perform ablution.' (Abu Dawud 60)

The Blessed Prophet ﷺ explained that purification for prayer was not just a case of getting washed. It had to be done specifically for the purpose of prayer, although one could elevate a normal bath into a *wudu'* by pronouncing the '*Bismillah*' ('In the name of Allah') before commencing. It is the intention to perform ablution that makes the washing into a *wudu'*.

Abu Hurayrah recorded: 'The prayer of a person who does not perform ablution is not valid, and the ablution of a person who does not mention the name of Allah is not valid.' (Abu Dawud 101)

WHEN ABLUTION IS NECESSARY

Prayer, to a Muslim, is such an integral part of everyday life, and the times it occurs and the circumstances surrounding preparation for it so intimate and private, that the *hadiths* on physical ablution might strike the non-Muslim as being rather too down-to-earth, and perhaps even shocking. However, it is not shocking to the Muslim, who knows that Allah has created and sees everything, and who is very well aware of the personal efforts of believers to be clean and pure in body as well as in thought at all times.

Ablution becomes necessary when a Muslim has been rendered ritually 'unclean' or 'impure' by certain specific things leaving the body—blood, semen, urine and faeces—and therefore *wudu'* is required after sexual intercourse or sexual emissions, during and after menstruation and childbirth, after going to the toilet, and after losing consciousness in sleep or illness. It is not generally considered compulsory for blood seeping from a wound, however.

It is therefore necessary to perform *wudu'* after visiting the toilet when one arises in the morning, and again during the day if any of the above things has happened. If the believer has passed from one prayer to another without any breaking action, say from the noon to afternoon prayer, then separate *wudu'* for the later prayer is not necessary. It is possible (though rather unlikely) to pass the entire day in a state of *wudu'* without renewing it.

The reader will bear in mind the primitive conditions under which the Blessed Prophet ﷺ and the early Muslims lived—there was no running water, and water was generally scarce. There were no such things as showers, toilet paper, detergents and so forth. When a *hadith* mentions cleansing after toilet using pebbles, bone or pieces of dried dung, one should consider similar congingency measures one might be obliged to use today if camping rough— one might use grass, leaves and so on.

On the other hand, it is easier to wash the body and feet when one wears just a simple garment, has slip-on sandals, and the water can simply fall on to the earth or on a tiled floor.

CLEANSING WOUNDS

Bleeding from wounds does not render a person ritually unclean, unless the bleeding is from the private parts. Sometimes a wounded person might desire to say the prayers, but be unable to cleanse either the wound, the dressing of the wound, or a bloodstained garment. Only the Hanafi school of Muslims claim that ablution becomes void by bleeding, however, and that *wudu'* must be performed.

Hadiths reveal that the Companions of the Prophet 🕌 used to offer prayer in the battle while their wounds were still bleeding and their garments were smeared with blood. The Prophet 🕌 never commanded them to take off these clothes or perform ablution. (see Abu Dawud 198 n. 94)

Jabir recorded one instance when a companion of the Blessed Messenger 🕌 was praying when an arrow struck him in the leg. (This brave soldier pulled out the arrow and continued to pray, without pausing to disturb his sleeping companion, or to ask for help). 'He took the arrow out and threw it away. (The enemy) then shot three arrows. Then he (the Muslim) bowed and prostrated and afterwards) awoke his companion... When the friend saw the man bleeding, he asked him: 'Glory be to Allah! Why did you not wake me up the first time he shot at you?' He replied: 'I was busy reciting a chapter of the Qur'an, and I did not like to leave it.' (Abu Dawud 198)

The Blessed Prophet 🕌 himself suffered wounds in battle, and yet continued to pray.

Sahl bin Sa'd as-Sa'idi was asked by the people: 'With what was the wound of the Prophet 🕌 treated?' He replied: 'None remains alive among the people who knows better than I. 'Ali brought water in his shield, and Fatimah washed the blood off his face. Then a straw mat was burnt and the wound filled with it.' (Bukhari 5.2.249)

CLEANSING DURING AND AFTER MENSTRUATION

Menstruation is an integral part of womanhood, the regular cycle of producing fertile eggs that are potential human beings. It should never be regarded as something evil or unnatural, but is part of the design of Allah for women.

'A'ishah recorded: 'We set out to perform *hajj*, and when we reached Sarif (a place six miles from Makkah) I began to menstruate. Allah's Messenger ﷺ came upon me while I was weeping. He said: 'What is the matter? Have you begun your period?' I replied: 'Yes.' He said: '(Don't be upset). This is something which Allah has laid down for all the daughters of Adam. So do what all the pilgrims do, with the exception of the circling of the Ka'bah.' (Bukhari 6.3.293)

However, while bleeding it is impossible for a woman to be ritually clean for prayer, so she is obliged to leave off *salah* until her periods finish.

'A'ishah recorded that the Prophet ﷺ said to her: 'Give up the prayer when your menses begin, and when it has finished, wash off the blood and start prayer (again).' (Bukhari 6.30.327)

Periods did not mean that a woman become in any way 'contaminating'. Although they could not pray *salah*, the Blessed Prophet ﷺ was quite content to pray beside a menstruating woman.

Maymunah (one of the Prophet's ﷺ wives) recorded: 'During my menses I never prayed, but I used to sit on the mat beside the praying-place of Allah's Messenger ﷺ. He used to offer the prayer on his sheet, and while bowing down some of his clothes used to touch me.' (Bukhari 6.32.329)

Continuous discharge of blood or other matter in between periods was not considered as menstruation, but classed as a wound or disease.

'A'ishah recorded that Fatimah bint Abu Hubaish came to the Prophet ﷺ and asked whether she should give up saying her prayers because she had continual bleeding from the uterus and could not become clean. Allah's Messenger ﷺ replied: 'No, because this is from a blood vessel and not the menses. So when your real menses begin, give up your prayers, and when it has finished wash off the blood and offer your prayers.' (Bukhari 4.67.228, Abu Dawud 282)

'A'ishah recorded: 'One of the Mothers of the Faithful (i.e. one of Muhammad's ﷺ wives) did i'tikaf while she was having bleeding in between her periods.' (Bukhari 6.12.308)

Umm Salamah (one of the wives of the Blessed Prophet ﷺ recorded that she once asked the Prophet ﷺ to give a decision about a woman who had a (continuous) issue of blood. He said: 'She should work out the number of days and nights during which she used to menstruate each month before she was afflicted with this trouble, and abandon prayer during that period each month. When those days and nights are over, she should take a bath, cover her private parts, and pray.' (Abu Dawud 274)

'A'ishah recorded that Sahlah bint Suhail had a prolonged flow of blood, and came to the Prophet ﷺ for advice. He commanded her to take a bath for every prayer. When it became hard for her, he commanded her to combine the noon and afternoon prayers with one bath, and the sunset and night prayer with one bath, and to take a bath separately for the dawn prayer.' (Abu Dawud 295)

WOMEN ARE NOT REQUIRED TO MAKE UP PRAYERS LOST THROUGH MENSTRUATION

Although women have to make up the days lost through menstruation in the fasting month of Ramadan (which is an annual event) it is not required for them to have the burden of making up for the daily prayers missed each month. This question was raised very early in the history of Islam in the town of Huraura where an extremist sect of Muslims had insisted that women should make up these prayers.

Muadha narrated that a woman asked 'A'ishah: 'Should I offer the prayers which I did not offer because of menstruation?' 'A'ishah said: 'Are you from the Huraura? We were with the Prophet 鹵 and used to menstruate, but he never ordered us to offer (the prayers missed).' (Bukhari 6.22.318, Muslim 660)

ISTANJA, OR CLEANSING AFTER TOILET

Before commencing *wudu'*, a person should first go to the toilet if they have need, and blow their noses, and then begin by cleansing those areas. In the morning, before *wudu'*, it is particularly necessary to rid oneself of matter that has built up in the body and nose during the night.

The Blessed Prophet 鹵 always prayed 'O Allah, I seek refuge in You' every time he entered a toilet. (Abu Dawud 4 etc.)

Zayd ibn Arqam recorded that the Messenger 鹵 said: 'These privies are frequented by the jinns and devils. So whenever any of you go there, you should say: 'I seek refuge in Allah from male and female devils.' ' (Abu Dawud 6, see also Muslim 729)

The Blessed Prophet 鹵 taught that out of respect one should never face or have one's back towards Makkah whilst going to the toilet.

Abu Ayyub al-Ansari recorded that he said: 'If any of you

goes to an open space to answer the call of nature, he should neither face nor turn his back towards the *qiblah*; he should either face east or west.' (Bukhari 4.11.146, Muslim 570)

In conditions where there is no toilet paper or running water, personal cleanliness is trickier than where there are modern conveniences of paper and water.

The Blessed Prophet ﷺ recommended that one should not handle one's private parts with the right hand.

Abu Qatadah recorded: 'Whenever any of you drinks water, he should not breathe into the drinking vessel, and whenever any of you goes to the toilet, he should neither touch his penis nor clean his private parts with his right hand.' (Bukhari 4.18.155, Abu Dawud 31)

Salman recorded that it was said to him: 'Your Prophet ﷺ teaches you about everything, even about excrement!' He replied: 'Yes. He has forbidden us to face the *qiblah* at the time of easing or urinating, or cleansing with the right hand, or cleansing with less than three stones, or with dung or bone.' (Abu Dawud 7, Muslim 504)

The Prophet ﷺ specified that one should wipe oneself with an odd number of times.

Abu Hurayrah recorded: 'When anyone wipes himself clean with pebbles he must make use of an odd number, and when he performs ablution he must snuff some water in his nose and clean it.' (Muslim 458). He added: 'When he wakes from sleep and performs ablution, he must clean his nose three times, for the devil spends the night up the nose!' (Muslim 462)

The Blessed Prophet ﷺ forbade urinating in public places, thoroughfares, under the shade of trees (where people liked to sit); and he forbade people showing their private parts while easing themselves. They should either be in private, or be covered with their garments. (Abu Dawud 15.25)

Although the Blessed Prophet 🕌 insisted on ablution before prayer if one had been to the toilet, it was not compulsory to wash every time one went to the toilet, although this was preferred.

'A'ishah recorded that (one day) the Prophet 🕌 urinated and 'Umar came up behind him with a jug of water. He said: 'What is this, 'Umar?' He said: 'Water for you to perform ablution with.' He said: 'I have not been commanded to perform ablution every time I urinate. If it were so, it would become a *sunnah*.' (Abu Dawud 42)

Normally, the Blessed Prophet 🕌 did take water and sprinkle his private parts with it. (Abu Dawud 166-168) It is interesting to note that the Prophet's nephew Anas ibn Malik usually had the job of seeing to the Prophet's 🕌 needs in this respect.

'Whenever the Prophet 🕌 used to answer the call of nature, I, along with another boy, used to carry a tumbler full of water and an *'anza* (spear-headed stick) which the Blessed Prophet 🕌 used for his cleansing' (Bukhari 4.15.152, 4.17.154). These lads got the nicknames Sahib an-Nalain and Sahib at-Tahur from their tasks of carrying the Prophet's 🕌 nalain (slip-on shoes) and tahur (water-pot).

CLEANSING AFTER INTERCOURSE

A person who has had sexual intercourse and has not yet taken a full bath is in the state called junub. People who are junub are not prevented from going out and about on their normal business, but they are expected to take a full and complete bath (known as *ghusl*) before prayer.

It is not necessary to take a full bath before sleeping, however. 'A'ishah recorded: Whenever the Prophet 🕌 intended to sleep while he was junub, he used to wash his private parts and perform ablution like that for the prayer (and then sleep). (Bukhari 5.28.286, Muslim 597)

Abdallah ibn Abul Qais recorded that he asked 'A'ishah what the Prophet ﷺ did after having sexual intercourse. Did he take a bath before going to sleep, or did he sleep before taking a bath? She said: 'He did all these. Sometimes he took a bath and then slept, and sometimes he performed ablution only and went to sleep.' (Muslim 603)

The Blessed Prophet ﷺ set a high standard of personal cleanliness for which his wives must have been grateful. He recommended ablution between repeated acts of sexual intercourse.

Abu Rafi recorded that one day the Prophet ﷺ had intercourse with all his wives (there were nine at that time!). He took a bath after each intercourse. I asked him: 'Messenger of Allah, why don't you make it a single bath?' He replied: 'This way is more purifying, better and cleaner.' (Abu Dawud 219, see also Muslim 605)

Other *hadiths* that suggest he did not always do this (e.g. Muslim 606, Abu Dawud 218—where he had sexual intercourse with (all) his wives in one day, with a single bath).

If a man has sexual intercourse with his wife but there is no emission, ablution as for *wudu'* is sufficient, and *ghusl* is not necessary before prayer.

Zayd bin Khalid al-Juhani asked 'Uthman ibn Affan about a man who had intercourse with his wife without emission. 'Uthman replied: 'He should perform ablution like that for the prayer, after washing his private parts.' 'Uthman added: 'I heard that from Allah's Messenger ﷺ.' (Bukhari 5.30.291)

A full description of the practice of the Blessed Prophet ﷺ

was supplied by his wives:

'A'ishah recorded that when Allah's Messenger ﷺ bathed because of sexual intercourse, he first washed his hands; he then poured water with his right hand on to his left hand and washed his private parts. He then performed ablution as for prayer. He then took some water and moved his fingers through the roots of his hair. When they were properly moistened, he then poured three handfuls of water on his head and poured water over his body, and finally washed his feet.' (Muslim 616)

Maymunah recorded: 'I placed the water for the Prophet ﷺ to wash himself after sexual intercourse. He lowered the vessel and poured water on his right hand. He then washed it two or three times. He then poured water over his private parts and washed them with his left hand. Then he put the pot on the ground and wiped it. He then rinsed his mouth and snuffed up water, and washed his face and hands. He then poured water over his head and body. Then he moved aside and washed his feet. I handed him a garment, but he began to shake the water off his body. I mention it to Ibrahim. They said that the Companions did not think there was any harm in using a garment (to dry off the water), but they didn't make a habit of it.' (Abu Dawud 245)

Ablution is necessary for a sexual emission as the result of a wet dream, or a small emission resulting from sexual thoughts even if the complete sexual act does not take place.

Umm Salamah (one of the wives of the Prophet ﷺ recorded that Umm Sulaim wife of Abu Talhah (the Prophet's ﷺ aunt) came to Allah's Messenger ﷺ and said: 'O Allah's Messenger! Truly Allah is not shy of the truth. Is it necessary for a woman to take a bath after she has had a wet dream?' Allah's Messenger ﷺ replied: 'Yes, if she notices a discharge.' (Bukhari 5.23.280, Muslim 607 etc. Abu Dawud 237)

It was similar for a man. Apparently the Prophet's ﷺ son-in-law had a particular problem with emission of semen even if he had not had full intercourse.

'Ali recorded: 'My fluid flowed excessively. I used to take a bath until my back cracked! I mentioned it to the Prophet ﷺ, or the fact was mentioned to him (by someone else). He said: 'Do not do this. When you find fluid, wash your penis and perform ablution as you do for prayer, and take a bath when you have (full) seminal emission.' (Abu Dawud 206)

Sahl ibn Hunaif, a companion with a similar problem, asked: 'What should I do if it smears my clothes?' He replied: 'It is sufficient if you take a handful of water and sprinkle it on your clothing where you find it has marked it.' (Abu Dawud 210)

When a full bath was taken after intercourse, it was not necessary for a woman with tightly plaited hair to undo it all in order to wash it. The Blessed Prophet indicated that it was sufficient to throw three handfuls of water on the hair, so long as it was all properly moistened.

Umm Salamah recorded that she said: 'Messenger of Allah, I have my hair in tight plaits—should I undo it for taking a bath after intercourse?' He said: 'No, it is enough for you to throw three handfuls of water on your head and then pour water over yourself, and you shall be purified.' (Muslim 643)

The Prophet ﷺ and his wives always performed ablution together, from the same vessel of water—and the Blessed Prophet ﷺ was usually courteous enough to let his wife bathe first.

Ibn Abbas recorded that Maymunah told him that she and the Messenger of Allah ﷺ took a bath from a single vessel; and that the Messenger took his bath from the water left over by Maymunah. (Muslim 631, 632)

Umm Salamah's daughter Zaynab recorded that Umm

Salamah and the Blessed Prophet ﷺ usually took their bath from the same vessel. (Muslim 633)

'A'ishah similarly recorded: 'I and the Messenger of Allah ﷺ took a bath from a single vessel, which was placed between us, and he would get ahead of me, so that I would say: 'Spare some water for me, spare some water for me!' (Muslim 630)

CLEANSING AFTER UNCONSCIOUSNESS

Whenever a person has slept deeply, fresh *wudu'* is necessary before prayer. (See Bukhari 4.37.183)

Ablution was not broken, however, by someone in the mosque who had merely dozed while sitting there.

Anas recorded that the people stood up for prayer and the Messenger of Allah was whispering to someone, and did not start the prayer until after some of the people of the people had dozed off (Muslim 731)

Qatadah recorded that he heard Anas say that the companion of the Prophet ﷺ dozed off and then offered prayer, but did not perform fresh ablution. (Muslim 733)

THE DESCRIPTION OF *WUDU'*

Having dealt with this necessary cleansing first, the Blessed Prophet ﷺ then laid down a particular pattern of performing *wudu'*. There are many traditions describing it in detail, as for example that of 'Uthman ibn Affan, recorded by his freed slave Humran:

'I saw 'Uthman ibn Affan when he performed ablution. He poured water over his hands three times and then washed them. He then rinsed his mouth and then cleansed his nose with water (three times). He then washed his right arm up to the elbow three times, then washed his left arm in similar manner; then wiped his

head; then his left foot in similar manner, then said: 'I saw the Messenger of Allah ﷺ performing ablution like this ablution of mine.' The he said: 'He who performs ablution like this ablution of mine, and then offers two *rak'ahs* of prayer without allowing his thoughts to be distracted, Allah will pardon all his past sins.' (Abu Dawud 106, Muslim 436)

Ata ibn Yasar recorded: 'Ibn Abbas performed ablution and washed his face (in the following way)—he ladled out a handful of water, rinsed his mouth and washed his nose with it by drawing in water and then blowing it out. He then took another handful of water and did like this (gesturing) joining both his hands, and washed his face, took another handful of water and washed his right forearm, then another handful and washed his left forearm, and passed wet hands over his head, and took another handful of water and poured it over his right foot (up to his ankles) and washed it thoroughly, and similarly took another handful of water and washed thoroughly his left foot (up to ankles), and said: 'I saw Allah's Messenger ﷺ performing ablution in this way.' (Bukhari 4.7.142)

It was important to wash thoroughly, especially the bits one might be tempted to be lazy over.

Abdallah ibn 'Amr recorded: 'Once Allah's Messenger ﷺ remained behind us on one journey, and caught us up while we were performing ablution for the 'asr prayer for which we were late. We were just passing wet hands over our feet (i.e. not washing them properly because they were in a hurry), so the Prophet ﷺ called to us in a loud voice and said two or three times: 'Save your heels from the fire!' (Bukhari 3.31.96)

Khalid recorded: 'The Prophet ﷺ saw a person offering prayer, and on the back of his foot a small place equal to the space of a dirham remained unwashed; the water did not reach it. The Prophet ﷺ commanded him to repeat the ablution and prayer.' (Abu Dawud 175)

The usual routine for performing ablution by believers is (a) to wash the hands up to the wrist, starting with the right hand,

(b) to rinse the mouth with water from the right hand

(c) to snuff water up the nose from the right palm, and squeeze it out with the left hand,

(d) to wash the forearms up to the elbows, starting with the right,

(e) to wash the face and head by splashing the face then wetting the hands and wiping the forehead, taking the fingers round to the nape of the neck and then bringing them back to the forehead,

(f) to clean the ears by inserting wet index fingers, twisting round the folds of the ears and passing the thumb behind the ears from the bottom upwards,

(g) and to wash the feet up to the ankles, starting with the right, making sure no part is left dry—particularly between toes.

Rubbing over the socks instead of washing the feet is permissible in certain circumstances, so long as the socks have been put on after performing an ablution earlier. Similarly, if there is wound covered by some medical dressing on any part of the body that needs ablution, it is permissible to just wipe over the dressing with a wet hand.

Other *hadiths* mention that it is sometimes permissible to wipe the hand over the turban if the head was clean previously and if it would cause difficulty to remove it. (Abu Dawud 147—165)

Many women wipe their hands over their hijab if their hair is clean beneath.

Al-Mughirah ibn Shubah recorded: The Messenger of Allah ﷺ performed ablution and wiped his forelock and turban. Another version says: The Messenger of Allah ﷺ wiped his socks and his forelock and his turban.' (Abu Dawud 150)

Ablutions remained valid for more than one prayer, providing that one remained in a condition of cleanliness.

Buraydah, on the authority of his father, recorded: The Messenger of Allah ﷺ performed five prayers with the same ablution on the occasion of the capture of Makkah, and he wiped over his socks. 'Umar said to him: 'I saw you doing a thing today that you never did.' He said: 'I did it deliberately.' (Abu Dawud 172)

Wudu' ends with *du'a* prayer:

'Ashhadu an la ilaha illalah wahdahu la shareeka lahu, wa ashhadu an-na Muhammadan abduhu wa rasuluhu.'

'I bear witness there there is no God except Allah Alone. He is One and has no partner. And I bear witness that Muhammad ﷺ is His servant and messenger.' (Muslim)

'*Allah hummaj 'alnee minat tawwabeen, waj 'alnee minal muta tah-hireen.*'

'O Allah, make me among those who are penitent and make me among the pure.' (Tirmidhi)

TAYAMMUM, IF NO WATER IS AVAILABLE

Washing before prayer is carried out either with water, or without water if there is none. The latter washing is to wipe over the same parts one would have washed with water with the dust or sand of the earth. It is known as *tayammum*.

'If you find no water, then take for yourselves clean sand or earth, and rub your faces and hands with it. God does not wish to place you in difficulty, but to make you clean, and to complete His favour to you, that you may know gratitude.' (*Sūrah* 5:7)

The background story to the revelation of that verse is quite touching, and reveals the Prophet's ﷺ great tenderness for his young wife 'A'ishah:

'A'ishah recorded: 'We went with the Messenger of Allah ﷺ on one of his journeys, and when we reached the place Baida or Dhat al-Jaish my necklace was broken, and the Messenger ﷺ and others stayed there searching for it. There was neither any water in that place, nor did they have any water with them. Some people came to my father Abu Bakr and said: 'Do you see what 'A'ishah has done? She has detained the Messenger of Allah ﷺ and those with him, and there is no water either here or with them.' So Abu Bakr came there while the Messenger of Allah ﷺ was sleeping with his head on my thigh. My father said: 'You have delayed the Messenger of Allah ﷺ and his companions, and there is no water here nor with them.' He scolded me and uttered what Allah wanted him to utter, and nudged my hips with his hand. Nothing prevented me from stirring but for the fact that the Messenger of

Allah ﷻ was lying on my thigh. The Messenger ﷺ slept until it was dawn in this waterless place. (It was) then Allah revealed the verses pertaining to *tayammum*, and they (all) performed *tayammum*. Usayd ibn al-Hudayr, who was one of the leaders, said: 'This is not the first of your blessings, O family of Abu Bakr!' Then we made my camel stand, and found my necklace beneath it!' (Muslim 714, see also Bukhari 4.32)

Some Muslims have made unnecessary burdens for themselves by believing it was impossible for them to pray in a certain situation because they had no water with which to wash. The Blessed Prophet ﷺ made it clear that the need to perform *wudu'* was not intended as a difficulty for anyone. Any available water would do equally well for the washing, and if there was no water, then *tayammum* was sufficient.

Imran ibn Husayn al-Khuzai recorded: Allah's Messenger ﷺ saw a person sitting aloof and not praying with the people. He asked him, 'O such-a-one! What prevented you from offering prayer with the others?' He replied: 'O Allah's Messenger, I am in unclean state, and there is no water.' The Prophet ﷺ said: 'Perform *tayammum* with clean earth—that will be sufficient for you.' (Bukhari 7.9.344)

The Prophet's ﷺ friend Ammar once wished to purify himself but could find no water, so he rolled himself in the dust 'just as a beast rolls itself.' He recorded:

'I came to the Messenger of Allah ﷺ and told him what I had done, and he said: 'It would have been enough for you to do thus,' and he struck the ground with his hands once and wiped his right hand with his left hand, and the exterior of his palms, and his face.' (Muslim 716)

The generally accepted method for the performance of *Tayammum* is to wipe the face once, and wipe the hands up to the elbows.

Ammar ibn Yasir recorded: 'They (the companions of the Prophet ﷺ) wiped with pure earth to offer the dawn prayer in the company of the Messenger of Allah ﷺ. They struck the ground with their palms and wiped their faces once. Then they repeated and struck the ground with their palms once again and wiped their arms completely up to the shoulders and up to the armpits with the inner sides of their hands.' (Abu Dawud 318— other chains also recorded this; Ibn Wahb did not mention the words 'shoulders' and 'armpits'.)

Sometimes the Prophet ﷺ struck a wall and not the earth (Abu Dawud 329-331). This happened when the Prophet ﷺ had just come out of a public toilet, and wished to purify himself before greeting someone he met on the street.

However, the Blessed Prophet ﷺ did not encourage people to use the *tayammum* when there was water available. On one occasion his friend Abu Dharr had been goat-driving, and had been in a state of sexual defilement for five or six days. When he came to the Blessed Prophet ﷺ he rebuked him and called for water to be brought for him:

'A black slave-girl... brought a vessel which contained water. She then concealed me by drawing a curtain and I concealed myself behind a she-camel and took a bath. I felt as if I had thrown away a mountain from me.' The Prophet ﷺ said: 'Clean earth is a means of ablution for a Muslim, even for ten years; but when you find water, you should make it touch your skin, for that is better.' (Abu Dawud 332)

WHAT KINDS OF WATER ARE CONSIDERED PURE?

The Blessed Prophet ﷺ included any water, even water that was not necessarily of the purest quality.

Abdallah ibn 'Umar said: The Prophet ﷺ was asked about water (in desert country) frequented by animals and wild beasts. He replied: 'When there is enough to fill two pitchers, it is not impure.' (Abu Dawud 63)

The well of Buda'ah sometimes suffered from unclean things such as dead animals and dirty cloths being washed into it by the flood of water during heavy rains. When questioned about using its water, the Blessed Prophet ﷺ replied:

'Truly water is pure, and is not defiled by anything.' (Abu Dawud 67)

Sea water was perfectly permissible for ablution (Abu Dawud 83), and so was a drink made from fruit soaked in water—although this was not recommended (Abu Dawud 84-87).

Water kept in receptacles in the house might have been used by more than one person, or even by an animal, and not be considered impure or defiled. Once the Prophet's ﷺ wife Maymunah saw her husband perform ablution from the water in a large bowl from which she had just cleansed herself after they had been intimate together.

Ibn Abbas recorded: The Prophet ﷺ and Maymunah (one of his wives) used to take a bath from a single pot.' (Bukhari 5.4.253)

Once again, the Blessed Prophet ﷺ claimed that water was not defiled. (Abu Dawud 68)

'A'ishah recorded: 'I and Messenger of Allah ﷺ took a bath from a single vessel while we were sexually defiled.' (Abu Dawud 77)

There are *hadiths* that men and women should not perform ablution from the same water, but as we have seen, this was not the practice during the lifetime of the Blessed Prophet ﷺ.

Ibn 'Umar recorded: 'Men and women used to perform

ablution from one vessel together during the lifetime of the Messenger of Allah ﷺ.' (Abu Dawud 79, 80; Bukhari 4.45)

'A'ishah recorded: 'The Prophet ﷺ and I used to take a bath from a single pot called 'Faraq'.' (Bukhari 5.3.250)

The Prophet ﷺ did specifically mention that if the water was not running water, (i.e. water in a bath or bowl or small pond), one thing would certainly make it unclean—and that was if anyone had urinated in it. Nobody should urinate in a bath, even by accident, and then expect to be made ritually clean by a wash in it!

Abu Hurayrah recorded: 'None of you should urinate in standing water, and then wash in it.' (Muslim 554, see also Abu Dawud 69-70)

Water was not made impure if a household pet had sipped at it. If a cat or dot licked from a bowl, it should be washed once for the cat, and seven times for the dog. (Abu Dawud 71-74)

On one occasion Abu Qatadah poured water into a vessel ready to perform his ablution, when a cat came and drank out of it. Instead of throwing it away, he allowed the cat to drink some more. He saw his niece looking at him and said: 'Are you surprised, my niece?' She said: 'Yes.' He then reported the Messenger of Allah ﷺ as saying:

'It is not unclean; it is one of those who live amongst us.' (Abu Dawud 75)

EXCESSIVE *WUDU'*

The Blessed Prophet ﷺ expected people to perform *wudu'* before prayer when they were in a state of impurity, and it did not matter if they did extra *wudu'* before a prayer when they had *not* actually become defiled in between the prayers. However, he did sound a warning that just as in private devotions certain people

would develop a fanatical and excessive tendency, so it could also apply to those seeking to excessively purify themselves.

Abdallah ibn Mughaffal recorded that his son had heard the Blessed Messenger ﷺ say: 'In this community there will be some people who will exceed the limits in purification as well as in supplication.' (Abu Dawud 86)

Excessive obsession with becoming ritually clean actually implies a lack of trust and faith in Allah rather than supreme faith and servitude; it implies that the person does not believe they have been granted cleanliness by Allah, and if they are in this state of mind because of some sin, it implies that they do not believe Allah will forgive them when they ask His forgiveness.

'Amr ibn Shuayb recorded: 'If anyone performs acts of ablution more than three times, he has done wrong, transgressed, and acted wickedly.' (Nisai, Ibn Majah)

The true Muslim knows that Allah is full of love and compassion, and does not seek our hardship or our suffering, and that human beings should never consider themselves to be impure or defiled beings, because:

'Truly, We have honoured the sons of Adam... and We have conferred upon them special favours, above a great part of Our creation.' (*Sūrah* 17:70)

It is the wrong beliefs and vicious acts of some humans that makes them truly 'defiled beings', and not natural things like the emissions from the body.

'O believers! Truly the pagans are unclean.' (*Sūrah* 9:28)

Abu Hurayrah recorded that one day he (saw) the Prophet ﷺ on a path leading to Madinah when he was in a state of defilement, and he slipped away and took a bath (instead of greeting him). The Messenger ﷺ went looking for him, and when he came he said: 'O Abu Hurayrah, where did you go?' He said: 'Messenger of Allah, I met you when I was defiled, and I did not like to (be) in your company before taking a bath.' Upon this, the Messenger of Allah 🕮 said: 'Glory be to Allah! Truly a believer is never defiled!' (Muslim 722)

On one occasion, the Blessed Prophet 🕮 was asked about two men who performed *tayammum* because there was no water, but before they actually prayed they did come across some water. One of the men then performed *wudu'* with the water, but the other did not. Which one was correct? The Blessed Messenger said to the first man: 'You followed the *sunnah*, and your first prayer was enough for you.' He said to the second man, who purified and prayed twice: 'For you there is double the reward.' (Abu Dawud 338)

Incidentally, it is perfectly permissible for a man who cares for his wife to kiss her before going off to prayers, even if he has already performed ablution. It does not break *wudu'*, and was the *sunnah* of the Blessed Prophet himself 🕮.

'A'ishah recorded: 'The Prophet 🕮 kissed me, and did not perform ablution' (Abu Dawud 178-180)

A COMPLETE BATH IS REQUESTED FOR FRIDAY PRAYERS

For Friday prayers, a complete bath was recommended instead of the simple *wudu'*. It was not obligatory, in the sense that a Friday prayer done without it would not be valid, but the Blessed Prophet 🕮 stressed its importance—particularly as during his lifetime the Muslims worked hard and wore woollen clothing which could become malodorous enough to be a distraction for others during public prayer. When one was praying one's own personal prayers, and not having to spend time sitting together listening to a sermon, it was less important—although the Prophet always stressed cleanliness and wearing clean garments for prayer.

The Prophet's wife Hafsah recorded: The Prophet said: 'It is necessary for every adult to go for Friday (prayer), and for everyone who goes, washing is necessary.' Abu Dawud 342)

'A'ishah was rather more blunt. She said: 'The people were workers, and they would come for Friday prayer in the same condition, so it was said to them: 'Would to God that you would wash yourselves.' (Abu Dawud 352)

'Amr ibn Abi 'Amr and Ikramah received the full explanation from Ibn Abbas: 'Some people came from Iraq and said: 'Ibn Abbas, do you regard taking a bath on Friday as obligatory?' He said: 'No, it is only a means of cleanliness, but it is better if one washes oneself. Anyone who does not take a bath, has not missed something compulsory. I will tell you how the bath commenced. The people were poor and used to wear woollen clothes, and would carry loads on their backs. Their mosque was small and its roof was low, it was a sort of trellis of vine. The Messenger of Allah once came out on a hot day and the people perspired profusely in the woollen clothes so much that foul smell emitted from them and disturbed each other. When that foul smell reached the Messenger he said: 'O people, anoint with the best oil and perfume you have.' Ibn Abbas then said: 'Then Allah the Exalted provided wealth to the people, and they wore clothes other than the woollen, and were spared from work, and their mosques became vast. The foul smell that caused trouble to them became non-existent.' (Abu Dawud 353)

Be that as it may, everyone knows the unpleasantness of being obliged to sit and move near a person who suffers from body odours. It does cause a distraction and is unpleasant for others, so attention should be paid to this.

WASHING CLEAN GARMENTS SPOILED BY STAINS

The Blessed Prophet ﷺ was always a very practical man, and did not go to extremes. If a garment was clean from dirt and stains, it was perfectly permissible to pray in it. When a person had a garment that was basically clean, but had become partially stained by some body fluid, the Prophet ﷺ considered it unnecessary to wash the entire garment if it was inconvenient—simply wetting the stained area and rubbing out the stain was sufficient. The Prophet ﷺ made this ruling for blood-stains, sexual emissions, and urine.

Umm Qais daughter of Mihsan reported that she came to the Messenger of Allah ﷺ with her little son who had not attained the age of solid food. The Messenger ﷺ sat him on his lap, and the little chap promptly urinated on his clothes. He sent for water and sprinkled it over his clothes, but did not wash them. (Abu Dawud 374, Muslim 563, Bukhari 4.63.222-223)

He did, however, differentiate between the urine of a male or female child.

Lubabah daughter of al-Harith recorded that Husayn (the Prophet's ﷺ grandson) was sitting on his lap and passed water on him. I said: 'Put on another cloth, and give me your wrapper to wash.' He said: 'The urine of a female child should be washed (thoroughly), but the urine of a male child needs only sprinkling over.' (Abu Dawud 375)

Abu al-Samh recorded: Once Hasan or Husayn (the Prophet's ﷺ grandsons) was brought to him and he passed water on his chest. I came to wash it. He said: 'It is only the urine of a female which should be washed; the urine of a male can be sprinkled over.' (Abu Dawud 376)

Scholars do disagree on this point, however, and many hold

that all sorts of urine are equal—and indeed they are both unpleasant on clothing!

Incidentally, there is a famous incident of a rather ignorant Bedouin coming into the mosque and urinating against the wall. The worshippers were outraged, but the Prophet 鬱 did not make a fuss or let anyone disturb or embarass him. When he had finished, he simply sent for a bucket of water and poured it over the place, and said to the offended Muslims: 'You have been sent to make things easy, and not to make them difficult!' (Bukhari 4.60.218; 4.61.219)

As regards other stains, menstruating women used to examine their clothing to see if there were any bloodstains on the garments. If they saw any stains they washed the garments. If there was just a small smear, it could be dampened and rubbed off, even perhaps by spitting on it to moisten it. That was enough.

Abu Nadrah recorded: 'The Messenger of Allah 鬱 spat on his clothes and rubbed part of it.' (Abu Dawud 389-390)

Asma ('A'ishah's sister) recorded: 'A woman came to the Prophet 鬱 and said: 'If any of us gets menses on her clothes, what should she do?' He replied: 'She should (take hold of the soiled place), rub it, and put it in the water and rub it in order to remove the traces of blood, and then rinse it. Then she can pray in it.' (Bukhari 4.67.227)

'A'ishah recorded: 'Each wife (of the Prophet) had a particular shirt which she would wear while menstruating or when sexually defiled. If she ever got a drop of blood on it she would simply rub it off by spitting on it (and rubbing it).' (Abu Dawud 364)

'A'ishah recorded: I was lying with the Messenger of Allah 鬱 and we had our garment over us, and we had put a blanket over it. When the day broke, the Messenger 鬱 took the blanket, wore it, and went out to offer the dawn prayer. He then sat (in the mosque among the people). A man told him: 'Messenger of Allah, I can see a spot of blood!' The Messenger ﷺ pulled it from around him and sent it to me folded in the hand of a slave, and said: 'Wash it and dry it and sent it back to me.' I sent for my vessel and washed it; I then dried it and returned it to him. When the Messenger ﷺ came at noon, he had the blanket over him.' (Abu Dawud 388)

The same applied to seminal fluid. If any of these markings was still fresh and fluid, it would be a simple matter to just rinse the affected area and wash it away.

'A'ishah recorded: 'I used to wash the traces of janaba (semen) from the clothes of the Prophet ﷺ and he would go off for prayers while they were still wet.' (Bukhari 4.68.229; 4.69.233)

Abdallah ibn Shihab al-Khaulani recorded that he stayed in the house of 'A'ishah, where he had a wet dream, so in the morning he washed his clothes. 'A'ishah's maid-servant saw this, and told her. She sent him a message: 'What prompted you to do that with your clothes?' He told her that he had seen in a dream what a sleeper sees. She said: 'Was there (any mark of the fluid) on your clothes?' He said: 'No.' She said: 'You need only have washed it if you found anything. Whenever I found anything dried up on the garment of the Messenger of Allah ﷺ, I used to scrape it off with my finger-nails!' (Muslim 572—See also Muslim 566-571)

The Blessed Prophet ﷺ disapproved of long robes that trailed on the ground, but if one happened to dirty one's garment in this way and there were marks, the person was not prevented from praying in it.

Umm Salamah recorded: 'The Messenger of Allah ﷺ said: 'What comes after it cleanses it.' (Abu Dawud 383)

If a person had trod on something and soiled his or her shoes, they were made clean again by rubbing them on earth. (Abu Dawud 385-7)

WASHING OVER THE SOCKS

The teaching of the Blessed Prophet's ﷺ nephew and son-in-law 'Ali revealed that sometimes the Prophet used to perform ablution while still wearing his shoes:

Mughira ibn Shuba recorded: I was on a journey with the Messenger of Allah ﷺ when he said: 'Mughira, take hold of this jar (of water).' I took it and went out with him. The Messenger ﷺ proceeded until he was out of my sight. He relieved himself and then came back, and he was wearing a tight-sleeved Syrian gown. He tried to get his forearms out, but the sleeve of the gown was very narrow, so he brought his hands out from under the gown and I poured water over (them), and he performed aboution for prayer, then wiped over his socks and prayed.' (Muslim 527, Bukhari 4.36.182)

Mughira's son Urwa added that his father had said: 'I bent down to take off his socks, but he said: 'Leave them, for my feet were clean when I put them on,' and he only wiped over them.' (Muslim 529, Abu Dawud 151)

Ibn Abbas recorded that 'Ali went into his house after he had passed water. He then called for water for ablution. We brought him a vessel containing water and placed it before him. He said: 'O Ibn Abbas, may I not show you how the Messenger of Allah ﷺ used to perform ablution?' I replied: 'Why not?' He then tipped the vessel over his hand and washed it. He then put his right hand in the vessel and poured water over the other hand and washed his hands up to the wrist. He then rinsed his mouth and snuffed up water. He then put both of his hands together into the water and threw it upon his face. He then inserted both of his thumbs in the front part of the ears. He did like that twice or thrice. He then took a handful of water and poured it over his forehead and left it running down his face. He then washed his forearms up to the elbows three times. He then wiped his head and the back of his ears. he then put both of his hands together in the water and took a handful of it and threw it upon his foot. He had a shoe on his foot which he twisted (or washed): 'Do you wash your foot while it is in the shoe?' He replied: 'Yes, while it is in the shoe.' This question and answer were repeated thrice.' (Abu Dawud 117)

'He then took a handful of water and sprinkled it over his right foot in his shoe and wiped the upper part of his foot with his one hand, and beneath the shoe with his other hand. He did the same with his left foot.' (Abu Dawud 137, on the authority of Ata ibn Yasar quoting Ibn Abbas.)

Abu Buraydah specifically mentioned the pair of 'black and simple socks' sent to the Blessed Prophet 變 by the Negus of Abyssinia, and that he 'performed ablution and wiped over them.' (Abu Dawud 155)

Washing over the socks after previous ablution was allowed for twenty-four hours after the first ablution, or for three days if one was on a journey.

It seems that sometimes the Blessed Prophet 變 even prayed while still wearing his sandals, so long as they were clean.

'Amr ibn Shuayb, on his father's authority, said that his grandfather reported: 'I saw the Messenger of Allah 變 praying both barefooted and wearing sandals.' (Abu Dawud 653)

Abu Maslamah asked Anas ibn Malik whether the Prophet 變 had ever prayed with his shoes on. He replied: 'Yes.' (Bukhari 8.24.383)

Abu Sa'id al-Khudri recorded: 'While the Messenger 變 was

leading the companions in prayer he took off his sandals and laid them on his left side; so when the people saw this they removed their sandals. When the Messenger ﷺ finished his prayer, he asked: 'What made you remove your sandals?' They replied: 'We saw you remove your sandals, so we removed ours.' The Messenger ﷺ then said: 'Gabriel came to me and informed me that there was dirt on them. When any of you comes to the mosque he should look; if he finds dirt on his sandals, he should wipe it off and pray in them.' (Abu Dawud 650) The implication was that it was not necessary otherwise.

ON NOT WEARING TOO MUCH SCENT

Muslim women are requested not to wear perfume when they go to the mosque, as their sweet scents prove a distraction to a man trying to pray. However, it is important to recognise that some of the heavy scents and attars worn by men can be just as disturbing, and sometimes so powerful as to be offensive.

The *hadiths* recommend the use of a touch of perfume—not so much as to be offensive or a distraction to others, but in order to freshen and lighten the atmosphere of the public prayer. It is not good practice to douse oneself in so much attar, (or after-shave or the many modern body-perfumes) so that other people can hardly breathe!

Abu Sa'id al-Khudri and Abu Hurayrah recorded: 'If anyone takes a bath on a Friday, puts on his best clothes, applies a touch of perfume if he has any, then goes to the congregational prayer, and takes care not to step over people, then prays what Allah has prescribed for him, then keeps silent from the time his Imam comes out until he finishes his prayer, it will atone for his sins during the previous week.' (Abu Dawud 343)

The Blessed Prophet ﷺ particularly disliked the scent made

from saffron known as khalq, which was generally used by women, but was often worn by men too.

Al-Rabi ibn Anas, quoting his two grandfathers, said: 'We heard Abu Musa say—the Messenger of Allah 🕮 said: 'Allah does not accept the prayer of a man who has any khalq on his body!' (Abu Dawud 4166)

Ammar ibn Yasir recorded: 'The angels do not come near three—the dead body of the unbeliever, one who anoints himself with khalq, and one who is sexually defiled except he performs ablution.' (Abu Dawud 4168 and 4164)

The Prophet 🕮 disliked it so intensely that he refused to touch anyone wearing it.

Al-Walid ibn Uqbah said: 'When the Prophet of Allah 🕮 had conquered Makkah, the people began to bring their boys and he would invoke a blessing on them and touch their heads. I was brought, but as I had been perfumed with khalq, he would not touch me.' (Abu Dawud 4169)

Anas ibn Malik recorded: 'A man came to the Messenger of Allah 🕮 and he had the mark of yellowness (of saffron). The Prophet 🕮 rarely mentioned anything he disliked in front of a person. When he went away, he said: 'Would you tell this man that he should wash this off him!' (Abu Dawud 4170)

GARLIC AND ONIONS

For the same reason, the Prophet 🕮 banned the eating of garlic or onions before coming to prayer.

Abu Hurayrah recorded: 'The Messenger of Allah 🕮 said: 'He who eats of this plant (garlic) should not approach our mosque and should not harm us with the odour of garlic!' (Muslim 1143)

Jabir recorded: 'The Messenger of Allah 🕮 forbade the

eating of onions and leeks before prayer. When we were over-powered by our desire (to eat them) we ate them. Upon this, he said: 'He who eats of this offensive plant must not approach our mosque; for the angels are harmed by the same things as men!' (Muslim 1145)

Abu Sa'id recorded: 'We, the companions of the Prophet ﷺ fell upon this plant (i.e. the garlic), because we were hungry. We ate it to our heart's content, and then made our way to the mosque. The Messenger ﷺ sensed its odour and said: 'He who takes anything of this offensive plant must not come near us in the mosque.' The people (therefore) said: 'Its use has been forbidden! Its use has been forbidden!' This reached the Prophet ﷺ and he said: 'O people, I cannot forbid (the use of a thing) which Allah has made lawful, but (this) is a plant the odour of which is repugnant to me.' (Muslim 1149) (see also Abu Dawud 3813-3820, Bukhari 12.78.814-815)

However, it must be made clear that it was the powerful smell of raw onions and garlic on the breath that the Prophet ﷺ objected to. He had nothing against the eating of those vegetables as such, and was quite happy to eat onions and garlic himself when they were properly cooked, as this took away the smell.

Mu'awiyah ibn Qurrah recorded: 'If it is necessary to eat them, make them 'dead' by cooking.' (Abu Dawud) 3818)

In fact, onions were included in the very last meal that the Prophet ﷺ ate on earth.

Khalid recorded: Abu Ziyad Khiyar ibn Salamah asked 'A'ishah about onions. She replied: 'The last food which the Messenger of Allah ﷺ ate was some which contained onions.' (Abu Dawud 3820)

Preparation For Prayer

············ ❦ ············

QIBLAH—THE DIRECTION OF PRAYER

When the Blessed Prophet ﷺ first came to Madinah, he offered his prayers facing the Baitul-Maqdis (the Holy Temple) of Jerusalem. This practice continued for sixteen or seventeen months, until a specific revelation gave him the direction of Makkah as qiblah.

Anas recorded: 'The Messenger ﷺ used to pray towards Bait-ul-Maqdis, when it was revealed (to him): 'Indeed, We see the turning of the face to heaven, wherefore We shall surely cause you turn towards a *qiblah* which shall please you. So turn your face towards the sacred mosque (i.e. the Ka'bah).' (*Sūrah* 2:144). 'A person from the Banu Salamah (went from there) and (found the people) in *ruku'* praying the dawn prayer, and they had said one *rak'ah*. He said in a loud voice: 'Listen! The *qiblah* has been changed!' And they all turned towards the (new) *qiblah* without getting up.' (Muslim 1075, 1071; Bukhari 2.31.39)

This was a change of far-reaching importance, because it made clear the difference between the Muslims and the Jews of Madinah who did not genuinely accept Islam. It tested and strengthened the loyalty of the Muslims towards Islam and the Prophet ﷺ. Nobody would have changed the *qiblah* of prayer had they not had absolute faith in the genuine nature of the revelations received by Muhammad ﷺ. Further revelation made Allah's motive very clear:

'We appointed not the *qiblah* which you have (for any reason other than) that We might distinguish the one who follows the Messenger from the one who turns back upon his heels and surely this was hard except for those whom Allah had guided aright.' (*Sūrah* 11:143)

Some Muslims were then worried about the prayers of their friends and relatives who had died before the new *qiblah* was announced. Were their prayers still to be considered valid? This was the type of pious question frequently asked by Muslims doing their best to serve Allah correctly through the rituals of Islam, without fully understanding the love of Allah and the Islam of the heart.

Al Bara recorded: 'Before we changed our direction towards the Ka'bah, some Muslims had died or been killed, and we did not know what to say about them (regarding their prayers). Allah then revealed: 'Allah would never make your faith to be lost!' (*Sūrah* 2:143) (Bukhari 2.31.39)

In other words, their prayers were perfectly valid.

When praying in a mosque, the direction of Makkah is always pointed out by a niche in the wall facing towards the Ka'bah, known as a mihrab. These are often beautifully decorated and tiled, but they should not be thought of as in any similar to the altars of pagan places of worship. They are there simply to point out the direction of *qiblah*. In the open, for example at many railway stations in Muslim countries, one can see an arrow pointing to *qiblah* on a prominent roof.

If a Muslim does not know the direction of Makkah, or is constantly changing direction whilst travelling, and so the *qiblah* keeps changing, the duty is simply to try to start the prayer in the direction of *qiblah*, or in what one thinks is the *qiblah*, and to go ahead with the prayer.

Once one *does* know the direction of *qiblah*, if one is praying behind an Imam, it does not matter if there is a 'barrier' of some description between the Imam and the believers.

Al-Hasan recorded: 'There is no harm in praying (even) if there is a river between you and the Imam.' Abu Mijaz said: 'One can follw the Imam even if there is a road or a wall between the Imam and the followers, providing the *takbir* is audible.' (Bukhari 11.79)

This is particularly important when women worshippers are placed behind a barrier or blocked off from view at the prayers. Such barriers were not the Prophet's *sunnah*, and it is important that women can follow the prayer properly.

PRAYING WITHOUT FACING *QIBLAH*, WHILE TRAVELLING

Sometimes the Blessed Prophet ﷺ made private prayers and supplications while he was travelling along, even while riding upon an animal. This did not apply to the *salah* prayers, which he always prayed with the full movements of *rak'ah*, but referred to many moments during the Prophet's ﷺ journeys when his mind became focussed upon Allah and he wished to think of Him or glorify Him or petition Him while he was travelling along.

Ibn 'Umar recorded: 'While travelling, the Messenger of Allah ﷺ would pray voluntary prayer on his riding-beast in whatever direction it turned... but he did not offer the obligatory prayers upon it.' (Abu Dawud 1220, Muslim 1497)

He also recorded that it was while the Blessed Prophet ﷺ was riding his camel, with his *back* to the *qiblah* in Makkah, that he received the revelation from Allah of *surah* 2:115. We know that the Prophet ﷺ frequently did receive verses in direct response to matters that had been troubling his mind, and this was possibly an example—whether it was necessary on a journey home to

Madinah to stop the camel and turn around for his voluntary prayer, or whether it was quite in order to say prayer in whatever direction one happened to be travelling. The same problem might trouble the mind of the modern traveller on a train or aeroplane or any other conveyance who wishes to pray *nafl* and think about Allah while they are travelling.

Ibn 'Umar recorded: 'The Messenger of Allah ﷺ used to say prayer on his camel while coming from Makkah to Madinah, in whatever direction his face had turned; and it was (in this context) that this verse was revealed: 'So in whatever direction you turn, there is the face of Allah.' (*Sūrah* 2:115). Muslim 1499)

Anas ibn Malik recorded: 'When the Messenger of Allah ﷺ was on a journey and wished to say a voluntary prayer, he made his she-camel face the *qiblah* and uttered the *takbir*, and then prayed in whatever direction his mount made him face.' (Abu Dawud 1221)

Abdallah ibn 'Umar recorded: 'I saw the Messenger of Allah ﷺ praying on a donkey, while he was facing Khaybar.' (Abu Dawud 1222, Muslim 1501)

Once Sa'id ibn Yasar was travelling along with Ibn 'Umar on the way to Makkah. Sa'id recorded: 'When I saw it was nearly dawn, I dismounted and observed witr prayer and then again joined him. Ibn 'Umar said to me: 'Where were you?' I said: 'I realised it was nearly dawn, so I dismounted and observed witr.' Upon this Abdallah said: 'Isn't your model pattern the Messenger of Allah ﷺ?' I said: 'Yes, by Allah!' Then he said: 'The Messenger of Allah ﷺ used to observe witr prayer on the camel's back.' (Muslim 1502)

Anas ibn Sirin recorded: 'We met Anas ibn Malik as he came to Syria at a place known as Ain al-Tamar, and saw him observing prayer on the back of his donkey with his face turned in that direction. Hammam, (one of the narrators) pointed towards the left of *qiblah*, so I said to him: 'You are observing prayer towards a direction other than that of *qiblah*.' Upon this, he said: 'Had I not seen the Messenger of Allah ﷺ (specifically) doing (it) like this, I would not have done so at all.' (Muslim 1507)

Incidentally, what about the five compulsory prayers whilst one is travelling? It is obviously impossible to remain facing *qiblah* whilst on a boat or train, or vehicle meandering about on a road, and so forth. Some Muslims, on the authority that these *hadiths* mention prayers of the Blessed Prophet ﷺ that were all *nafl*, have concluded that it is wrong to observe obligatory prayers in trains or aeroplanes—but the jurists unanimously agree that prayer can be said on a boat; therefore, it is quite logical to extend permission to other modes of transport. One could comment that the Muslim should also bear in mind the words of *surah* 2:115, the flexibility of the times of prayer, and not make their personal piety an excuse to inconvenience other passengers in a crowded place. It would be ridiculous, for example, to claim the right to pray properly on a crowded bus—far better manners to wait until the bus stopped somewhere for a length of time.

DRESS FOR PRAYER

The correct clothes for a Muslim man to pray in are those that are clean from stains, and that cover the body at least from the navel to the knees. In other words, it would not be suitable to pray in shorts or bathing-trunks or a loin-cloth. It is also preferrable that the shoulders should be covered.

Abu Hurayrah recorded: 'None of you should pray in a single garment of which no part comes over the shoulder.' (Muslim 1047)

The extreme simplicity of the way of life of those early

Muslims was recorded by Abu Hurayrah on the subject of whether it was more fitting for a man to pray in two garments as opposed to a single robe. The Blessed Prophet ﷺ retorted: 'Have you all got two garments?' (Muslim 1043) How times have changed!

Women should wear something that covers the whole body from head to foot, leaving only the face and hands visible. Many Muslim women keep a clean chador or prayer-shawl with which to cover themselves, and others keep handy a prayer 'suit' consisting of elasticated white full-length skirt and long head-veil, which is easily carried in a bag, and easy to slip on over the everyday clothes, or to change into completely. However, this is not compulsory so long as the woman's clothing covers her body.

The clothing should be Islamic—that is to say, it should not be so tight-fitting that it shows the shape of the body, or transparent. The Blessed Prophet ﷺ used to call women who wore clothes like this 'naked, even though they were clothed' (see

Muslim 1486).

It is always preferable to wear fresh clean garments, but this is not always possible. The Prophet ﷺ did not object to prayer said in the ordinary clothes of the day (or even of the night) so long as they were not soiled by stains. The ordinary dust of the day or the wayside did not make the clothes unsuitable for prayer.

As always in Islam, the rule of necessity allows concessions when a person finds it impossible for some reason to fulfil the usual procedures. The Muslim tries to pray in the most *perfect* way, and this involves a rule of dress. However, the prayer is more important than the clothing, and God understands every situation and motivation, and is the Compassionate and Merciful, Oft-forgiving.

ON WAITING POLITELY FOR THE IMAM

If the Imam has not yet arrived for the prayer, the people should sit down and wait patiently. (Abu Dawud 539)

They should not give the impression of impatience or clock-watching, and they should not indulge in activities that disturb those who are in a prayerful frame of mind—i.e. no intrusive conversations, or loud recitations, and so forth. Keep to your own privacy.

Abdallah ibn Abi Qatadah recorded that Allah's Messenger ﷺ said: 'If the *iqamah* is pronounced, do not stand for the prayer until you see me (in front of you), and then do it calmly.' (Bukhari 11.23.611)

Bilal used to give the *adhan*, and wait before giving the *iqamah* until he saw the Prophet ﷺ come out of the house.

Jabir ibn Samurah said: 'Bilal would call the *adhan*, then he used to wait. When he saw the Prophet ﷺ come out (of his house) he would pronounce the *iqamah*.' (Abu Dawud 537)

Once the Imam was on his way, believers should quietly take up their positions in straight rows. This is the practice known as sumud. (Abu Dawud 543 n. 233)

Abu Hurayrah recorded: 'Iqamah was pronounced and we stood up and made rows straight till he (the Holy Prophet -ﷺ) stood at his place of worship before takbir tahrima. He suddenly remembered something, and went back out saying that we should stand at our places and not leave them. We waited till he came back to us, and he had made wudu' and water trickled from his brow as he led us in prayer.' (Muslim 1256)

It was considered bad manners, however, to wait pointedly, standing up in the rows in such a way as to draw attention to one's earliness or one's own piety, and thereby to imply criticism of others—either those not standing, or the Imam who is late arriving.

As if to make this point, on one occasion the Blessed Messenger ﷺ remained talking to somebody in the corner of the mosque long after the iqamah had been pronounced. He put the person's problem first, and did not come to lead the prayer until the people began to doze. (Abu Dawud 544—on the authority of Anas)

The Blessed Prophet ﷺ varied his practice.

Abu al-Nadr recorded: When the iqamah was pronounced and the Messenger ﷺ saw that they (the people) were few in number, he would sit down and not pray; but when he saw a large number, he would pray.' (Abu Dawud 545; also recorded by 'Ali and others). This saying implied that he was giving an extra chance for late-comers to arrive in time:

PRAYING BEHIND A SCREEN OR BARRIER

A screen or sutrah is something that worshippers place in

front of them in the direction of the Ka'bah, so that other people and animals can pass in front of them without disturbing their prayer. It is considered bad manners for someone to pass in front of a person who is praying, but if this is likely to happen, then after putting some kind of screen or some object to act as a 'block', it does not matter. It depends where the prayer is taking place. If it is in a mosque, facing a *qiblah* wall, it is unlikely that anyone would pass in front. However, it is very likely if the prayer is in the open or in the home.

Talhah ibn Ubaydullah recorded: 'When you place in front of you something such as the back of a saddle, then there is no harm if someone passes in front of you.' (Abu Dawud 685)

Musa ibn Talhah recorded: 'When one of you places in front of himself something such as the back of a saddle, he should pray without caring who passes on the other side of it.' (Muslim 1006)

Ibn 'Umar recorded that the Prophet himself used to bring a lance and set it up in the ground in front of him and pray in its direction. He did this while on journeys, or for Eid prayers.

Ibn 'Umar recorded: When the Messenger ﷺ went out for Eid day, he ordered to carry a spear, and it was fixed in front of him, and he said prayer towards it.' (Abu Dawud 687, Muslim 1010, Bukhari 9.1.473)

Abu Hurayrah recorded: 'When one of you prays, he should put something in front of his face; and if he can find nothing, he should set up his staff; but if he has no staff; he should draw a line— then what passes in front of him will not harm him.' (Abu Dawud 689).

When the Blessed Prophet ﷺ drew a line, he did it either in a curved shape like a crescent moon or a straight line. The crescent is the normal shape of a *qiblah* niche, or the design on a prayer mat.

Abu Dawud recorded: I heard Ahmad ibn Hanbal, who was

questioned many times about how the line should be drawn. He said: 'In this way, flat on the ground in a round semi-circular form like the crescent, that is, a curve.' (Abu Dawud 690)

Sufyan ibn Uyainah recorded that he saw Sharik, who led them in the afternoon prayer during a funeral ceremony. He placed his cap in front of him for saying the obligatory prayer, the time of which had come.' (Abu Dawud 691)

Sometimes the Blessed Prophet ﷺ used the side of his own camel. (Abu Dawud 692)

Ibn 'Umar recorded: 'The Prophet ﷺ used to pray facing his camel.' (Abu Dawud 692)

Nafl recorded: 'I saw Ibn 'Umar praying while taking his camel as the sutrah in front of him, and he said: 'I saw the Prophet ﷺ doing the same.' (Bukhari 8.49.422)

If he used an object like his spear, the Blessed Prophet always had it opposite his right or left eyebrow, and never directly in front of him—in case there was any danger of the practice being likened to the bowing down in front of idols—which were frequently stones or standing pillars or sacred trees and the like. (Abu Dawud 693)

The Blessed Prophet ﷺ recommended leaving a small space between the sutrah and the leader of the prayer.

Sahl ibn Sa'd al-Sa'idi recorded: Between the place of worship where the Messenger of Allah ﷺ prayed and the sutrah, there was a gap through which a goat could pass.' (Muslim 1029, see also Bukhari 9.2.475)

When he was not praying in rows in a mosque, the Blessed Prophet ﷺ used to like to pray behind a column or pillar. It is the normal practice of many Muslims to pray at least two *rak'ahs* on arrival at the mosque, and other *rak'ahs* according to their choice. They do not do this in rows, but in any convenient place. To pray behind a pillar meant that no-one could pass in front of you and disturb you—and also that you were unlikely to be in the way of anyone or a nuisance to anyone.

Yazid ibn Abi Ubayd recorded that he used to accompany Salamah ibn al-Akwa, and he used to pray behind the pillar which was near the place where the Qur'ans were kept. He said: 'O Abu Muslim! I see you are always seeking to pray behind this pillar.' He replied: 'I saw Allah's Messenger 🕮 always seeking to pray near that pillar.' (Bukhari 9.6.481)

Anas recorded: 'I saw the most famous amongst the companions of the Prophet 🕮 hurrying towards the pillars at the *maghrib* prayer, before the Prophet 🕮 arrived.' (Bukhari 9.6.482)

'Umar once saw a person praying between two pillars and brought him close to a pillar and told him to pray behind it. (Bukhari 9.6.481 comment) This indicates that 'Umar felt the worshipper was probably blocking the way of others coming in.

However, this was not a compulsory matter—the Prophet 🕮 also offered many non-congregational prayers between the pillars.

Ibn 'Umar recorded that the Prophet 🕮 entered the Ka'bah along with Usamah bin Zayd, "Uthman ibn Talhah and Bilal, and they remained there for a long time. When they came out, I was the first to enter the Ka'bah. I asked Bilal: 'Where did the Prophet 🕮 pray?' Bilal replied: 'Between the two front pillars.' (Bukhari 9.7.483). Of course, the space between the front pillars is not in the way of those coming in behind.

SHOULD YOU PRAY IF SOMEONE IN FRONT OF YOU IS TALKING OR ASLEEP?

It was not considered a good thing to pray with a person talking or sleeping in front of you:

Abdallah ibn Abbas recorded: 'Do not pray behind a sleeping or a talking person.' (Abu Dawud 694—but the chain of this tradition is weak). This applies particularly to a spacious and public place where there is room to choose. It did not apply in other conditions, and did not break the prayer.

There are many *hadiths* recorded from 'A'ishah that she frequently lay in bed and the Blessed Prophet prayed while facing her, and was therefore between the Prophet 🕮 and the *qiblah* on many, many occasions.

'A'ishah said: I was sleeping in front of the Prophet 🕮 with my legs between him and the *qiblah*.' (Abu Dawud 710—and many other references)

Urwah reported on the authority of 'A'ishah: 'The Messenger of Allah 🕮 used to pray at night and she would lie between him and the *qiblah*, sleeping on the bed on which he would sleep. When he wanted to offer the witr prayer, he would awaken her and she also offered the witr prayer.' (Abu Dawud 711, Muslim 1036)

A highly personal insight into their intimate relations was reported in all three major collections:

She added: 'When he knelt in prostration, he pinched me and I pulled back my legs, and when he stood up, I stretched them out again.' (Muslim 1040, see also Abu Dawud 712, Bukhari 8.22.379)

ARE PRAYERS 'CUT OFF' BY DONKEYS, DOGS AND WOMEN?

Some *hadiths* indicate that the prayer would be 'cut off' if a woman, donkey or black dog passed in front of the person praying. The black dog, in particular, was treated with dislike.

Abu Dharr recorded that the Messenger of Allah 🕮 said: 'When any of you stands for prayer and there something before him like the back of a saddle, that covers him; and in case there is not anything like the back of a saddle in front of him, his prayer would be cut off by (the passing of an) ass, woman and black dog.' I said: 'O Abu Dharr, what feature is there in a black dog that distinguishes it from the red or yellow dog?' He said: 'O son of my brother, I asked the Messenger of Allah the very same question, and he said: 'The black dog is a devil.' (Abu Dawud 702, Muslim 1032) (Incidentally this last phrase is not intended to be taken literally, it was just a figure of speech—the same the Prophet 🕌 used even of human beings who were a nuisance. (See Muslim 1023, 1024)

As regards the inclusion of women in this list, there is controversy about it. 'A'ishah was certainly very indignant about this saying when she heard of it.

Urwa ibn Zubayr recorded that 'A'ishah asked: 'What disrupts the prayer?' We said: 'The woman and the donkey.' Upon this she remarked: 'Is the woman an ugly animal? I used to lie (without moving) in front of the Messenger of Allah 🕌 like the bier of a corpse, and he said prayer!' (Muslim 1037)

Masruq recorded that it was mentioned before 'A'ishah that prayer was invalidated (by the passing) of a dog, a donkey and a woman. Upon this 'A'ishah said: 'Now you liken us to asses and dogs! By Allah! I saw the Messenger of Allah 🕌 saying prayer while I lay on the bed between him and the *qiblah*. When I felt the need (to move for any reason), I did not like to sit in front of and disturb the Messenger of Allah 🕌, and I quietly moved out from under its legs (i.e. the bedstead).' (Muslim 1038)

A variant version recorded by al-Aswad reports 'A'ishah as saying:

'You have made us (women) equal to the dogs and asses, whereas I used to lie on the bedstead while the Prophet 🕌 would come and stand in the middle of the bed to say prayer. I did not like to take the quilt off me (in that state), so I used to slip away slowly and quietly from the foot of the bed and thus got out of my blanket.' (Muslim 1039, Bukhari 9.10.486, see also 9.13.490, 9.16.493, 9.19.498)

Some authorities, still trying to maintain the tradition, claimed it meant when the woman was menstruating and therefore unclean. However, even this is contradicted by several *hadith*:

Maymunah, the wife of the Messenger 變 recorded: The Messenger 變 said prayer, and I (lay) opposite to him while I was in my menses. Sometimes his clothes touched me when he prostrated.' (Muslim 1041)

'A'ishah recorded: The Messenger 變 said prayer at night, and I was by his side in a state of menses, and I had a sheet pulled over me a portion of which was on his side.' (Muslim 1042)

Abu al-Sahba recorded a time when he and another boy came riding a donkey while the Messenger 變 was at prayer and left it tethered in front of the row of worshippers, and the Prophet 變 did not pay any attention. (Abu Dawud 715)

He also, apparently, paid no attention to a pair of girls who started fighting in front of the praying people (Abu Dawud 716) and a she-ass and bitch that started playing in front of them. (Abu Dawud 717)

In fact, Abu Sa'id recorded; 'Nothing interrupts prayer, but prevent as much as you can anyone who passes in front of you, for he is just a devil.' (Abu Dawud 718, see also Muslim 1023 etc.)

Abu Salih al-Samman recorded what he heard and saw from Abu Sa'id al-Khudri: 'One day I was with Abu Sa'id and he was saying prayer on Friday, turning towards a thing which concealed from the people, when a young man from Banu Mu'ait came there and tried to pass in front of him. He turned him back by striking his chest. He looked about, but finding no other way to pass except in front of Abu Sa'id, he made a second attempt. He turned him away by striking his chest more vigorously than the first time. He stood up and had a scuffle with Abu Sa'id. Then the people gathered there. He came out and went to Marwan and complained to him about what had happened to him. Abu Sa'id also came to Marwan, and Marwan said to him: 'what has happened to you and to the son of your brother, that he came to complain against you?' Abu Sa'id said: 'I heard from the Messenger of Allah ﷺ—'When anyone of you prays facing something which conceals him from people, and anyone tries to pass in front of him he should be turned away; and if he refuses, he should be forcibly stopped from (doing) it, for he is a devil.' (Muslim 1024)

In fact, the unseemly scuffle reported here gives a revealing example of the different types of Muslim. Abu Sa'id was so concerned about the prayer being valid he was prepared to break off and fight an ill-mannered person. Others might feel that it would have been more tactful and proper to cover that man's fault and ignore it. Muslims know that *nothing* can ever really come between a believer and Allah, for Allah is He Who is closer than one's neck vein.

The concern about non-compulsory sunnahs is well-meant, but unnecessary.

'When My servants ask you concerning Me, I am indeed close to them; I listen to the prayer of every suppliant when he (or she) calls on Me; let them also lisen to My call with a will, and believe in Me, that they might walk in the right way.' (*Sūrah* 2:186)

'It was We Who created humanity, and We know what dark suggestions his soul makes to him; for We are nearer to him than his jugular vein.' (*sūrah* 50:16)

The Good Manners of Prayer

IF ONE FEELS THE CALL OF NATURE, OR FEELS HUNGRY

The Blessed Prophet ﷺ taught that one should have total devotion and peace of mind while offering prayer. It is therefore incorrect to try to pray whilst suffering from the pangs of hunger, or the desire to relieve oneself.

Urwah recorded that one day when Abdallah ibn al-Arqam was leading them in the dawn prayer, he said to them: 'One of you should come (and take over).' He then went away to relieve himself. He explained: 'I heard the Messenger of Allah ﷺ say: 'When any of you feels the need to relieve himself (even if) the congregational prayer is ready, he should go and relieve himself.' (Abu Dawud 88)

Thawban recorded: 'The Messenger of Allah ﷺ said: 'Three things are forbidden; supplicating Allah specifically for oneself and ignoring others while leading people in prayer; looking inside a house without permission; and saying prayer while one is feeling the call of nature, until one relieves oneself.' (Abu Dawud 90)

'A'ishah recorded: 'Prayer should not be offered in the presence of meals, nor at the moment when one is struggling with two evils (i.e. feeling the call of nature).' (Abu Dawud 89)

Anas ibn Malik recorded that the Messenger of Allah ﷺ said: 'When the supper is placed before you, and it is also the time to say prayer, first take food before saying the evening prayer, and do not hasten (leaving aside the food).' (Muslim 1135)

This letter advice is kind on two counts—firstly it is kind to the hungry believer himself or herself, by allowing them to satisfy the hunger pangs before attempting to concentrate on prayer; secondly it is kind and considerate manners to the person who has prepared the food, who would be hurt and perhaps offended if their effort was wasted and the food spoiled if the person for whom it was intended suddenly hurried off just as it was ready. It is yet another example of the Blessed Prophet's ﷺ courtesy and consideration for female Muslims, whose service towards helping Muslim men is so often taken for granted.

ON FINDING THE RIGHT ATMOSPHERE IN THE MOSQUE

If a person arrived early for Friday prayer, he or she should not be made to feel uncomfortable or intrusive by finding the place in use for public teaching on this occasion. The Blessed Prophet ﷺ wished the atmosphere to be one of welcome and prayerful readiness, and did not want any-one to feel embarrassed or guilty.

'Amr ibn Shuayb reported: 'The Messenger of Allah ﷺ prohibited buying and selling in the mosque, announcing aloud about a lost thing, the recitation of a poem in it, and prohibited sitting in a circle on Firday before the prayer.' (Abu Dawud 1074)

Sitting in a circle refers to the way the people used to sit around to receive religious instruction. As the Prophet ﷺ wanted people to come early for the Friday prayer, he did not want them to feel inhibited by being obliged to sidle in feeling they were interrupting people who were studying, and therefore being made to feel guilty (or perhaps, even, inferior). It was important to keep the heart clear for prayer and worship—therefore the other things forbidden were also prohibited; the categories included secular business or trading, personal announcements, and listening to recitations (or concerts, or performances or talks). All these things were perfectly permissible in their place and at the right time—but just before Friday prayers was not the right time or place!

Sulayman ibn Buraydah recorded on the authority of his father that when the Messenger of Allah ﷺ had said the prayer a man stood up and cried out: 'Who has lost a red camel?' (Upon this) the Messenger of Allah ﷺ said: 'May it not be restored to you! Mosques are built for what they are intended for!' (Muslim 282)

COME TO PRAYER IN A TRANQUIL FRAME OF MIND

Allah requested that believers should hasten towards prayer eagerly, and not hang back. The true believer is always eager to be in the company of other believers, and should look forward to Friday prayer in congregation in particular.

'When the call to prayer is made on Friday, hasten to the remembrance of Allah, and leave off your business.' (*Surah* 62:9)

The Blessed Prophet ﷺ, however, disapproved of people 'hastening' if it meant rushing to the mosque at the last moment, and arriving breathless and in disarray. He advised walking calmly, even if a little late, and arriving in a calm and tranquil frame of mind. One should never come bursting in making a noise, drawing attention to yourself and disturbing others.

Abdallah ibn Qatadah recorded that his father said: 'While we were praying with the Prophet ﷺ he heard the noise of some people. After the prayer he asked: 'What was the matter?' They replied: 'We were hurrying (to be in time) for the prayer.' He said: 'Do not rush for the prayer, but whenever you come to it, you should come with calmness, and pray whatever you get (with the people) and (afterwards) complete the rest that you missed.' (Bukhari 11.20.608, Muslim 1253)

Abu Hurayrah recorded: 'When the *iqamah* has been called for prayer, do not go running to it, but go walking in tranquillity, and pray what you are in time for, and complete what you have missed (afterwards); for when people are preparing for prayer, they are in fact already engaged in prayer.' (Muslim 1250)

THE FRONT ROWS

Many Muslims regard it as being an act of merit to be early in the mosque, and to have the seats in the front rows of the worshippers.

The Blessed Prophet ﷺ acknowledged that those who came early and sat near the Imam and paid attention were surely amongst the believers to be commended:

'Allah the Exalted and Mighty sends blessings and the angels invoke blessings for those who are nearer to the front rows. No step is more liked by Allah that one which takes a worshipper to join the row (of the prayer).' (Abu Dawud 543)

Abu Hurayrah recorded: 'If you were to know what excellence lies in the first rows, there would have been drawing of lots (for filling them). (Muslim 880)

Abu Hurayrah recorded: 'The best of the men's rows is the first and the worst of them is the last; but the best of the women's rows is the last and the worst of them is the first.' (Abu Dawud 678, Muslim 881)

The Blessed Prophet ﷺ was thinking about the *niyyah* or motivation of his followers. To be at the front showed a commitment and eagerness to be there on time, ready to serve God, and therefore the first rows of men were recommended. For a woman, however, it was also commendable to show modesty and consideration, this was possibly the reason why the last row of the women was recommended above the first. It might also be because the women at the back tend to be motherly, keeping an eye on the youngsters. However, we could also comment that this *hadith* recorded by Abu Hurayrah may be another that would have annoyed 'A'ishah!

When women are also responsible for small children during the prayers, it is particularly commendable if they are able to concentrate upon their worship of God as well. The Blessed Prophet ﷺ always took note of his congregation, and never prolonged the compulsory prayers when there were aged and infirm worshippers, or mothers struggling with crying babies. Lengthy prayers belonged to the times of private devotions, prayers which were over and above those laid down as compulsory.

The Blessed Prophet ﷺ particularly liked to be surrounded by those of a similar temperament to himself at prayer times, and did not wish to be disturbed in his prayer by people who were unable to sit still and concentrate. He preferred those to be further back.

Abu Mas'ud recorded: 'Let those of you who are calm and conscientious be near me, then those who are next to them, then those who are next to them.' (Abu Dawud 674, Muslim 870)

However, when he recommended the first rows, he did not mean by this that the prayer of those further back in the place of prayer was any less valid. Every person who prays in the mosque in congregation has made the effort to be there, when they might have been elsewhere, and is always to be recommended. There is no reason for anyone to feel that their prayer is not as perfect or acceptable to Allah as the prayers made by those at the front!

Occupying the front rows for the prayer does not of itself make a person into a pious Muslim. If the people who have taken position in the front rows have done so for the wrong reasons, they have misunderstood the spirit of Islam. A selfish desire to 'get there first' or to 'push in', and thus gain 'points of merit' for themselves at the expense of others is hardly the correct attitude of mind or *niyyah*! Such an attitude would probably earn them 'points of demerit' not the rewards they foolishly craved.

The Blessed Prophet ﷺ heartily disapproved of an unseemly scramble for position. His phrase for those who made a point of acting in a superior manner, or clambering past others to get to the front rows was 'stepping over the necks'.

'Whoever washes himself on a Friday and applies perfume and wears good clothes, and does not step over the necks of people, and does not indulge in idle talk during the sermon, that will atone (for his sins) between the two Fridays. But he who whispers or chats, and steps over the necks of people, that (Friday) will be for him (no more than) a noon prayer.' (Abu Dawud 347, 343)

Indeed, the Companions understood this very well, and it is worth pointing out to misguided modern zealots that they usually behaved in a very quiet and modest manner, taking their seats at the back. They were actually so reticent to push themselves forward that the Blessed Prophet ﷺ was frequently obliged to encourage them to move to the front, remembering their responsibilities as future leaders.

Abu Sa'id al-Khudri recorded: The Messenger saw a tendency among his Companions to go to the back. He said to them: 'Come forward and follow my lead; and let those who come after you follow your lead. If people continue to keep to the back, Allah will put them to the back!' (Abu Dawud 680)

STRAIGHT ROWS

The Blessed Prophet ﷺ thought it was important for the people to pray in straight lines, and to complete one line before starting another. Anas reported the Messenger ﷺ as saying: 'Complete the first row, then the one that comes next, and if there is any incompleteness, let it be in the last row.' (Abu Dawud 672)

Jabir ibn Samurah recorded the Messenger ﷺ saying: 'Why do you not stand in rows as the angels do in the presence of their Lord?' We asked: 'How do the angels stand?' He said: 'They make the first row complete and keep close together in the row.' (Abu Dawud 661)

He liked the people to be close together, shoulder to shoulder, in companionable spirit and not stiff or haughty, or unsociable, shrugging the neighbour away.

It helped people not to 'look down their noses' at brothers they might have considered inferior; or to be abashed by those they felt to be superior. It also helped to heal rifts and arguments that might have arisen. The physical contact was not just symbolic, but an important aid.

Ibn Abbas recorded: 'The best of you are those whose shoulders are soft in prayer.' (Abu Dawud 672) The neighbour was not stiffly kept at a distance, but welcomed.

It was also very important to the Blessed Prophet ﷺ that the rows were straight and regular, and disciplined.

Abu Mas'ud recorded: 'The Messenger of Allah ﷺ used to touch our shoulders in prayer and say: 'Keep straight! Don't be irregular, for there will be dissensions in your hearts. Let those of you who are sedate and prudent be near me, then those who are next to them, then those who are next to them.' (Muslim 868)

Anas ibn Malik recorded: 'The Messenger of Allah ﷺ said:

'Straighten your rows, for the straightening of rows is part of the perfection of prayer.' (Muslim 871)

Al-Numan ibn Bashir said: 'The Prophet ﷺ used to straighten us in rows as the arrow is straightened, until he thought that we had learned it and understood it. One day he turned towards us, and when he saw a man whose chest projected out of the row he said: 'You must straighten your rows, or Allah will certainly put your faces in contrary directions!' (Abu Dawud 663, Muslim 875)

Abdallah ibn 'Umar recorded: 'Set the rows in order, stand shoulder to shoulder, close the gaps, be pliant in the hands of your brethren and do not leave openings for the devil. If anyone joins up a row, Allah will join him up, but if anyone breaks a row, Allah will cut him off!' (Abu Dawud 666)

Anas ibn Malik recorded: 'Stand close together in your rows, bring them near one another, and stand neck to neck for by Him in Whose hand is my soul, I see the devil creeping in through openings in the row just like a little black sheep!' (Abu Dawud 667)

Anas ibn Malik also recorded that he used some words familiar to every teacher: 'Straighten your rows, for I can see you behind my back.' He added—Every one of us used to put his shoulder against the shoulder of his neighbour, and his foot against the foot of his neighbour.' (Bukhari 11.75.692)

The Blessed Prophet used to straighten the rows before he prayed, by pointing with his stick.

Muhammad ibn Muslim ibn al-Sa'id recorded that one day he prayed by the side of Anas ibn Malik. He said: 'Do you know why this stick is placed here?' I said: 'No, by Allah.' He said: 'The Messenger of Allah ﷺ used to put his hand upon it and say: 'Keep straight, and straighten your rows'.' (Abu Dawud 669)

Anas ibn Malik recorded that when the Messenger of Allah

ﷺ stood for prayer he took (the stick) in his right hand and turning (to the right side) said: 'Keep straight, and straighten your rows'. He then took it in his left hand and said: 'Keep straight, and straighten your rows.' (Abu Dawud 670)

EYES IN THE BACK OF HIS HEAD!

The Blessed Prophet ﷺ warned his congregation not to behave badly behind his back, for he could see them—like a teacher with 'eyes in the back of his head'.

Abu Hurayrah recorded: 'Do you think that my face is turned towards *qiblah*? By Allah, neither your submissiveness nor your bowing is hidden from me; surely I see you from my back!' (Bukhari 8.40.410, 2.40.410, Muslim 853-856)

Anas ibn Malik recorded: The Prophet ﷺ led us in prayer and then got up on the pulpit and said: 'In your prayer and bowing, I certainly see you from my back as I see you (while looking at you).' (Bukhari 8.40.411)

Anas also recorded: 'Straighten your rows, for I see you behind my back!' (Bukhari 11.70.686, Muslim 872)

ON NOT RUSHING THE PRAYERS OR ADOPTING UNDIGNIFIED POSITIONS

The Blessed Prophet ﷺ disapproved of people rushing through the prayers or being disruptive or selfish in their movements.

Anas recorded: 'I did not offer prayer behind anyone more concise than the one offered by the Messenger of Allah ﷺ, or one that was more perfect. When he said: 'Allah listens to him who praises him', he stood so long that we thought he had omitted something; then he would say *takbir* and prostrate, and would sit between the two prostrations so long that we thought he had omitted something.' (Abu Dawud 852)

In other words, he did not insist on reciting long *sūrahs* at every prayer, but he never hurried along the various parts of the prayer in an unseemly manner.

Abdal Rahman ibn Shibi recorded: 'The Prophet of Allah ﷺ prohibited pecking like a crow, spreading the forearms like a wild beast, and fixing a place in the mosque like a camel which fixes its place.' (Abu Dawud 861—the wording of Qutaibah)

What he was referring to by 'pecking like a crow' were the people who bobbed quickly up and down during their prostrations, instead of taking time to actually pray and think the words, and be tranquil. 'Fixing a place like a camel' referred to people taking their places with a great fuss, shunting and shuffling about disturbing other people, and drawing attention themselves. This was not considered to be the correct respectful attitude.

If the person praying was uncomfortable, for example because of small pebbles on the ground, he or she should not make a distraction out of smoothing the ground.

Mu'aiqib recorded: 'Do not remove pebbles while you are praying; if you do it out of sheer necessity, do it only once.' (Abu Dawud 946)

The Blessed Prophet ﷺ did not like 'slavish' positions that were not dignified, either. Some people, when prostrating, placed their arms flat on the ground in front of them and rested their heads on the earth. The Prophet ﷺ called this 'stretching like a dog.'

Anas ibn Malik recorded: 'Adopt a moderate position when prostrating yourselves, and see that none of you stretches out his forearms (on the ground) like a dog!' (Abu Dawud 896, see also Bukhari 12.59.785)

When the Blessed Prophet ﷺ made his prostration, he did

not grovel but kept his arms clear of the earth, and those praying behind him reported they could see his armpits.

Maymunah recorded: 'When the Messenger ﷺ prostrated himself, if a lamb wanted to pass between his arms, it could pass.' (Muslim 1002)

Abdallah ibn Malik ibn Bujainah recorded: 'When the Prophet ﷺ prostrated, he spread out his arms so that the whiteness of his armpits was visible.' (Muslim 1000)

CONCERNING ANYONE WHO COMES LATE TO PRAYER

So often in Islam, the Blessed Prophet ﷺ took an incident or something said, and turned what people thought about it on its head. For example, everyone knows the situation of being at prayer in unison when the door opens and in comes a latecomer. It is human nature for those already at prayer to have their thoughts disturbed by this, and to be irritated by the late person.

Some Muslims might even think that if a person is late for the prayer, it is no longer valid. However, this is not what was taught by the Blessed Prophet ﷺ, who looked not at the actual late arrival, but at the intention in the late one's heart, and took into consideration the reasons why he was late. Obviously he himself would not know those reasons, but the Blessed Prophet ﷺ never forgot that Allah always knew what he did not, and it was not for him to judge. He therefore took a kind and gentle view of the matter.

Anas ibn Malik recorded that once, while the Prophet was praying, 'a man came panting to join the row of worshippers, and said 'Allah is Great: praise be to Allah, much praise, good and blessed.' When the Messenger of Allah ﷺ finished his prayer, he asked: 'Which of you is the one who spoke those words? He said nothing wrong.' Then the man said: '(It was) I; I came and had difficulty in breathing, so I said them.' He said: 'I saw twelve angels racing against one another to be the one to take them up to Allah!' (Abu Dawud 762, Muslim 1247)

By these encouraging words, the Blessed Prophet showed that not only should the embarrassed worshipper not be rebuked or looked down on by those who were not late, but that he should be recommended for taking the point of view that it was far better to arrive late than not come at all! The man had made effort, and hurried, and his intention was really to get there on time, and that intention was the one with which Allah would be pleased.

It was not recommended, however, that a person should have the idea that it was acceptable to get into the habit of being late, or to linger and then be obliged to come running for prayer in an over-heated and breathless state. However, the person who arrived late for prayer (who had obviously made the effort to get there) should not feel that the prayer was not valid, or that he or she had 'missed' it.

The Blessed Prophet's ﷺ instructions were quite clear, and simple, and practical. The narrator Humayd, in commenting on the above *hadith*, stated:

'When any of you comes for prayer, he should walk as usual; then he should pray as much as he finds it (i.e. along with the Imam), and should offer the part of the prayer himself (when the prayer is finished) which the Imam had offered before him.' (Abu Dawud 762)

ENTERING THE MOSQUE

The Blessed Prophet ﷺ taught that a person should not come running to the mosque, and enter it breathlessly and noisily. It was important to preserve the atmosphere of tranquillity, even if the person was late.

Abu Hurayrah recorded: 'Come to prayer with calmness and tranquillity.' (Abu Dawud 573)

'When the words of the *iqamah* are pronounced, do not come to prayer running, but go with tranquillity; pray what you are in time for, and then complete what you have missed.' (Muslim 1250-55)

It is traditional for the Muslim to enter the mosque with the right foot.

'A'ishah recorded: The Prophet ﷺ used to start everything from the right (for good things) whenever it was possible in all his affairs; for example, in washing, combing or putting on his shoes.' Abdallah ibn 'Umar commented that he always used to enter the mosque by putting his right foot first, and while leaving he put his left foot first.' (Bukhari 8.47.418)

When a Muslim enters the mosque, he or she should pray a blessing on the Prophet ﷺ and say: 'O Allah, open for me the gates of Your mercy.'

When leaving one should say: 'O Allah, I ask You (to bless me) out of Your abundance.' (Abu Dawud 465)

It is usual practice to offer two *rak'ahs* on arrival before sitting down to wait for the congregational prayer. This prayer is known as *tahayyat al-masjid* or 'respect of the mosque'.

Abu Qatadah recorded that Allah's Messenger ﷺ said: 'If any of you enter a mosque, you should pray two *rak'ahs* before sitting.' (Bukhari 8.60.435)

ON NOT DISTURBING THE PEACEFUL ATMOSPHERE

The atmosphere of the praying-place in the mosque should always be one of peace and prayful serenity. People should not allow their children to run around in the mosque, or speak loudly themselves or shout out—for example, if they have lost some-

thing, or have a message for someone, or wish (these days) to bring someone to the telephone. Mobile phones should be switched off.

Abu Hurayrah recorded: 'I heard the Messenger of Allah ﷺ say: 'If anyone hears a man crying out in the mosque about something he has lost, he should say—May Allah not restore it to you, for the mosques were not built for this.' (Abu Dawud 473)

One should never speak loudly, or hold conversations that would disturb others. The place of prayer should be treated with respect, and one's behaviour be quiet and appropriate, even if nobody is there praying. If somebody *is* there, it is obviously important.

Every Muslim knows well the irritation caused to the devout by people who sit in the mosque talking, sometimes even during the services. It doesn't matter if they happen to be talking in a whisper, it is just as annoying. Muslims should always be conscious of the atmosphere of prayer and serenity.

COUGHING, SPLUTTERING AND SPITTING

Similarly, one should try not to disturb others by loud coughing and spluttering, or the need to spit. If Muslims have a cough or cold, they should have a cloth or handkerchief available with them. If they are attending a sermon and they know there is great likelihood of a coughing spasm, it would be good manners to take a position at the back, so that one could easily slip away and perhaps take a sip of water or medicine, and then return quietly without disturbing anyone.

Apparently, in mosques which are praying-places on bare earth and in societies where spitting is not regarded as gross bad manners, there is a great temptation for some people to spit, but this was strongly discouraged by the Prophet ﷺ. The following hadiths all refer to praying places on the natural ground. Obviously, if one is in an enclosed mosque, or one with a tiled floor, or carpeted, or with other flooring, one should not spit on it at all!

Anas ibn Malik recorded: 'Spitting in the mosque is a sin; its (only) expiation is to bury it.' (Bukhari 8.37.407, Abu Dawud 474)

In absolute necessity, if a person had coughed up phlegm and needed to be rid of it, the Prophet ﷺ recommended:

'A faithful believer while in prayer is speaking in private to his Lord, so he should neither spit in front of him nor to his right side. But he could spit either on his left or (bury it) under his foot.' (Bukhari 8.36.405, Muslim 1123—on the authority of Anas, see also Abu Dawud 478 etc.) Even this would not be pleasant. Always remember there are people on your left side too.

Abu Hurayrah recorded that the Messenger of Allah ﷺ saw some spittle in the direction of the *qiblah* in the mosque. He turned towards the people and said: 'How is it that someone amongst you stands before his Lord and then spits out in front of him? Would any of you like it if you were standing in front of someone, and then he spat in your face? So, if any of you spits, he must do it on his left side under his foot. If there is no space, he should do it like this.' Qasim (one of the narrators) then spat in his cloth, and then folded it and rubbed it.' (Muslim 1121; see also Abu Dawud 480) This is obviously by far the better practice, and offends no-one. A worshipper with a cold, or problem with phlegm, should make sure they are carrying a handkerchief! Sadly, some peoples' manners are pretty offensive, even in a place of worship.

It is hard to believe, but people who attended prayer with the Propeht ﷺ himself occasionally defiled the mosque. The Prophet ﷺ, rather than making a fuss about it, gave an example of direct action. Several *hadiths* record that when the Blessed Prophet ﷺ saw spittle on the wall of the mosque, he removed it with his own hands and made the place clean. (e.g. Bukhari 8.33.399)

Abu Sahlat al-Saib ibn Khallad recorded the Prophet's ﷺ disgust: A (certain) man was lending the people in prayer. He spat towards *qiblah* while the Messenger of Allah ﷺ was looking at him. The Messenger ﷺ said of him when he finished his prayer: 'He should not lead you in prayer (after this).' After that, when this man intended to lead them in prayer, they forbade him and told him of the prohibition of the Messenger ﷺ. He then mentioned it to the Messenger ﷺ who explained to him: 'You gave offence to Allah and to His Messenger!' (Abu Dawud 482).

ON NOT TALKING DURING THE PRAYER

Sometimes people come in late to the prayer, thereby causing some disturbance; at other times, people whisper to those sitting near them. This distracts the other worshippers, and also the Imam if he is praying or giving the sermon. The Blessed Prophet ﷺ thoroughly disapproved of such bad manners. He said:

'When someone sits in a place where he can listen (to the sermon) and see (the Imam), keeps silence and does not interrupt, he (or she) will get double reward. If he (or she) sits far away in a space where they cannot hear, yet still keeps silence and does not interrupt, they get the single reward for it. If he (or she) sits in a place where they can listen and look, but do not keep silence, they will have the burden of it. (Let) anyone tell the companion sitting beside him (or her) to be silent, it is idle talk. Those who interrupt will get nothing on that Friday!' (Abu Dawud 1046—narrated by 'Ali; see also Bukhari 13.34.56)

On one occasion, a person's sneeze nearly started an 'incident'.

Mu'awiyah ibn al-Hakim recorded: While I was praying with Allah's Messenger 鐵, a man in the company sneezed. I said: 'Allah have mercy on you!' The people (then) started at me with disapproving looks, so I said: 'Woe to me, why are you staring at me like that?' They began to strike their hands on their thighs, and when I realised they were urging me to observe silence (I became angry) but I said nothing. When the Messenger of Allah 鐵 had said the prayer (and I declare that neither before nor since have I seen a leader who gave better instruction, than he for whom I would give my father and mother as ransom!), I swear that he did not scold, beat or revile me, but said: 'Talking to persons is not fitting during the prayer...' (Muslim 1094)

HOW TO FOCUS THE EYES DURING PRAYER

The Blessed Prophet 鐵 disapproved of people raising their eyes to heaven whilst praying, or shutting their eyes tight, or focussing on some holy picture or statue like the pagan worshippers. He recommended simply withdrawing one's attention from the world by focussing on the place on the prayer mat on which one would place one's head during prostration.

Jabir ibn Samurah recorded: The Messenger of Allah 鐵 said: 'The people who lift their eyes towards the sky in prayer should avoid it, or they will lose their sight!' (Muslim 862)

Many pagans worshipped the 'heavenly bodies' such as the sun, moon and stars as if they were gods. Others mistakenly believed that God was to be found somewhere 'up in the sky'. This is not the teaching of Islam—God is to be found everywhere, in every place, and in particular stirring the human heart.

'To Allah belong the East and the West; in whatever direction you turn, there is the Presence of God. For God is All-Pervading, All-Knowing.' (*Sūrah* 2:115)

'Truly, We are never absent (from any time or place).' (*Sūrah* 7:7)

Concentrating on anything which is *not* God as if it is intimately connected with God—as for example gazing at the sky as if that was where God lived, results in spiritual blindness and loss of understanding.

Abu Hurayrah recorded: 'People should avoid lifting their eyes towards the sky while supplicating in prayer, otherwise their eyes would be snatched away.' (Muslim 863, see also Bukhari 12.11.717)

RAISING THE HANDS FOR *TAKBIR*

'Ali recorded that when the Messenger stood up for prayer, he raised his hands opposite his shoulders at the *takbir*, and again when he finished the recitation of the Qur'an and was about to bow, and again when he raised his head after bowing. He did not raise his hands in prayer while he was sitting. When he stood at the end of two *rak'ahs* he raised his hands in a similar way and uttered the *takbir*.

Wail ibn Hujr recorded that he saw the Messenger of Allah ﷺ raising his hands at the time of the beginning of the prayer, and reciting *takbir*, and the hands were lifted opposite to his ears. He then wrapped his hands in his cloth and placed his right hand over his left hand. And when he was about to bow down, he brought out his hands from the cloth and then lifted them, and then recited *takbir* and bowed down, and when (he came back to the erect position) he recited: 'Allah listens to him who praises Him.' And when he bowed down, he prostrated between the two palms.' (Muslim 792)

ON NOT MUTTERING PRAYERS ALOUD IN CONGREGATION SO AS TO DISTRACT OTHERS

Some Muslims feel it is a commendable practice to join in with the Imam when he recites familiar passages, by whispering the words aloud. Some people do not even confine themselves to a whisper, but join in quite audibly. No doubt the motive is one of piety and devotion, but it is misguided. It can actually be a distraction to others, particularly to the person leading. Anyone who has done this job will tell you that no matter how familiar the words, the mind can slip or go blank, and words be forgotten. Imams do not usually have a written text in front of them. When the worshippers in the rows are whispering, muttering, or praying aloud, it can be very distracting, and might actually cause the Imam to forget or stumble in the words.

Ubadah ibn al-Samit recorded that he was behind the Messenger of Allah ﷺ once during the dawn prayer, and while he was reciting the passage even he stumbled over it. When he had finished the prayer, he turned to the congregation and asked if they had also recited behind him. They replied that it was indeed so. The Blessed Prophet then requested them not to do so, except for the words of *al-Fatihah*. (Abu Dawud 822)

Ubadah recorded: 'The Messenger of Allah ﷺ led us in a certain prayer in which the Qur'an was recited aloud, but he became confused during the recitation. When he finished he turned his face to us and said: 'Are you reciting (with me) while I recite the Qur'an aloud?' Some of us said: 'We do so: (He said:) 'This is why I asked myself what had confused me (in the recitation of) the Qur'an. Do not recite anything from the Qur'an while I recite it aloud, except the Umm al-Qur'an (this is *al-Fatihah*).' (Abu Dawud 823).

Imran ibn Husayn recorded that the Prophet ﷺ led them in the noon prayer, and when he finished it he said:

'Which of you recited the *sūrah* 'Glorify the name of your Lord, the Most High (*Sūrah* 86)?' A man said: 'I'. He said: 'I knew that one of you had confused me in it!' (Abu Dawud 828, see also Muslim 783)

THE HANDS, DURING SUPPLICATION

The Blessed Prophet ﷺ taught three special positions for the hands during moments of private prayer. He did not advise clenching the hands, or wringing them, or placing palms together like the Christians.

Ikramah quoted Ibn Abbas as saying: 'When asking for something you should raise your hands opposite your shoulders; when asking for forgiveness you should point with one finger; and when making an earnest supplication you should spread out both your hands.' (Abu Dawud 1484)

'Supplicate Allah with the palms of your hands; do not supplicate Him with their backs upwards. When you finish your supplication, wipe your faces with them.' (Abu Dawud 1480— a tradition reported on several chains, but all of them weak.)

Salman recorded: 'Your Lord is munificent and generous, and is ashamed to turn away empty the hands of His servant when he raises them to Him.' (Abu Dawud 1483)

Al-Sa'ib ibn Yazid recorded on the authority of his father: 'When the Prophet ﷺ made supplication to Allah, he would raise his hands and then wipe his face with his hands.' (Abu Dawud 1487)

ON NOT GESTURING WITH THE HANDS DURING THE SALUTATION

Jabir ibn Samurah recorded: 'When we said prayer with the Messenger of Allah ﷺ we pronounced: 'Peace be upon you and mercy of Allah, peace be upon you and mercy of Allah', and made gesture with the hand on both the sides. Upon this, the Messenger of Allah ﷺ said: 'What do you point out with your hands, as if they are the flicking tails of head-strong horses? It is enough that you should place your hands on your thigh and then pronounce the salutation on your neighbour on the right side then on the left.' (Muslim 866)

A variant version concludes:

'He should only turn his face towards his companion and should not make gestures with his hand.' (Muslim 867)

MODERATION IN PRAYERS

Many Muslims attempt to go to all sorts of extremes in their devotions, for many reasons. They try to copy the *sunnah* of the

Blessed Prophet ﷺ, sacrificing themselves more and more in the attempt. One of the ways in which this is done is in the multiplication of lengthy prayers, taking the private practice of the Blessed Prophet ﷺ as their example. Of course, Allah is always pleased when we remember Him, and spend our time in contemplation of Him and devotion towards Him. However, excessive devotions can result in several things which are not desired either by Allah or his Prophet ﷺ.

Firstly, it should be made clear that it is a false piety to imagine that one can imitate the Blessed Prophet too closely. He was a very special person, and had a special strength. Alqamah once asked 'A'ishah if the Messenger of Allah ﷺ kept up his demanding routine all the time, or whether perhaps he performed his prayer devotions exclusively on particular days and not on others. She confirmed that what he did was normal for him, it was his regular practice, not just laid on for special occasions.

She said: 'He performed his actions regularly. Which of you has the strength as much as the Messenger of Allah ﷺ had?' (Abu Dawud 1365)

However, when the Blessed Messenger ﷺ was aware of others trying to imitate his practice, he warned them of their other responsibilities, to take care of their own health and also think of the wellbeing of their families, who might suffer from neglect and deprivation, if they spent too much time on their devotions. He did not wish their personal relationships to become rushed, or stressed, or maybe irritable.

'A'ishah recorded him saying: 'Choose such actions as you are capable of performing (without difficulty); Allah does not grow weary but you do. The acts most pleasing to Allah are those which are done as regular practice, even if they amount to little.' She added: 'Whenever he began an action, he would do it regularly.' (Abu Dawud 1363, Muslim 1710)

One reason why excessive efforts were not approved of was because the Prophet ﷺ knew only too well the extent to which human endurance could go, and did not wish believers to strain themselves to the limits. People would not be able to keep that up forever, and then when they gave up they would feel that they had failed. They would not have failed Allah at all, merely the unrealistic limits they had set themselves. And if their extreme practice had been public and observed by others, they might well feel foolish and embarassed by knowing looks. Allah loves the keen young worshippers as the teacher loves the earnest pupil—but the wisdom of 'those in the know' always advises moderation. Nothing is more unpleasant, of course, then a bumptious zealot happy in the conceited thought that he or she is more devout or saintly than others. This is *not* the hallmark of the saint at all!

Urwah ibn Zubayr recorded that 'A'ishah had told him that one Hawlah bint Tuwayt passed by her on one occasion while she was with the Prophet ﷺ. She said: 'That is Hawlah bint Tuwayt, and they say that she (prays so much that she) does not sleep at night.' Upon this the Messenger ﷺ said: 'She does not sleep at night! Choose an act which you are capable of doing (regularly). By Allah, Allah never grows weary, but you will grow weary.' (Muslim 1716, see also Abu Dawud 1363)

'A'ishah recorded: Once the Prophet ﷺ came while a woman was sitting with me. He said: 'Who is she?' I replied: 'She is so-and-so,' and told him about her (excessive) praying. He said disapprovingly: 'Do (good) deeds which are within your capacity (without your being overtaxed by your effort), as Allah never gets weary, but (surely) you will get weary; the best deed in the sight of Allah is that which is (able to be) done regularly.' (Bukhari 2.33.41)

ON KEEPING PUBLIC PRAYERS BRIEF

The Blessed Prophet 鑗 used to spend many long hours in private prayer, but he believed there was a vital difference between the motivation of people who prayed at length in private and those who did so in public. Public prayers involve a responsibility towards others. An Imam or prayer-leader has no right to impose a burden that might not be acceptable to those praying behind him.

The guiding principles of the Blessed Prophet 鑗 were always those of practicality and kindness, for he was very well aware that not everyone can sit comfortably on the floor, and many believers would be uncomfortable because they were aged or infirm, or were looking after infants. Others had all sorts of duties to attend to, businesses to go to, and all the daily chores and responsibilities that people normally have.

One famous *hadith* reveals the Prophet's 鑗 great, and perhaps unexpected, consideration for others—even when concentrating upon his prayer. Abu Qatadah recorded the Messenger as saying:

'I stand up to pray and intend to pray at length: but when I hear the cry of a child I shorten it for fear that his mother might be distressed.' (Abu Dawud 788, Muslim 952, Bukhari 11.64.675-676)

There are usually children, or mothers with children, present at most of the prayers—and usually the mothers who .wish to concentrate on their prayers properly have little choice but to care for their children at the same time, so that the men might be free from this distraction. Every mother knows how embarrassing it is to have a child that insists on crying or making some sort of disturbance. The Blessed Prophet 鑗 knew it too, and when he heard mothers in difficulties because of their children, he cut short

long prayers or recitations in order not to distress them any more than necessary.

In fact, it is the public *duty* of the Imam or prayer-leader to be aware of the personal problems and limitations of his congregation, and to lead in such a way that none of the participants feel tired or become bored; and shorten it if there is any incident during the prayer.

It is recorded that the Blessed Prophet ﷺ once rebuked Mu'adh ibn Jabal, who was leading the people in the sunset prayer. He said:

'O Mu'adh, do not become a trouble, because the aged, the weak, the needy and the traveller pray behind you.' (Abu Dawud 791, Muslim 936)

Abu Mas'ud al-Ansari recorded: A person came to the Messenger of Allah ﷺ and said: 'I stay away from the morning prayer on account of such-and-such, because he keeps us so long.'

I never saw Allah's Messenger ﷺ more angry than he was that day. He said: 'O people, some of you are frightening others away—so whoever leads in prayer he must be brief, for behind him are the weak, the aged, and those who have business to attend.' (Muslim 940, Bukhari 3.29.90, 11.61.670 etc.)

A *hadith* recorded by Abu Hurayrah made it crystal clear:

'When one of you leads the people in prayer, he should be brief, for among them are the weak, the sick and the aged. But when any of you prays by himself, then he may pray for as long as he likes.' (Abu Dawud 794, 795; Muslim 942–946)

ON NOT NEGLECTING ONE'S HOUSEHOLD

The Blessed Prophet ﷺ was always pleased if Muslims managed to get to a mosque for the five compulsory prayers, but he disapproved of Muslim men spending so long in the mosques that they neglected their families and their other duties.

The Muslim men (or women) who wished to spend long times in personal prayer should not be selfish in their devotions, but should bear other people in mind too. This is particularly important to stress for men who enjoy the company of their male friends, and stay away from their wives and families for such prolonged periods that their loved ones are neglected or distressed.

The Blessed Prophet ﷺ recommended:

'Offer some of your prayers in your houses, and do not make them graves.' (Abu Dawud 1038 and 1443—recorded by Ibn 'Umar; see also Muslim 1703, Bukhari 8.52.424 etc.)

The Blessed Prophet ﷺ was speaking with gentle irony. Graves were places where he had specifically forbidden prayers to be said. The saying therefore encouraged Muslim men to bring the atmosphere of prayer into their homes, to keep and preserve their homes as clean and pure places of happiness where Allah was respected and not resented, and not to neglect them.

The Blessed Prophet ﷺ actually made it quite clear that prayers other than the compulsory five earned more 'reward' if said at home with the family, than if they were said in the mosque.

'The prayer a man offers in his house is more excellent than his prayer in this mosque, except for obligatory prayer.' (Abu Dawud 1039—recorded by Zayd ibn Thabit)

A famous *hadith* underlined the fact that it was also a good thing to pray even the compulsory prayer at home from time to time—so that a Muslim did not get the idea that prayer in congregation at the set five times was compulsory. The following *hadith* reveals the claims the general public made on the Prophet ﷺ, and his occasional chiding them for trying to take things too far.

Zayd ibn Thabit said: 'The chamber of the Messenger of Allah ﷺ was built in the mosque. He used to come out at night and pray. They (the people) also prayed along with him. They would come every night. If on any night the Messenger of Allah ﷺ did not come out, they would cough, raise their voices, and throw pebbles and sand on his door. The Messenger of Allah ﷺ came out to them in anger, and said: 'O people, you have done this so often that I have (started to) think it is compulsory for you! Offer your prayers in your houses, for a man's prayer is better in his house except the obligatory prayer!' (Abu Dawud 1442, Muslim 1708, Bukhari 21.4.229)

It is important to stress that although the Blessed Prophet ﷺ remarked that 'the angels invoke blessings on anyone who remains sitting or standing at the place where he says his prayer, (i.e. in the mosque), even if he is not in *wudu*', saying: 'O Allah, forgive him (or her); O Allah, have mercy on him (or her).' (Abu

Dawud 469), he nevertheless did not approve of a Muslim man remaining long hours in the mosque if it was to the neglect and sadness of his wife and family—even if it was for the purpose of prayer. Many Muslim men miss this point, and their private devotions away from their homes cause their wives and families loneliness, grief and distress.

Needless to say, the Blessed Prophet ﷺ would hardly approve if excessive time was spent there merely for socialising and playing games! The reason has to be genuinely for prayer, and even then the Blessed Prophet ﷺ considered that private prayers were better said at home.

Abu Hurayrah recorded: 'One is considered to be at prayer so long as one is detained by prayer; nothing (else) should prevent a person from going home to one's family, except prayer.' (Abu Dawud 470)

It is all too easy for a devout man to consider that he is earning credit with Allah for his long times spent in devotion, but forget that if he is genuinely hurting or depressing those who love him by doing this, then his long prayer becomes a selfish act and the so called 'credit' he has earned will have to be 'paid back' to those he has hurt, when he faces Judgement Day.

Abu Hurayrah recorded that the Messenger of Allah said: 'Do you know who is the real destitute and bankrupt person?' The companions said: 'Anyone who does not have money, property, or means of subsistence.' He said: '(No,) The really poor person is the one amongst my followers who will bring forth on the Day of Judgement his good record of *salah*, *zakah* and other forms of worship, but who will also have in his record of deeds such sins as reviling and slandering others, misappropriating someone's property, or murdering unjustly, and so forth. The good deeds of the person will be distributed amongst the aggrieved parties, and when all his good deeds are exhausted, the misdeeds and sins of the aggrieved persons will be thrust upon him, and consequently he will be cast into hell-fire.' (Muslim)

Needless to say, it was the Blessed Prophet's ﷺ own practice to return speedily to his house, where he blessed his private quarters and made his wives happy with his prayerful presence.

On one occasion the Blessed Prophet ﷺ actually rebuked 'Uthman ibn Mazun, not for being a bad man, but because he spent so much time on his private devotions that his wife was neglected and his normal family life suffered. The Prophet ﷺ disapproved of anything that made others suffer. He advised him to make sure that he found adequate time for his wife, for entertaining friends, and for looking after and enjoying his own self and interests.

'A'ishah recorded: 'The Prophet ﷺ called 'Uthman ibn Mazun. When he came to him, he said: "Uthman, do you dislike my practice?' He said: 'No, by Allah, but I seek (to emulate) your practice.' The Prophet ﷺ said: 'I sleep, I pray, I keep fast, I leave fast, and I marry women. Fear Allah, 'Uthman, your wife has a right on you, your guest has a right on you, your self has a right on you; you should keep fast and leave fast, and pray and sleep.' (Abu Dawud 1364; see also Bukhari 62.90.127)

Sometimes, it was the other way round, and it was a devout wife who neglected her husband and had to be rebuked:

Abu Sa'id recorded that an aggrieved woman came to the Prophet ﷺ expecting him to support her against her husband. She said: 'Messenger of Allah, my husband Safwan ibn al-Muattal beats me when I pray, and makes me break my fast when I keep fast, and he does not offer dawn prayer until the sun rises.' He asked Safwan, who was present there, about what she said. He replied: 'Messenger of Allah, as for her statement 'he beats me when I pray', she recites two *surahs* and I have forbidden her.' The Prophet ﷺ said: 'If one *surah* is recited, that is sufficient.' Safwan continued: 'As regards her saying 'he makes me break my fast', she (will) keep on fasting; I am a young man, I cannot withhold myself.' (Perhaps it should be explained that sexual intercourse is not allowed whilst one is fasting). The Prophet ﷺ said on that day: 'A woman should not fast except with the permission of her husband.' Safwan said: 'As to her statement that I do not pray until the sun rises, we are a people belonging to a (certain) class, and (our profession of supplying water) is already known about us. We do not awake until after sun-rise.' The Prophet ﷺ said: 'Offer your prayer when you awake.' (Abu Dawud 2453) (Water-carriers supplied people until almost the end of the night, and therefore found it impossible to rise for prayer before sunrise)

If you read Abu Sa'id's *hadith* again, you will see how both husband and wife in a case like this will have to be more caring to the other if their marriage is to survive. Both are good Muslims, who fast and pray. But her husband should not beat or harass his wife for her devotion towards Allah; and on the other hand, the wife should not make her devotions an excuse for neglecting her husband.

Incidentally, night-workers should take comfort from this *hadith*, and accept the mercy of Allah for when they are unable to pray at the proper time due to their special sleep-patterns.

Problems

............🌿............

EASED CONDITIONS ALLOWED FOR THE ELDERLY OR THOSE IN PAIN

The point of view of the Blessed Prophet ﷺ was that if there was nothing wrong with the person praying, then they should offer their prayer in the correct position. However, if a person was aged or infirm, or suffering from some disability, there was nothing wrong with praying in a sitting position, or even lying down.

Imran ibn Husayn recorded that he had a fistula, and so he asked the Prophet ﷺ about this. The Prophet ﷺ said:

'(Normally) offer prayer in a standing position; if you are unable to do this, then from a sitting position; if you are still unable, then on your side (i.e. lying down). (Abu Dawud 952)

'A'ishah commented: 'I never saw the Messenger of Allah ﷺ reciting the Qur'an in his prayer at night in the sitting position until he became old. Then he used to sit in it, and recite the Qur'an until forty or thirty verses remained, then he stood and recited them and then prostrated himself.' (Abu Dawud 953, Muslim 1590) She added that 'when he prayed standing he bowed standing, and when he prayed sitting, he bowed sitting.' (Abu Dawud 955)

Sometimes, when he became old, he leaned upon a staff during the recitation:

Umm Qais, daughter of Mihsan, said that when the Messenger of Allah ﷺ became aged and the flesh grew increasingly upon him, he took a prop at his place of prayer and rested on it.' (Abu Dawud 948)

The Prophet ﷺ did not approve of people making themselves ill in their efforts to carry out their prayers. If they were weak and the prayer was long, they were allowed to sit down if they needed. One interesting incident involved his gentle rebuke of one of the daughters of Jahsh—either his wife Zaynab or her sister Hamnah.

Anas said: The Messenger of Allah ﷺ entered the mosque (and saw that) a rope was tied between two pillars, He asked: 'What is this rope for?' The people told him: 'This is for Hamnah ibn Jahsh who prays here. When she is tired, she reclines on it.' The Messenger of Allah ﷺ said: 'She should (only) pray as much as she has strength (to do). When she is tired, she should sit down.' (Abu Dawud 1307. The version of Ziyad names Zaynab as the woman and adds: 'When she becomes fatigued, or is tired, she holds it.' He said: 'Undo it. You should pray in good spirits. When one is fatigued or tired, one should sit down.' (Abu Dawud 1307, Muslim 1714)

ON TENDERNESS AND ENCOURAGEMENT TO CHILDREN DURING PRAYER

There are several *hadith* that record the Blessed Prophet's ﷺ tenderness towards children during moments of prayer. He did not exclude them, or regard them as distractions. For example, Abu Qatadah recorded one occasion when the Prophet ﷺ came to the mosque carrying his grand-daughter Umamah (daughter of Zaynab and Abu'l-'As) on his shoulder:

'The Messenger of Allah ﷺ led the people in prayer while she was (leaning against) his shoulder. When he bowed he put her down, and picked her up again when he got up. He kept on doing so until he had finished his prayer.' (Abu Dawud 918, Muslim

1107, Bukhari 9.17.495)

How lovely to visualise our Prophet ﷺ performing his devotions with his little granddaughter in his arms. Mind you, this *sunnah* is not copied by many men, who prefer to leave the little ones with the women. In any case, if a man was carrying a child, it would be polite to take a position at the back and not where others would be distracted.

Once his grandsons Hasan and Husayn came toddling in: Abdallah ibn Buraydah recorded: 'The Messenger of Allah ﷺ was preaching a sermon to us when his grandsons Hasan and Husayn came toddling in wearing red shirts. He (broke off his sermon), came down from the pulpit and lifted them up (in his arms) and went back to the pulpit carrying them. He then said: 'How true, what Allah said! 'Your property and your children are a trial to you!' (*Sūrah* 64:15). I saw these two, and I could not wait.' After (saying that) he resumed his speech.' (Abu Dawud 1104)

The Blessed Prophet ﷺ was always aware if there were children with their mothers in the congregation, and bore this in mind by keeping his sermons brief.

Anas ibn Malik recorded: 'The Messenger of Allah ﷺ would take note of the crying of a lad in the company of his mother during prayer, and he would recite a short *sūrah*.' (Muslim 951)

ON PRAYING AT HOME IN BAD WEATHER

Although the Blessed Prophet ﷺ was always pleased whenever Muslims took themselves to the mosque to pray alongside other Muslims, he did not expect the call to the Mosque to cause suffering. There are traditions that he excused believers when the weather was bad, either through cold or rain.

Nafi narrated on the authority of Ibn 'Umar that whenever there was a cold or rainy night, the Messenger of Allah ﷺ

commanded the announcer to tell the people to pray in their dwellings. (Abu Dawud 1055, Muslim 1487, Bukhari 11.18.605; 11.40.635 etc.)

Ibn 'Umar made the call to prayer at Dajnan (a place between Makkah and Madinah) on a cold and windy night. He added the words at the end of the call: 'Lo! Pray in your dwellings! Lo! Pray in your dwellings!'. He then said: 'The Messenger of Allah ﷺ used to command the mu'adhdhin to announce 'Lo! Pray in your dwellings!' on a cold or rainy night during journeys.' (Abu Dawud 1057)

Ibn 'Umar also recorded that the announcer of the Messenger of Allah ﷺ used to announce people to pray in their homes at Madinah on rainy days or cold mornings.

Ibn Sirin recorded that Ibn Abbas said to his mu'adhdhin on a rainy day: 'When you have uttered the words 'I testify that Muhammad is the Messenger of Allah', do not say 'Come to prayer' but say 'Pray at your homes.' The people were very surprised by this announcement. He said: 'One who was better than me did it. The Friday prayer is an obligatory duty; but I did not wish to put you to hardship by making you walk in mud and rain.' (Abu Dawud 1061, Bukhari 11.10.590)

Obviously, with the modern situation of paved roads and cars and so forth, the majority of Muslims are hardly put to hardship by most weather conditions. However, there are still a few days during the year when conditions really *are* horrendous— and on these days no Muslim should feel unnecessarily guilty if he or she could not get to the Mosque. Prayer in the home, or wherever one happens to be, is quite appropriate at those times.

It is also quite appropriate for consideration to be shown towards anyone who is aged or infirm, or who would have difficulty in walking, and so on.

This is affirmed also by the *hadith* that the congregational prayer is not compulsory in any case for four categories of people—slaves, women, children, or sick people. (Abu Dawud 1062)

COMBINING PRAYERS

Ibn Abbas recorded: The Messenger of Allah ﷺ combined the noon and afternoon prayers, and the sunset and night prayers at Madinah, without being in a state of fear or on a journey. Sa'id (one of the narrators) asked Ibn Abbas why he did that, and he replied that the Prophet ﷺ wanted that no-one among his *Ummah* should fall into (unnecessary) hardship.' (Abu Dawud 1207, Muslim 1516)

This practice was considered permissible if a person was submerged in some task and unable to offer the separate prayers in normal fashion; but it was not recommended to do this in normal circumstances, or to get into the habit of it. (Abu Dawud 1207 n. 628)

The Prophet thought it quite permissible to do this during journeys, or in times of battle, or if there was heavy rain—although the *hadith* quoted above specified that it was not a time of rain.

'Short' prayers, limited to two *rak'ahs fard* for *zuhr*, *'asr* and *isha'*, are known as qasr prayers. It is expected that travellers will be able to pray *fajr* and *maghrib* prayers as usual. He called this practice a 'gift' from Allah.

Yala ibn Umayyah said: 'I told 'Umar ibn al-Khattab that Allah had said: 'You may shorten the prayer only if you fear that those who are unbelievers may harm you.' (*Sūrah* 4:101), whereas the people are now safe.' He replied: 'I also wondered about that, so I asked the Messenger ﷺ and he said: 'It is an act of charity which Allah has granted to you, so accept His charity.' (Muslim 1461)

Abdallah ibn Shaqiq reported that Ibn Abbas was speaking to the believers one afternoon, and he still had not finished when the sun disappeared and the stars came out; the people (grew restless and) began to say 'Prayer, prayer!' A certain person from Banu Tamim was there, who refused to stop or back down, but (continued crying) 'Prayer, prayer.' Ibn Abbas said: 'May you be deprived of your mother! Do you teach me *sunnah*?' And then he said: 'I saw the Messenger of Allah ﷺ combining the noon and afternoon prayers and the sunset and *isha'* prayers.' Abdallah ibn Shaqiq said: 'Some doubt was created in my mind about it, so I came to Abu Hurayrah and asked him, and he testified that this was true.' (Muslim 1523)

According to Anas ibn Malik, the Blessed Prophet ﷺ used to pray qasr prayers when he went on a journey of three miles or over (Muslim, Ahmad, Abu Dawud, Baihaqi and Talkhees ibn Hajr), although others suggest nine miles or a day's journey to be more appropriate.

Other *hadiths* suggest that it depended on what time the Prophet ﷺ actually began his journey:

Anas ibn Malik recorded that whenever the Prophet ﷺ used to start on a journey before noon, he used to delay the *zuhr* prayer until the time of the *'asr* prayer, and then he would dismount and pray them together; and whenever the sun declined before he started the journey he used to offer the *zuhr* prayer and then ride.' (Bukhari 20.16.213)

Qasr prayers can continue for as long as the person is on the journey, for an unlimited length of time. During temporary stays in one place on the journey, the same 'gift' applies.

Jabir ibn Abdallah recorded one incident when the Blessed

Prophet 🕮 and his friend 'Umar ibn al-Khattab both missed the 'asr prayer on the day of the Battle of the Ditch. 'Umar said: 'Messenger of Allah, I could not say the 'asr prayer before the sun set.' Upon this the Messenger 🕮 said: 'By Allah, I too have not observed it.' So we went to a valley. The Messenger 🕮 performed ablution and we did too, and then he said the 'asr prayer after the sun had set, and then said the evening prayer after it.' (Muslim 1318)

In fact, there are two types of combining of prayers—the real or *haqiqi*, and formal or *suwari*. In *haqiqi* combination, the two prayers really are combined, but in suwari the combination means nothing more than delaying one prayer until the last moment of its time, and then praying the next prayer at the first moment of its time; in this way, both are really offered at their correct times. Abu Dawud 1202 n. 626, Muslim 1514 n. 962)

IF THE IMAM FORGETS A PRAYER

Sometimes, through sheer familiarity with the prayers, the leader can unconsciously make a mistake. For example, it is quite possible to forget the number of *rak'ahs* done. In this case, it is the duty of the congregation to tactfully inform the leader so that the extra *rak'ahs* can be added.

Nobody is above this kind of human error, not even the Blessed Prophet himself 🕮.

Abu Hurayrah (and many other narrators) recorded one such incident:

'The Messenger of Allah 🕮 led us in one of the evening prayers. He led us in two *rak'ahs*, and then gave the salutation(i.e. finished the prayer two *rak'ahs* early). Then he got up and walked to a wooden bar which was placed in the front part of the mosque and placed his hands upon it, one on the other, with a disturbed expression on his face. The people came out hastily muttering: 'The prayer has been shortened! The prayer has been shortened!' Abu Bakr and 'Umar were among these people, but they were too shy to speak to him about it. Eventually a man called Dhu al-Yadain stood up (asking him): 'Did you forget, Messenger of Allah, or has the prayer been shortened?' He said: 'I did not forget it, nor did I shorten it.' The man insisted: 'Messenger of Allah, you did forget.' The Messenger of Allah ﷺ turned towards the people and asked: 'Does Dhu al-Yadain speak the truth?' They signalled that it was so. The Messenger of Allah ﷺ then returned to his place and prayed the remaining two *rak'ahs*, and then gave the salutation. He then uttered the *takbir* and prostrated himself as usual or longer. He then raised his head and uttered the *takbir*, then he uttered the *takbir* and made the prostration as usual or longer. Then he raised his head and uttered the *takbir*.' (Abu Dawud 1003, Muslim 1184, Bukhari 22.23.321)

Prayers for forgetfulness are known as sajdah sahev. They are allowed if a person forgets how many *rak'ahs* they have performed, or get up after the second *rak'ah* having forgotten to pray *tashahhud*, or fall short of the number of *rak'ahs* they intended to do. In these cases, when one is not sure, it is allowed to do two sajdah *rak'ahs* either before or after the salutation, and the prayer is still valid.

However, the prayer is not considered valid if any of the key parts of it has been ommitted, for example the *qiyam*, *ruku'* or either sajdahs.

Abdallah ibn Jafar recorded: 'Anyone who has become confused and doubtful in his (or her) prayer should do two extra sajdahs after the salutation.' (Ahmad, Abu Dawud, Nisai, Ibn Khuzaimah).

Islamic jurists differ in their opinions as to whether one

should offer prostration due to forgetfulness before or after the salutation; for example, the Abu Hanifah school suggests after and the al-Shafi'i school before.

What matters is that it is not a matter for censure or blame, and that no member of the congregation has the right to sneer at or abuse the leader, but they do have the duty to remind the leader and see to it that the matter is swiftly put right, whether before or after the salutation.

Imran ibn Husayn recorded: 'The Messenger of Allah ﷺ gave the salutation at the end of three *rak'ahs* in the afternoon prayer, then went into the apartment (according to the version of Maslamah). A man called al-Khirbaq who had got long arms got up and said: 'Has the prayer been shortened, Messenger of Allah?' He came out angrily trailing his cloak, and said: 'Is he telling the truth?' They said: 'Yes.' He then prayed that *rak'ah*, then gave the salutation, then made two prostrations, then gave the salutation.' (Abu Dawud 1013)

Sometimes the error could be that of making one *rak'ah* too many. Abu Allah ibn Mas'ud recorded:

'The Messenger of Allah ﷺ prayed five *rak'ahs* in the noon prayer. He was asked whether the prayer had been extended. He asked what they meant by that. The people said: 'You prayed five *rak'ahs*.' Then he made two prostrations after having given the salutation.' (Abu Dawud 1014, Muslim 1168)

The version of the narrator Ibrahim added the Blessed Prophet's ﷺ gentle and humble words:

'When he finished the prayer he turned his face to us and said: 'Had anything new happened in prayer, I would have informed you. I am only a human being, and I forget just as you do; so when I forget, remind me; and when any of you is in doubt about his prayer, he should aim at what is correct, and complete his prayer in that respect, then give the salutation and afterwards make two prostrations.' (Abu Dawud 1015)

The general advice of the Prophet was that if a person was not sure whether he or she had performed the correct number of *rak'ahs*, they should not agonise in their mind about it, but perform two more anyway; that way the missing ones would be completed, and if the worshipper ended up doing too many, it could only count to his or her credit.

Abu Sa'id al-Khudri recorded: 'When any one of you is in doubt about his (or her) prayer and does not know how much has been prayed, three or four (*rak'ahs*), he (or she) should cast aside doubt and base the prayer on what he (or she) is sure of, then perform two prostrations before giving salutation. If he has prayed five *rak'ahs*, they will make his prayer an even number for him, and if he has prayed exactly four, they will be humiliation for the devil.' (Muslim 1166)

The mention of the devil was not without its humourous side! As we have seen so many times in these *hadiths* the Prophet ﷺ had a very colourful turn of phrase on occasions.

Abu Hurayrah recorded him saying: 'When any of you stand up to pray, the devil comes to you and confuses you so that you do not know how much you have prayed.' (Muslim 1159). 'When there is a call to prayer the devil runs back breaking wind so that he may not hear the call, and when the call is complete he comes back. And when the *takbir* is pronounced he again runs back, and when *takbir* is over he comes back and distracts a person saying 'Remember such-and-such, referring to something the person did not have in their mind, with the result that he (or she) does not know how much he has prayed; so when any one of you is not sure how much he (or she) has prayed, perform two prostrations while sitting.' (Muslim 1161)

ON INTERRUPTING PRAYER

Normally, once a person has started saying the prayer, they do not stop for any interruption and polite people wait quietly until the prayer is finished rather than disturb them. However, this was not regarded by the Blessed Prophet ﷺ as a compulsory matter, but he judged the circumstances. Sometimes, for example, when praying in the house, people can arrive, interruptions take place, the telephone rings, and so on. Should one just ignore them and make them wait, or break off and then start the prayer all over again?

'A'ishah records what the Prophet ﷺ did:

'Once the Messenger of Allah ﷺ was praying with his door bolted, when I arrived and knocked to have the door opened. He walked to the door and opened it for me, and then returned to his place of prayer.' (Abu Dawud 922)

If people spoke to him while he was praying, sometimes he acknowledged them and sometimes he did not.

Abdallah ibn Mas'ud said: 'We used to salute the Messenger of Allah ﷺ while he was engaged in prayer, and he would respond to our salutation; but when we returned from the Negus we saluted him and he did not respond to us. He said: 'Prayer demands one's whole concentration.' (Abu Dawud 923, Muslim 1096)

Ibn 'Umar recorded on the authority of Suhaib: 'I passed by the Messenger of Allah ﷺ who was praying. I saluted him, and he returned it by making a sign... with his finger.' (Abu Dawud 925)

Once the Blessed Prophet ﷺ was praying whilst on his camel. Jabir recorded that when he tried to talk to him, the Prophet ﷺ just made a sign with his finger, and when he had finished the prayer spoke to him, asking for the details of the mission on which Jabir had been sent. He said: 'Nothing prevented me from talking to you except that I was praying.' (Abu Dawud 926, Muslim 1102)

It is obviously not good manners for someone to try to insist on getting a response from anyone who is praying unless it is a real emergency. Normally, you should wait quietly until they have finished. For example, if the phone rings for someone and you call them to come but there is no response, just think if it is prayer time and remember the Muslim could be praying. Ask the caller to try again later, rather than disturb them.

ON CATCHING THE ATTENTION OF THE IMAM DURING PRAYER

If anything happens during prayer and the people behind the Imam wish to attract his attention, the Prophet ﷺ recommended that a man might say 'Glory be to Allah', whereas a woman should not speak but gently tap the outer part of her left hand with the inner part of her right hand (the position in which she will have her hands during he prayer), (Abu Dawud 940), or with two fingers of her right hand. (Abu Dawud 942). (see also Muslim 845, 850)

MISHAPS

It is always necessary to be in *wudu'* before performing the *salah* prayers.

Abu Hurayrah recorded: 'The prayer of a person who does hadath is not accepted until he performs the ablution.' A person from the Hadramaut asked him: 'What is hadath?' Abu Hurayrah replied: 'Hadath means the breaking of wind from the anus.' (Bukhari 4.2.137)

Sometimes a person involved in prayer is suffering from indigestion, or a cough, or has a weak bladder. The performance of the prayer movements of bowing and sitting could sometimes have embarrassing consequences. The believers wondered if breaking wind would break *wudu'* or not, and whether anyone to whom this happened should leave the row and perform another ablution, and whether or not if they did they should complete the prayer they had interrupted, or repeat it afresh.

'Ali ibn Talq recorded that the Prophet ﷺ said: 'When any of you breaks wind during prayer, he should withdraw, perform ablution and repeat the prayer.' (Abu Dawud 205)

However, matters were occasionally in doubt, and in these cases, the Prophet ﷺ took an understanding and sympathetic attitude:

Abbad ibn Tamim recorded from his uncle that a person raised the matter with the Messenger ﷺ that he was not sure as to whether or not something had happened to him to break his ablution. The Holy Prophet ﷺ said: 'He should not break off his prayer unless he hears a sound or perceives a smell (of passing wind).' (Muslim 702, Abu Dawud 176, Bukhari 4.4.139)

Abu Hurayrah recorded: 'If any one of you has pain in his abdomen, but is not sure whether or not anything has issued from him, he should not leave the mosque unless he heard the sound or perceived a smell.' (Muslim 703)

As regarded a fit of coughing, the Blessed Prophet did not consider this to be a matter for which fresh ablution was necessary, although it was certainly inconvenient and a disturbance of the prayer:

Abdallah ibn Sa'ib recorded: 'The Messenger of Allah ﷺ led us in the morning prayer in Makkah and began surat al-Muminun (23), but when he came to the mention of Moses and Aaron (verse 45) or to the mention of Jesus (verse 50), a cough got the better of him, and he bowed.' (Muslim 918). Abd al-Razzaq's version stated: 'He cut short the recitation and bowed.'

Friday Mid-Day Prayers

······ ❦ ······

THE IMPORTANCE OF FRIDAY PRAYERS

The prayer said by the gathered community of Muslims at zuhr on Friday is regarded as particularly important. Even if worshippers cannot get to a mosque for the other set prayers, they are expected to make a special effort to gather together for this prayer on Fridays. The Friday prayer is different from all the other prayers in that it is specifically intended to draw the whole Muslim community of worshippers together. Indeed, it is accepted as traditional in Islam that the Friday prayer is valid only if it is said in congregation. If a Muslim misses the congregation for some reason, then they may pray the noon prayer alone, but they have missed the Friday prayer.

The number of persons required to form a congregation is disputed by the various schools of Islam; the school of Abu Hanifah accepts that if three persons are gathered together, with an Imam, then that is valid as a congregational prayer. Other schools insist that the minimum number for a congregation should be forty persons ('Awn al-Mabud 1.412.415)

Unless a city or town has a very high population of Muslims, it is recommended that all the Muslims in the region should go and offer the Friday prayer in one place, even if they usually support several different mosques.

Where a place has only a small community of Muslims, their congregation should still be considered valid, on the grounds that

the Qur'an gave an unconditional and absolute order to hold the
prayer, without mentioning whether it should be in a city or not.
The school of thought that requires a large number to form a
congregation based its reasoning on a tradition reported by 'Ali,
that no Eid day supplications or Friday prayers were valid except
in a city. However, this was not a statement of the Blessed Prophet
ﷺ, and against this it can be pointed out that 'Umar wrote to the
people of Bahrain to 'Offer Friday prayer wherever you might
be', and there is a *hadith* in Baihaqi that the Prophet ﷺ said:

'The Friday prayer is obligatory on the people of every
village, although there live (there only) four persons.'

Although it was not compulsory for women to attend Friday
prayers at the mosque, nevertheless we know from the *hadith* that
many women did so. For example, Umm Hisham, bint al-Harith
ibn al-Numan commented that she actually memorised *sūrah* al-
Qaf from the mouth of the Messenger ﷺ.

Umrah, daughter of Abd al-Rahman reported on the authority of her sister: 'I memorised *sūrah* al-Qaf from the mouth of
the Messenger of Allah ﷺ; he used to recite it on every Friday.'
(Abu Dawud 1097)

Many aspects of the Muslim life involve struggle and self-
denial and sacrifice, as well as inner peace and joy. To arrive at the
'climax' of the week and share it in the company of the other
Muslims is a great blessing. The Blessed Prophet ﷺ indicated that
lovely feeling of calm and satisfaction which should flow from the
Muslim way of life and prayer; the drawing on of evening after the
afternoon prayer and before the close of night feels especially
blessed:

Jabir ibn Abdallah reported: 'Friday is divided into twelve
hours. Amongst them there is an hour in which a Muslim does not
ask Allah for anything but He gives it to him. So seek it in the last

hour, after the afternoon prayer.' (Abu Dawud 1043)

Other authorities recorded other sayings about this time of peace and blessing.

Ka'b said (referring to the Hour of Blessing): 'It is on one day every year.' So I said: 'It is on *every* Friday.' Ka'b read the Torah and said: 'The Messenger of Allah has spoken the truth.' Abdallah ibn Salam said: 'I know what time it is.' Abu Hurayrah said: 'I asked him: Tell me about it.' Abdallah said: 'It is at the very end of Friday.' I asked: 'How can it be when the Messenger of Allah ﷺ said, 'No Muslim finds it while he is praying...' and this is a moment when no prayer is offered? Abdallah said: 'Has the Messenger of Allah ﷺ not said: If anyone is seated waiting for the prayer, he is engaged in the prayer until he observes it?' I said: 'Yes, it is so.' (Abu Dawud 1041)

The author of 'Fath al-Bari' quoted no less than forty-two opinions. Some believe that the purpose of not revealing the hour is so that Muslims shall remain prayerful throughout the entire day. Others believe it starts when the Imam starts his khutbah (sermon) and lasts until the end of the *zuhr* prayer.

Muslims recognise the Friday prayer as a very important focus of their week, and a vital part of the building-up of the spirit of community. All male Muslims are expected to attend, and if a Muslim misses the prayer for more than a couple of weeks, it is a matter of concern.

Al-Ja'd al-Damri, one of the Companions, recorded: 'He who misses the Friday prayer for three (consecutive) Fridays for no reason other than slackness, Allah will mark his heart.' (Abu Dawud 1047)

However, as for all prayers, the *niyyah* or intention of the worshipper is always the key to what takes place, and whether or not blessing is really received.

Abdallah ibn 'Amr recorded that the Blessed Prophet ﷺ said: 'Three types of people attend Friday prayer: one is present in a frivolous way, and that is all he gets from it; another comes with a supplication, which Allah may grant or refuse as He wishes; another is present silently and in quiet, without stepping over a Muslim or annoying anyone—and that is atonement for his (or her) sins till the next Friday and three days more, the reason being that Allah, the Exalted, says: 'He (or she) who does a good deed will have ten times as much. (*Surah* 6:160)' (Abu Dawud 1108)

Incidentally, people with no knowledge of Arabic are often confused as to the name of the Friday prayer. Sometimes it is called the jumah prayer, and sometimes it is referred to as jama'ah. The world 'jumah' simply means Friday, and denotes the day of the obligatory assembly. The word 'jama'ah' means congregation or assembly, and describes the fact that on this occasion at least as many Muslims as possible must gather together for the prayer.

Many Muslims try to pray other prayers together in the mosque, some even attempting to be there for all five; but whereas this may be commendable, it is not practicable for most men, and it certainly not compulsory. However, it is quite feasible for most men to be able to attend this one weekly and compulsory service.

COMING LATE TO THE SERMON

If someone comes in late to the prayer, perhaps even while the Imam is actually in the process of giving the sermon, should they just slip in quietly without fuss, or what? Some people seem very disapproving if a latecomer prays the two *rak'ahs* of 'respect to the mosque' before sitting. The Blessed Prophet ﷺ advised that even if other people noticed, it was still better that he or she should pray two *rak'ahs*, and then sit down.

Jabir and Abu Salih recorded: Sulaik al-Ghatafani came while the Messenger ﷺ was giving the sermon. He asked him: 'Did you pray something?' He said: 'No.' He said: 'Offer two *rak'ahs* of prayer, and make them short.' (Abu Dawud 1111)

It is interesting to notice that as Imam on this occasion the Prophet ﷺ interrupted himself to clarify the position with the latecomer. According to the version of Jabir ibn Abdallah, the Prophet ﷺ then turned to the people and said:

'When any of you come while the Imam is preaching, he (or she) should pray two *rak'ahs* and make them short.' (Abu Dawud 1112)

Abu Qatadah recorded: 'I entered the mosque, when the Messenger of Allah ﷺ had been sitting among the people, and I also sat down among them. Upon this, he said: 'What prevented you from offering two *rak'ahs* (of *nafl* prayer) before sitting down?' I said: 'Messenger of Allah, I saw you sitting and the people sitting (around you, and I, I therefore, also sat down). He said: 'Whenever any of you enters the mosque, he should not sit down until he has observed two *rak'ahs*.' (Muslim 1541)

However, the Blessed Prophet ﷺ always disliked behaviour that was disruptive and rude. Another occasion when he interrupted his sermon in order to speak to someone was when, according to Abdallah ibn Busr:

'A man came and stepped over the people (seeking to sit in a particular place instead of just slipping in quietly at the back) while the Prophet ﷺ was giving the sermon on Friday. The Prophet ﷺ said: 'Sit down! You have disturbed (the people)'. (Abu Dawud 1113)

The one circumstance in which the Blessed Prophet ﷺ condoned a person moving about the changing his or her position during the sermon was if they were in danger of actually falling asleep.

Ibn 'Umar recorded: 'When any of you dozes in the mosque, he (or she) should change his place.' (Abu Dawud 1114)

This would fully wake the person and restore alertness. The Prophet ﷺ considered this quite acceptable, and even commendable—for the urge to sleep during the congregation was sometimes to be attributed to the wiles of the devil! (Abu Dawud 1114, n. 568)

ON NOT MAKING THE SERMON TOO LONG

The Blessed Prophet ﷺ used to be very considerate of his congregation. One *hadith* records how he noticed a friend sitting down at a distance, and called him over.

Jabir recorded: 'When the Messenger of Allah ﷺ seated himself on the pulpit on a Friday, he said: 'Sit down.' Ibn Mas'ud took it literally and sat down at the door of the mosque, and when the Messenger of Allah ﷺ saw him, he said: 'Come here, Abdallah ibn Mas'ud.' (Abu Dawud 1086)

Jabir also commented: 'The prayer offered by the Messenger of Allah ﷺ was moderate, and the sermon given by him was also moderate. He would recite a few verses from the Qur'an, and exhort the people.' (Abu Dawud 1096)

The Prophet ﷺ wished to instruct the people and bring them closer to Allah, but he did not wish them to become bored. It is doubtful whether any sermon given by the Blessed Prophet ﷺ himself could *ever* have been boring; but he knew human nature very well, and may have experienced for himself the long rambling speeches of those who enjoy the sound of their own voices, those who seem quite incapable of realising the discomfiture of those listening to them, who might not have quite the same estimation of their talents or the worth of what they are saying!

Abu Mas'ud al-Ansari recorded: 'Someone came to the Messenger of Allah ﷺ and said: 'I keep away from morning prayer on account of such and such a man, because he keeps us so long.' I never saw Allah's Messenger ﷺ more angry when giving advice then he was that day. He said: 'O people, some of you are scaring people away, so whoever of you leads the people in prayer, he must be brief, for behind him are the weak, the aged, and people who have business to attend to!' (Muslim 940, Bukhari 3.29.90)

'Ammar ibn Yasir recorded: 'The Messenger of Allah ﷺ commanded us to shorten the speeches.' (Abu Dawud 1101)

Jabir ibn Samurah al-Suwai recorded: 'The Messenger of Allah ﷺ would not lengthen the sermon on Friday. He would say a few words (only).' (Abu Dawud 1102)

Shaqiq recorded: We were sitting at the door of Abdallah ibn Mas'ud, waiting for him (to come out and deliver a sermon to us). It was at this time that Yazid ibn Mu'awiyah happened to pass by. We asked him to inform Abdallah of our presence there. He went in and Abdallah lost no time in coming out to us and said: 'I was informed of your presence here, and nothing hindered my coming out to you but the fact that I did not like to bore you (by stuffing your minds with sermons) as Allah's Messenger ﷺ did not deliver sermons on certain days fearing that it might prove boring for us.' (Muslim 6775)

Ramadan

.............🌿.............

TARAWIH PRAYERS DURING RAMADAN

Ramadan is such a special month to Muslims that it is natural for them to withdraw from the world more and more to spend long periods in thoughtful meditation and prayer. Most Muslim men will go to the mosque every night during Ramadan, even if they did not do so during the rest of the year.

The special nightly *rak'ahs* in the mosque are known as tarawih prayers. Authentic and sound traditions indicate that the Blessed Prophet 🌿 used to pray eleven *rak'ahs* in this worship—that is, eight *rak'ahs* for tarawih and three for witr. However, the schools of Abu Hanifah, Malik, al-Shafi' and Ahmad recommend twenty *rak'ahs*—although there is evidence supporting both points of view, the majority feel that the traditions supporting twenty *rak'ahs* is weak. (Awn al-Mabud) 1, 521-22)

Whatever, the Blessed Prophet 🌿 did not wish people who could not or chose not to attend the mosque for some reason or other to feel guilty or downhearted about it. The prayers were certainly highly recommended, but they were not to be considered as compulsory duties, like the five *fard* daily prayers.

Abu Hurayrah recorded: 'The Messenger of Allah 🌿 used to commend prayer at night during Ramadan, but he did not command it as a duty.' (Abu Dawud 1366, Muslim 1663 etc.)

'A'ishah made this clear to the people. Abu Dawud 1368 reveals:

'A'ishah, wife of the Prophet ﷺ offered tarawih prayer in the mosque, and the people also prayed along with him. He then prayed on the following night, and the people gathered in large numbers. They gathered on the third night too, but the Messenger of Allah ﷺ did not come out to them. When morning came, he said: 'I saw what you did, and nothing prevented me from coming out to you except that I feared that this (prayer) might (then) be considered compulsory for you.' (That was in Ramadan.' (Abu Dawud 1368, Muslim 1666)

Incidentally, this same passage points out that it is perfectly permissible for women to accompany the men to tarawih prayer if they so wish. It was the practice of the Blessed 'A'ishah to do so, and when they prayed in the house she seems to have been particularly close to her beloved husband ﷺ as his helpmate and fellow worshipper.

'A'ishah said: 'The people used to pray (tarawih) in the mosque during Ramadan individually. The Messenger of Allah ﷺ commanded me (to spread a mat). I spread a mat for him, and he prayed upon it. The Prophet ﷺ said: O people, praise be to Allah, I did not pass my night without caring, nor did your position remain hidden from me.' (Abu Dawud 1369)

In other words, he was perfectly well-aware of the fact that people were in the mosque expecting him, but he established the practice of praying in the home as well, so that his followers might not come to believe it was compulsory to be in the mosque. Towards the end of 'Umar's caliphate, 'Umar urged the Muslims to come to congregation, calling it a 'good innovation'; and that is why the schools of Abu Hanifah, al-Shafi' and Ahmad and many others now regard it is more commendable to offer tarawih in congregation. However, according to Yusuf and Malik it is better to offer this prayer alone in the house. (Abu Dawud 1366, n. 722)

Zayd ibn Thabit recorded: Allah's Messenger ﷺ made a small room (with a palm leaf mat). He came out of his house and prayed in it. Some men came and joined him in his prayer. Then again the next night they came for the prayer, but Allah's Messenger ﷺ delayed and did not come out to them. So they raised their voices and knocked the door with small stones (to draw his attention). He came out to them in a state of anger saying: 'You are so insistent on doing this (i.e. making tarawih prayer together in the mosque) that I thought this prayer (i.e. tarawih) might become (regarded as) compulsory for you. So you people, offer this prayer in your homes, for the best prayer of a person is the one which he offers at home, except the compulsory (congregational) prayer.' (Bukhari 72.75.134)

Wherever they are said, the performance of tarawih prayers during Ramadan is a great blessing of Allah for any person who has sinned and fallen short. It gives a chance to make up for those shortcomings, and 'wipe the slate clean' again, in order to make a fresh start.

'He would say: 'If anyone prays during the night in Ramadan because of faith and seeking his reward from Allah, his previous sins will be forgiven to him.' When the Messenger of Allah ﷺ died, this was the practice, and it continued thus during Abu Bakr's caliphate and the early part of 'Umar's.' (Abu Dawud 1366, Muslim 1662)

The saying was transmitted by numerous people. The version of Uqail is slightly different—it recommends the one who fasts during Ramadan and prays during the night; but this is obviously what is implied in the first passage, since a Muslim who was not fasting would be unlikely to be performing the extra prayers!

LAYLAT-AL-QADR

Laylat al-Qadr is perhaps the most important night of the Muslim year, because it was on this night that the Blessed Prophet ﷺ first received his revelations of the Qur'an.

'We have indeed revealed this (message) in the Night of Power. And what will explain to you what the Night of Power is? The Night of Power is better than a thousand months. On it the angels and the spirit came down by God's permission, on every errand; Peace... This until the rising of the Morning.' (*Sūrah* 97)

There is a lot of discussion amongst scholars as to which night in Ramadan is the specific night on which it falls, but it is generally established that is on one of the odd numbers during the last ten days of Ramadan. The Blessed Prophet ﷺ did not pinpoint it exactly, so it is not known for certain to this day. However, it is such a blessed night that many Muslims consider prayers and worship on this night to be worth more than any amount of other worship, some say 'than the worship of a thousand months'. Many Muslims regard the night of the twenty-seventh as the special night:

Ubayy ibn Ka'b recorded: 'By Allah, it is the twenty-seventh night of Ramadan, without any reservation.' I (Zirr ibn Hubaysh) said: 'How do you know that, Abu al-Mundhir (Ubayy)?' He replied: 'By the sign of which the Messenger of Allah informed us.' I asked: 'What is that sign?' He replied: 'The sun rises like a vessel of water in the morning following that night; it has no ray until it rises high up.' (Abu Dawud 1373)

One can tell by the poetic words of the sign mentioned that the tradition is still not fixed. The 27th Ramadan occurs at any season of the year as the Muslim calendar is a lunar one.

Abdallah ibn Unays recorded a different tradition:

'I was present in the gathering of Banu Salamah, and I was the youngest of them. They said: 'Who will ask the Messenger of Allah ﷺ for us about Laylat al-Qadr?' This was on the twenty-first of Ramadan. I went out and said the sunset prayer along with the Messenger of Allah ﷺ, and I then stood at the door of his house. He passed by me and said: 'Come in.' I entered the house, and the dinner was brought for him. I was prevented from taking food myself as there was so little. When he finished his dinner, he said to me: 'Give me my shoes.' He then stood up, and I also stood up with him. He said: 'Perhaps you have some business with me?' I said: 'Yes. Some people of Banu Salamah have sent me to you asking about Laylat al-Qadr.' He asked: 'Which is the night today?' I said: 'Twenty-second.' He said: 'This is the very night.' He then withdrew and said: 'Or the following night,' referring to the twenty-third.' (Abu Dawud 1374)

Muhammad Ibrahim later asked Abdallah ibn Unays's son what his father's practice was for this night. The son recorded that his father had said to the Messenger ﷺ: 'I have a place in the desert where I live and in which I pray, with the praise of Allah; but give me command as to which night I should come to the mosque.' He replied: 'Come on the twenty-third night.' Abdallah ibn Unays used to enter the mosque when he had offered the afternoon prayer, and did not leave it for any purpose until he prayed the morning prayer. Then, when he had prayed it, he found his riding beast at the door of the mosque, mounted it, and went back to the desert.' (Abu Dawud 1375)

Abu Dharr recorded: 'We fasted along with the Messenger of Allah ﷺ during Ramadan, but he did not make us get up at night for prayer at any time during the month until seven nights remained; then he made us get up for prayer till a third of the night had passed. When the sixth remaining night came, he did not make us get up for prayer. When the fifth remaining night came, he made us get up for prayer until a half of the night had gone. I said: 'O Messenger of Allah, I wish you had led us in voluntary prayers for the whole of the night!' He said: 'When a person prays with an Imam until he leaves, it is counted as having spent the whole night in prayer.' On the fourth remaining night, he gathered his family, his wives, and the people and prayed with us till we were afraid we would miss the 'falah'. I said: 'What is the 'falah?' He said: 'The meal before daybreak.' Then he did not make us get up for prayer during the remainder of the month.' (Abu Dawud 1370)

It is probable that he prayed on the twenty-third, twenty-fifth and twenty-seventh night of Ramadan because they are the odd numbers.

'A'ishah recorded: 'When the last ten days of Ramadan came, the Prophet ﷺ kept vigil and prayed during the whole night,... and awakened his family to pray during the night.' (Abu Dawud 1371)

Ibn Abbas recorded the Prophet ﷺ as saying: 'Seek Laylat al-Qadr in the last ten nights of Ramadan; when nine nights remain, when seven remain, when five remain.' (Abu Dawud 1376)

Obviously people who pass whole nights in prayer are not going to be able to perform the humdrum day time duties of their normal work. The work of the Blessed Prophet ﷺ *was* to pray and preach and lead the people, and it is well known that he had enormous spiritual reserves in any case. This is one reason why he did not wish the Muslims to regard long full nights of prayer as in any way compulsory—for many Muslims are in the position of having to carry on their normal working days during Ramadan, despite the fast, and there is little point in making oneself ill, which only results in abandoning the fast.

One can find examples of people wishing to put others under pressure from very early times, and this was disapproved of. For example, Zirr ibn Hubaysh recorded that he asked Ubayy ibn Ka'b to tell him about Laylat al-Qadr, because he had previously asked Ibn Mas'ud about it and been told that 'anyone who gets up for prayer every night all the year round will hit upon it!' Ubayy retorted: 'May Allah have mercy on Abd al-Rahman (Ibn Mas'ud)! By Allah, he knew that it was in Ramadan, but he didn't like people to content themselves with that night alone.' (Abu Dawud 1373, Muslim 1668)

I'TIKAF, OR SECLUSION DURING THE LAST DAYS OF RAMADAN

'A'ishah recorded that when the last ten nights of Ramadan came, 'the Blessed Prophet ﷺ kept awake at night (for prayer and devotion), wakened his family, and prepared himself to observe prayer (with more vigour)... He used to exert himself in devotion during these last ten days to a greater extent than at any other time.' (Muslim 2643-44)

Many Muslims spend the whole of the last ten days of Ramadan in seclusion, set aside from the world, doing nothing but prayer, reading and studying the Qur'an. This is known as i'tikaf, from the word 'akafa' meaning 'to retire, to devote, to be bent on something,' or literally 'to stay in a place.' The person observing i'tikaf is known as mu'takif. I'tikaf does not have to be for ten days; the Prophet ﷺ actually recommended a night and a day. (See Abu Dawud 2468)

Ibn 'Umar recorded: 'The Prophet ﷺ used to observe i'tikaf during the last ten days of Ramadan. Nafi said: Abdallah (ibn 'Umar) showed me the place in the mosque where the Messenger of Allah ﷺ used to observe i'tikaf.' (Abu Dawud 2459, Muslim

2637)

Abu Hurayrah recorded: 'The Prophet ﷺ used to observe *i 'tikaf* during ten days of Ramadan every year. But in the year that he died, he observed twenty days.' (Abu Dawud 2460)

'A'ishah recorded: 'The Messenger of Allah ﷺ used to observe *i 'tikaf* in the last ten days of Ramadan until Allah called him back (i.e. he died). Then his wives observed *i 'tikaf* after him.' (Muslim 2640, Bukhari 33.1.243)

The main object of keeping fasts is to purify oneself from evil, and for high spiritual advancement it is a good thing to take some moments when one is devoted exclusively to the remembrance of Allah and His worship. This is not possible when a person is engaged in the normal routine, and therefore a Muslim tries to withdraw from home, family and daily routine and retire completely into contemplation of Allah. Many men take themselves to the mosque, and live and sleep there either for a day (usually Laylat ul-Qadr) or even for the last ten days.

Surprisingly, there is a great divergence of opinion on who should be in the mosque, and in which mosques the *i 'tikaf* is valid. The schools of Malik, al-Shafi'i, Ahmad ibn Hanbal, Dawud and most scholars hold that women should be allowed to spend *i 'tikaf* in the mosque also, but those following Abu Hanifah maintain that women should observe it in their homes, and that their *i 'tikaf* in the mosque would not be valid! Some Maliki and Shafi'i scholars hold that it is permissible for both men and women to observe *i 'tikaf* in their own houses.

Furthermore, Al-Shafi'i, Malik and the majority of scholars hold that *i 'tikaf* is allowed in every mosque, whereas according to Abu Hanifah and Ahmad it should only take place in mosques where prayers are offered in congregation; others say it should only be in a great mosque where Friday prayers are offered; and the companion Hudhayfah ibn al-Yaman maintained that it was only really valid in three mosques—the Sacred Mosque at Makkah, the Mosque of the Prophet ﷺ at Madinah and the great mosque at Jerusalem ('Awun al-Mubad 11, 308-9)

Once in the state of i'tikaf, the Prophet ﷺ did not break it for casual social reasons. He only left the mosque for 'necessary purposes.' 'A'ishah recorded: 'The sunnah for one who is observing i'tikaf is not to visit a patient, or to attend a funeral, or touch or embrace one's wife, or go out for anything but necessary purposes. There is no i'tikaf without fasting, and there is no i'tikaf except in a congregational mosque.' (Abu Dawud 2467) This hadith suggests that visiting sick friends and attending funerals was not considered important enough a reason—but we must bear in mind the social nature of these events in the Prophet's society. He is not talking about ignoring suffering and distressed friends in real emergencies but just breaking off what would have been his normal kind social routine with acquaintances.

Certainly, mu'takifs (i.e. people observing i'tikaf) were not supposed to break their seclusion for the usual social round. However, there was nothing to prevent them inquiring after a patient, or paying respects at a funeral. Indeed, 'A'ishah put on record, according to Ibn Isa, that the Prophet ﷺ did sometimes visit patients while observing i'tikaf—(Abu Dawud 2466). There is no hadith referring to his attending a funeral, but surely one cannot imagine that the Prophet ﷺ would have refused to attend the funeral of someone dear to him, had such a death occasioned while he was in i'tikaf.

The following example shows the true Muslim spirit of love and kindness taught by the Prophet: Abdallah Ibn Abbas was once sitting in i'tikaf in the mosque in Madinah when someone came and sat down next to him, with tears streaming down his face. Ibn

Abbas asked him gently what the matter was. He said: 'I owe a person some money, and by the Lord of this grave, I am not able to repay it.' Ibn Abbas consoled him by stating that he would go and speak to the claimant on his behalf. He got up, and as he was about to leave the mosque, the man reminded him that he was sitting in i'tikaf. 'Perhaps you had forgotten?' he said. 'No, I had not forgotten,' replied Ibn Abbas, 'but—and it seems like only yesterday I heard the Prophet say—(and tears came into the eyes of this Prophet's 🕌 companion and cousin as he spoke)—'to do one's best to help one's brother is better than spending ten whole years in i'tikaf.' (Baihaqi)

As regards one's intimate relations with a spouse, the word used in the *hadith* recorded by 'A'ishah for touching the wife refers to actual sexual intercourse, and only the schools of Malik and Abu Hanifah take it to mean not even greeting one's wife with a tender kiss or embrace. It does not mean one has to avoid *all* contact with one's wife. The following hadith shows clearly that being in i'tikaf does not necessitate sitting aloof in the role of a 'holy man', refusing all normal communication with dear ones because one was 'concentrating only on God'. Allah *never* requires us to ignore or hurt our loved ones.

'A'ishah recorded: 'When the Messenger of Allah 🕌 observed i'tikaf, he used to bend his head towards me, and I would comb his hair; but he entered the house only to fulfil human needs (i.e. to relieve himself).' (Abu Dawud 2461, Bukhari 33.2.245, 33.3.246)

The rule laid down by Allah in the Qur'an makes this quite clear: 'While you are in i'tikaf in the mosques, do not have sexual relations with your wives; these are the limits set by Allah, so do not approach them (for sexual relations).' (2:187) Of course, a loving relationship at night was perfectly permissible on the other nights of Ramadan. The Prophet did not disapprove, or advocate a month's abstinence! On the contrary, he felt that expression of love during this month was a blessed thing.

Once, some people of ill intent jumped to wrong conclusions about the Blessed Prophet ﷺ, when they saw him leaving the company of a woman.

Safiyyah bint Huyayy, a wife of the Prophet ﷺ recorded: 'When the Messenger ﷺ was observing i'tikaf in the mosque, I used to go to him and visit him. I had a talk with him, and then stood up. I then returned, and he also stood up to accompany me (to my house). Two men from the Ansar passed, and when they saw the Prophet ﷺ, they hurried up to him. The Prophet ﷺ said: 'Be at ease! This is (my wife) Safiyyah, daughter of Huyayy.' They said: 'Glory be to Allah, Messenger of Allah!' He said: 'Satan runs in man like blood. I feared he might have put some (evil) thought into your mind.' (Abu Dawud 2464, see also Bukhari 33.8.251, 33.11.254) (Incidentally, a sub-narrator asked Sufyan: 'Did Safiyyah visit him at night?' He replied: 'Of course, at night.'—Bukhari 33.12.255)

This passage shows clearly that the Prophet ﷺ did not ignore his wives during i'tikaf (as some of today's zealots feel they should), but treated them with love and courtesy. Men who believe they are doing right when they cut their wives and families off completely should bear this in mind.

Moreover, Muslims who are intent on preventing women from observing in the mosque should remember the hadith of 'A'ishah which stated clearly that not only did the Blessed Prophet's ﷺ wives perform i'tikaf alongside their dear husband, but one of them, Umm Salamah, was even allowed to do this in the mosque with him, even whilst she had a flow of blood (although there is discussion as to whether this was menstruation

or from some other cause).

'A'ishah recorded: 'One of the wives of the Messenger of Allah ﷺ observed i'tikaf along with him (in the mosque). She would see yellowness and redness. Sometimes we would place a washbasin while she prayed.' (Abu Dawud 2470, Bukhari 33.10.253)

To observe i'tikaf while fasting in Ramadan is *sunnah*, but it is not obligatory. Moreover, this seclusion does not *have* to be the last ten days of Ramadan—it can be done at other times. The Prophet once did it in the month of Shawwal to prove this point. Incidentally, the following *hadith* also shows that he realised, from the eager desire of his wives and other believers to copy him, that the practice would soon be in danger of being regarded as compulsory, and might then be imposed as a burden, and he wished to make it quite clear for all believers that it was *not* compulsory.

'A'ishah recorded: 'When the Messenger ﷺ intended to observe i'tikaf, he prayed the dawn prayer and then entered his place of seclusion. On one occasion he intended to observe i'tikaf during the last ten days of Ramadan. He ordered me to pitch a tent for him, and it was pitched. The other wives of the Prophet ﷺ also ordered to pitch tents for them, and they were pitched. When he offered the dawn prayer, he saw the tents and said: 'What is this? Did you intend this as an act of virtue?' She said: 'He then ordered to demolish his tent, and it was demolished. Then his wives also ordered to demolish their tents, and they were demolished. He then postponed i'tikaf until the first ten days of Shawwal.' (Abu Dawud 2458)

We should note here that the reason for the tent was because the Prophet ﷺ wished to be alone. His home was the mosque, and his wives had small rooms alongside the courtyard. The

Blessed Prophet ﷺ actually had no private room of his own. Putting a tent in the mosque courtyard gave him a little privacy. However, since the wives had the seclusion of their own rooms, tents were not all necessary for them, and although he accepted their desire to please Allah and copy him, he did not wish to start the fashion of filling the mosque with tents and people camping there. The principle of i'tikaf is to withdraw oneself and be alone with God; it defeats the object if one's place of seclusion becomes full of other people.

(According to the version of 'Amra bint Abdur-Rahman in Bukhari: 'A'ishah recorded that the Prophet ﷺ used to practise i'tikaf in the last ten days of Ramadan, and she used to pitch a tent for him, and after offering the morning prayer, he used to enter the tent. 'A'ishah asked his permission to let her practise i'tikaf too, and he allowed her; and so she pitched her tent in the mosque. When Hafsah heard of it, she also pitched a tent (for herself), and when Zaynab (bint Jahsh) saw it, she too pitched another tent. When, in the morning, Allah's Messenger ﷺ had finished the morning prayer, he saw four tents and asked: 'What is this?' He was told of the whole situation. Then he said: 'What made them to do this? Is this righteousness? Remove the tents, for I do not wish to see them.' So the tents were removed. The Prophet ﷺ therefore abandoned the i'tikaf in that month and practised it for ten days in the month Shawwal.' (Bukhari 13.14.257, see also 33.6.249, 33.7.250, 33.18.261). In the version of Muslim, it was his wife Zaynab who first pitched a tent to follow his practice, and then 'A'ishah and Hafsah followed her—Muslim 2641-1)

The last ten days of Ramadan is not a compulsory time for retreat. Abu Sa'id al-Khudri recorded that Allah's Messenger ﷺ used to practise i'tikaf sometimes in the *middle* ten days of Ramadan, and once he stayed in i'tikaf till the night of the twenty-first. He said: 'Whoever is in i'tikaf informed (of the date) of the Night (Laylat ul-Qadr), but I have been caused to forget it. (In a dream) I saw myself prostrating in mud and water in the morning of that night. So, look for it in the last ten days, and in the odd ones of them.' It rained that night, and the roof of the mosque dribbled, as it was made of leaf-stalks of date palms. I saw with my own eyes the mark of mud and water on the forehead of the Prophet ﷺ.' (Bukhari 33.1.244, 33.9.252, 33.13.256)

I'tikaf does not actually *have* to include fasting, although the schools of Malik, Abu Hanifah and others maintain that it does. The school of al-Shafi'i maintains that fasting is not a necessary condition.

It is important, too, to remember that when a Muslim retires for i'tikaf, he or she has to be supported by others, who will see to their food arrangements at night and take care of the normal things the Muslim would have done on the days of withdrawal. I'tikaf is not something that should be undertaken selfishly, without consultation with those who will have to cope in the absence of the 'withdrawn' person, or those on whom the 'withdrawn' person depends. A mu'takif requires a 'support team,' and they are all seen and rewarded for their intention by Allah— whether they are the person in i'tikaf, or the ones who support that person.

EID (FEAST-DAY) PRAYERS

The two Eids, Eid-ul-Fitr and Eid-ul-Adha, are the two great festivals sanctioned in Islam. The first is celebrated at the end of the month-long fast of Ramadan, and the second on the tenth day of Dhu'l-Hijjah—to commemmorate the sacred memory of the Blessed Ibrahim's willingness to offer up his son Isma'il.

They were considered to be the best of days on which to do

good deeds:

Ibn Abbas recorded that the Blessed Prophet ﷺ said: 'No good deeds done on any other days are superior to those done on these (first ten days of Dhu'l-Hijjah).' Then some companions said: 'Not even jihad?' He replied: 'Not even jihad, except that of a man who puts himself and his property in jeopardy and loses all these things.' (Bukhari 15.11.86)

The first thing the Blessed Prophet used to do before going out to Eid prayers was to eat a simple meal of dates:

Anas ibn Malik recorded that Allah's Messenger ﷺ never proceeded (for the prayer) on the Day of Eid-ul-Fitr unless he had eaten some dates. Anas also narrated that the Prophet ﷺ used to eat an odd number of dates.' (Bukhari 15.4.73)

If someone intended to slaughter an animal for the sacrificial meal, he should do it after the Eid prayer and not before.

Anas ibn Malik recorded: 'If anyone slaughtered his sacrifice before the Eid prayer, he should slaughter again.' (Bukhari 15.4.74)

Abu Burda ibn Niyar, the uncle of al-Bara, said: 'O Allah's Messenger! I have slaughtered my sheep before the Eid prayer and I thought of today as a day of eating and drinking, and I wanted my sheep to be the first to be slaughtered in my house. So I slaughtered my sheep and took my food before coming to the prayer.' The Prophet ﷺ said: 'Tne sheep which you have slaughtered is just mutton (and not a nusuk—or sacrifice),' Abu Burda said: 'O Allah's Messenger! I have a young she-goat which is dearer to me than two sheep. Will that be sufficient as a nusuk on my behalf?' The Prophet ﷺ said: 'Yes, it will be suficient for you, but it will not be sufficient for anyone else after you.' (Bukhari 15.5.75, 15.10.85)

One way in which the Eid prayer was different from the usual ones was in the fact that there was no *adhan* called, nor *iqamah*.

Ata recorded that during the days of Ibn az-Zubayr, Ibn Abbas had sent him a message telling him that the *adhan* for the Eid prayer was never pronounced (in the lifetime of Allah's Messenger 鷹, and the khutbah used to be delivered after the prayer.' (Bukhari 15.7.78)

Another difference is that for Eid prayers local congregations are encouraged to gather together, to create the largest congregation possible. In order to do this, the prayer is sometimes held in an available open space such as a park, a field, or even a car-park, rather than the usual mosque.

The Blessed Prophet 鷹 used to set up a small spear (harba) or spear-headed stick (*anza*) as his sutrah, and then pray.

Ibn 'Umar recorded that the Prophet 鷹 used to proceed to the Musallah (the place of *salah*) and an *anza* used to be carried before him and planted in the Musallah in front of him, and he would pray facing it. (Bukhari 15.14.90)

Unlike the usual concession of allowing ladies to pray at home (because of their family commitments), the Blessed Prophet 鷹 actually commanded women to come to the Eid prayers, even if they were unable to pray because of menstruation. They were encouraged to come to the congregation nevertheless.

Umm Atiyya recorded that the Messenger of Allah 鷹 commanded them to 'bring out the young women, women in seclusion, and even menstruating women—provided these latter kept back from prayer but participated in goodness and supplication of the Muslims.' (Muslim 1934, Bukhari 15.15.91, Abu Dawud 1135) The incident referred to by Umm Atiyyah was when a group of Ansari women had gathered together in one house, and the Prophet 鷹 actually sent 'Umar to fetch them.

Both Eids are occasions for religious joy and thanksgiving,

and have a deep spiritual meaning behind them. They are marked by two *rak'ahs* of congregational prayer in the morning, followed by a khutbah or sermon.

The number of *takbirs* is different in an Eid prayer, and there are numerous schools of thought concerning how many there should be.

'A'ishah recorded that the Messenger of Allah ﷺ used to say the *takbir* seven times in the first *rak'ah* and five times in the second on the day of the breaking of the fast and on the day of sacrifice. (Abu Dawud 1145)

This is the view held by the majority of scholars. The schools of Ibn Mas'ud, Abu Musa, Abu Mas'ud al-Ansari, al-Thawri and Abu Hanifah have three takbirs in the first *rak'ah* before the recitation of the Qur'an, and three in the second *rak'ah* after the recitation. It is usual to raise the hands for these takbirs, not based on traditions directly reported from the Prophet ﷺ but from the statements and practice of his companions. (Muslim 1145, n. 588)

The recommended passages from the Qur'an for recitation at Eid prayers are *surahs* 50 ('By the glorious Qur'an) and 54 (The Hour drew near and the moon was rent asunder'). (Muslim 1936-7, Abu Dawud 1150)

After the prayer came the khutbah, or sermon—but this was not a compulsory part of the proceedings. After the prayer, people with pressing needs were free to depart if they wished.

Abdallah ibn al-Saib recorded that he attended the Eid prayer along with the Messenger of Allah ﷺ. When he finished the prayer he said: 'We shall (now) deliver the sermon; the one who wishes to sit to listen to it may sit, and the one who wishes to leave may leave.' (Abu Dawud 1151)

The Prophet ﷺ also used the occasion of this sermon to appeal to people to be generous and give charity to others.

Ibn Abbas recorded that he participated in the Eid-ul-Fitr prayer with the Messenger of Allah ﷺ, Abu Bakr, 'Umar and 'Uthman; all of them observed the prayer before the sermon, and then the Prophet ﷺ delivered the sermon. Then the Messenger ﷺ descended (from the pulpit) and (as if he were seeing him now), he commanded the people with his hand to sit down. He made his way through their assembly until he came to the women. Bilal was with him. He then recited this verse: 'O Prophet, when believing women come to you giving you a pledge that they will not associate anything with Allah' (Sūrah 60:12), till he finished this section to them. Then he said: 'Do you conform to this?' Only one woman among them replied: 'Yes, Messenger of Allah,' but none else spoke. He (the Prophet ﷺ then urged them to give charity. Bilal stretched out his cloth and called: 'Come forward with alms, let my father and mother be taken as ransom for you!' And they began to throw their rings and bracelets into Bilal's cloth.' (Muslim 1293, Bukhari 15.19.95)

Jabir ibn Abdallah's version records that it was also on this occasion that the Blessed Prophet ﷺ took the opportunity to chide women, in his usual humourous manner (so often misunderstood by serious-minded zealots!):

Jabir ibn Abdallah recorded that he observed prayer with the Messenger of Allah ﷺ on the Eid day. He commenced with prayer before the sermon without adhan or iqamah. He then stood up leaning on Bilal, and commanded them all to be on their guard (against evil for the sake of) Allah, and he urged their obedience to Allah; he preached to the people and encouraged them. He then walked down to where the women were, and preached to them and encouraged them, and asked them to give alms, for most of them were (destined to be) the fuel of Hell. A woman with a mole on her cheek stood up and said: 'Why is that so, Messenger of Allah?' He said: 'Because you grumble all the time, and are ungrateful to your husbands!' And immediately they began to take off their ornaments such as their earrings and rings, which they threw into Bilal's cloth.' (Muslim 1926)

Incidentally, it is worth commenting here how unfortunate it is that so many male Muslims have missed an awareness of the Prophet's sense of humour, and colourful turn of phrase. If you think about it, it is obvious that most of the praying, believing, generous Muslim women sitting in front of the Prophet on that occasion were *not* destined for Hell. Why should our dear Prophet make such a remark? I respectfully suggest he was joking with them, as his reply to the woman indicates; those who quote this hadith out of context to the detriment of female Muslims are misinformed and lacking in understanding.

Eid is a joyful day, of laughing, loving and giving.

To make the day all the more joyful, the Blessed Prophet ﷺ recommended going home after the Eid prayer by a different route—so that the more people would be blessed by meeting him and receiving his blessing. He took the opportunity to greet the greatest possible number of people.

Jabir ibn Abdallah recorded that 'on the Day of Eid the Prophet ﷺ used to return (after offering the Eid prayer) through a way different from that which he went.' (Bukhari 15.24.102, Abu Dawud 1152)

If anyone missed the Eid prayer, it was recommended that they should pray two *rak'ahs*—(Bukhari 15.25). If the Imam himself missed the Eid day, (for example, if he had not sighted the new moon), he should go and offer the Eid prayer on the following day. (Abu Dawud 1153)

FESTIVITIES AND MUSIC AT EID

All sorts of festive activities were encouraged, and, what surprised (and still surprises) those who disapproved of music and light-hearted enjoyments, this included the singing of songs (devoid of bawdiness or indecent or unsuitable content of course), playing of musical instruments and drums, and taking part in physical sports and feats of valour.

One occasion was recorded when the Prophet ﷺ enjoyed listening to some young girls singing when he went home after the Eid prayer. Abu Bakr was surprised, but the Blessed Prophet ﷺ encouraged them.

'A'ishah recorded: 'Abu Bakr came to see me while I had two Ansari girls with me, and they were singing what the Ansar recited to one another at the Battle of Bu'ath. They were not, however, (professional) singing girls. Seeing this, Abu Bakr (her father) said: 'What! (The playing of) this wind instrument of Satan in the house of the Messenger of Allah, and on Eid day, too!' Upon this, the Messenger of Allah ﷺ said: 'Abu Bakr, everybody has a festival, and this is our festival—(so let them play on).' (Muslim 1938, Bukhari 15.3.72)

In another version 'A'ishah recorded that the Messenger of Allah ﷺ came (into her apartment) while there were two girls with her singing the songs of the Battle of Bu'ath. He lay down on the bed, and closed his eyes (i.e. listened). But when Abu Bakr (her father) came, he scolded her and said: 'Oh! This musical instrument of the devil in the house of the Messenger of Allah!' The Messenger turned towards him and said: 'Leave them alone.' It is not recorded whether Abu Bakr then sat and listened too, although one would imagine that he did, and did not just get up and walk out again after just arriving on his visit. 'A'ishah continued her narration: 'And when he lost interest, I dropped hints to the girls and they went out; and it was the Day of Eid, and Abyssinians were there playing with shields and spears. I do not remember whether I asked the Messenger ﷺ or whether he asked me if I wanted to see their sport. I said: 'Yes.' I stood behind him with his face parallel to my face, and he said: 'O Banu Arfada (the Abyssinians), keep going (in your sport) until she is satisfied.' He (then) said to me: 'Is that enough?' I said: 'Yes.' Upon this, he asked me to go.' (Muslim 1942, Bukhari 15.2.70)

The 'face parallel to my face' seems an odd phrase until one realises the tenderness of the scene.

In another version, she said: 'I placed my head upon his shoulder and began to watch their sport, until it was I who turned away from watching them.' (Muslim 1943)

Abu Hurayrah recorded that while these Abyssinians were playing with their weapons in the presence of the Messenger of Allah ﷺ, 'Umar ibn al-Khattab arrived. He bent down to take up pebbles to throw at them (in order to make them go away). The Messenger of Allah ﷺ said to him: 'Umar, leave them alone!' (Muslim 1946)

Surprisingly, although it was actually disapproved of to carry arms on Eid day, especially in the sanctuary, these Abyssinians performed sport with their weapons. One assumes that the Prophet ﷺ allowed them to do this as a special dance or performance for the festival—they were presumably visitors.

Al-Hasan recorded: 'It was forbidden (in the lifetime of the Prophet ﷺ to carry arms (anywhere) on the Day of Eid, except if there was a fear of the enemy.' (Bukhari 15.9.)

Sa'id ibn Jubayr recorded that he was once with Ibn 'Umar in Mina when a spearhead pierced the sole of his foot and his foot stuck to the paddle of the saddle and he got down and pulled his foot out. Al-Hajjaj heard of it and came to inquire about his health and said: 'Alas! If only we could know the man who wounded you!' Ibn 'Umar said: '*You* are the one who wounded me.' Al-Hajjaj said: 'What do you mean?' Ibn 'Umar said: 'You have allowed arms to be carried on a day on which nobody used to carry them, and you allowed arms to be carried in the *Haram* even though it was not allowed before.' (Bukhari 15.9.83)

Concerning the Imam

······💛······

WHAT SORT OF PERSON SHOULD BE CHOSEN AS IMAM

It is very important that the Imam chosen by a community is a reliable and responsible person. He has the duty of leading the prayers, and should not be late at the place of congregation. If the Imam does come late, then the people waiting cannot be held at fault if their prayer is not on time.

Uqbah ibn Amir recorded: 'He who leads the prayer and does so at the right time will receive the reward. He who delays from the appointed time will be responsible (for this delay) and not those who are led in prayer.' (Abu Dawud 580)

Politeness is very important when choosing someone to act as Imam for a group.

Abu Mas'ud al-Badri recorded: 'The one of you who is most versed in the Book of Allah should act as Imam for the people; and the one who is best in reciting; if more than one are equally versed in reciting, it then it should be the one who emigrated earliest to Madinah (this obviously applied to the time of the Prophet ﷺ). If they emigrated at the same time, then the most senior of them. But no man should lead another in prayer in that other man's house, or where the latter has authority, or sit in his place of honour without his permission.' (Abu Dawud 582)

This means that in a person's own home, the owner of the house is more entitled to act as Imam than the outsider, providing he is competent. It is not polite for a visitor, no matter how

eminent, to assume that he should put himself in the place of the leader of that household—unless, of course, he is invited to do so.

Although some scholars have disputed whether or not it is permissible for a child to lead the prayer, the Blessed Prophet ﷺ allowed competency and knowledge to overrule the question of age. There is a lovely *hadith* recorded by 'Amr ibn Salamah, who as a boy had a particularly good memory and was very devout. His father and a group of his clan went to the Prophet ﷺ to be taught prayer, and the Prophet ﷺ told them that the one with the most knowledge of the Qur'an should act as Imam.

'I knew the Qur'an better than most of them because I had memorised it.' (Said 'Amr) 'They, therefore, put me in front of them, and I would lead them in prayer. I wore a small yellow mantle which, when I prostrated myself, went up on me, and a woman of the clan said: 'Cover the backside of your leader from us!' So they brought me an 'Ammani shirt, and I have never been so pleased about anything after embracing Islam as I was about that shirt! I used to lead them in prayer, and I was only seven or eight years old.' (Abu Dawud 585)

Those scholars who dispute the practice of allowing a very young Imam (Ata, al-Shabi, Malik, al-Thawri, al-Awzai and Abu Hanifah) maintain that the Prophet ﷺ did not know about this instance.

Malik ibn a-Huwayrith recorded: 'When the time of prayer comes, call the *adhan*, then call the *iqamah*, then the one who is oldest among you should act as your leader.' (Abu Dawud 589)

The Blessed Prophet ﷺ did not think it right for a person to insist on performing as Imam if he was not the genuine choice of the people, or if he was a habitual latecomer, or if he revealed a fault in his character by bringing anyone into slavery.

Ibn 'Umar recorded: 'There are three types of people whose

prayer is not accepted by Allah—one who goes in front of people when they do not like him; a man who comes too late; and a man who takes into slavery a free man or woman.' (Abu Dawud 593)

THE IMAM SHOULD NOT BE RAISED UP FOR PRAYER

The Imam should be a humble person, and should not glorify himself in his position. It is not correct for the Imam to be raised up on a level higher than those praying behind him.

Hammam recorded: Hudhayfah led the people in prayer in al-Madain standing on a bench. Abu Mas'ud took him by the shirt and brought him down. When he finished his prayer, he said (to Hudhayfah): 'Do you not know that people were forbidden to do that?' He said: 'Yes—I remembered when you pulled me down.' (Abu Dawud 597)

Adi ibn Thabit al-Ansari recorded that once when he heard the *iqamah* called for prayer, Ammar came forward and stood on a bench and prayed while the people prayed on a lower place than he. Hudhayfah came forward and took him by the hands, and Ammar followed him till Hudhayfah brought him down. When Ammar finished his prayer, Hudhayfah said to him: 'Did you not hear the Messenger of Allah ﷺ say—'When a man leads the people in prayer, he must not stand in a position higher than theirs?' Ammar replied: 'That is why I followed you when you took me by the hand.' (Abu Dawud 598)

The Blessed Prophet ﷺ used to preach from the pulpit and even recite from it, but when he prostrated himself, he got down and bowed upon the earth.

Abu Hazim ibn Dinar recorded that Sahl bin Sa'd was asked about the Prophet's ﷺ pulpit, as to what it was made of. He said: 'By Allah, I know of what it was made. I saw it the first day it was placed there, and the first day when the Messenger of Allah ﷺ sat on it. The Messenger of Allah ﷺ sent for a woman whom Sahl named, and asked her: 'Order your boy, the carpenter, to construct me a wooden pulpit so that I may sit on it when I deliver a speech to the people. So she ordered him, and he made a pulpit of a wood called tarfa taken from al-Ghabah (a place nine miles from Madinah). He ordered that it be placed here. I saw the Messenger of Allah ﷺ praying on it. He said: 'Allahu Akbar', he then bowed while he was on it; then he came down and prostrated at the base of the pulpit; he then went back (on to the pulpit). When he finished the prayer he addressed himself to the people and said: 'O people, I did this so that you might follow me and know my prayer.' (Abu Dawud 1075, see also Bukhari 8.18.374)

Ibn 'Umar added that the pulpit had two steps (Abu Dawud 1076), and Salamah ibn al-Akwa commented that the space between the pulpit and the wall of the mosque was such that a goat could pass. (Abu Dawud 1077)

IF THE IMAM LEADS THE PRAYER WHILE UNABLE TO STAND

If an Imam has been hurt or wounded, it is permissible for him to continue to lead the people from a sitting position. Once the Blessed Prophet ﷺ himself was thrown from a horse, and injured his right side. He then led the prayers while sitting, and the people prayed behind him also sitting.

Jabir recorded: The Messenger of Allah ﷺ rode a horse in Madinah. It threw him off at the root of a date palm, and his foot was injured. We visited him to inquire about his illness and found him praying sitting in 'A'ishah's apartment. We, therefore, stood (praying) behind him. He kept silent. We visited him again to inquire about his injury. He offered the obligatory prayer sitting. We stood praying behind him, but he made a sign to us and we sat down. When he finished the prayer, he said: 'When the Imam prays sitting, pray sitting; and when he prays standing, pray standing, and do not act as the people of Persia used to act with their chiefs (i.e. the people stood while they sat). (Abu Dawud 602)

The version in Muslim is slightly different:

Jabir recorded: The Messenger of Allah ﷺ was ill and we said prayer behind him while he was sitting. And Abu Bakr was making his *takbir* audible to the people. As he paid his attention towards us he saw us standing, and (directed us to sit down) with a gesture. So we sat down and said our prayer with his prayer, in a sitting posture. After uttering salutation, he said: 'You were at this time about to do an act like that of the Persians and the Romans—they stand before their kings, while they (the kings) sit; so don't do that. Follow your Imams. If they say prayer standing you should do so too, and if they say prayer sitting, you should also say prayer sitting.' (Muslim 824)

Other strong *hadiths* were recorded by Anas ibn Malik and 'A'ishah:

Anas ibn Malik recorded: The Messenger of Allah ﷺ fell down from a horse and his right side was grazed. We went to him to inquire after his health when the time of prayer came. he led us in prayer in a sitting position, and we said prayer behind him sitting; and when he finished the prayer he said: 'The Imam is appointed only to be followed; so when he recites *takbir*, you should also recite it, when he prostrates, you should also prostrate; when he rises up, you should also rise up, and when he says 'God listens to him who praises Him' you should say 'Our Lord to You be the praise'; and when he prays sitting, all of you should pray sitting.' (Muslim 817, Bukhari 11.51.656)

'A'ishah recorded: The Messenger of Allah ﷺ fell, and some

of his companions came to inquire after his health. The Messenger of Allah ﷺ said prayer sitting, while his companions said it behind him standing. He directed them by his gesture to sit down, and they sat down (in prayer). After finishing the (prayer) he said: 'The Imam is appointed to be followed, so bow down when he bows down, and rise up when he rises up, and say (prayer) sitting when he says (it) sitting.' (Muslim 822)

Strangely enough, at the very well-known event of the last prayer of the Prophet ﷺ during his illness, he led the prayer sitting while the people were standing behind him.

Ubaydallah ibn Abdallah recorded that he visited 'A'ishah and asked her to tell him about the illness of the Messenger of Allah ﷺ. She agreed, and said: The Messenger ﷺ was seriously ill, and he asked whether the people had prayed. We said: 'No, they are waiting for you, Messenger of Allah.' He said: 'Put some water in the tub for me.' We did so, and he took a bath, and when he was trying to move, with difficulty, he fainted. When he came round, he again said: 'Have the people said prayer?' We said: 'No, they are waiting for you.' He again said: 'Put some water for me in the tub.' (To lose consciousness breaks the ritual state of *wudu'*). We did accordingly, and he took a bath, but when he was about to move, with difficulty, he (again) fainted. (This happened again). The people were staying in the mosque and waiting for the Messenger ﷺ to lead the last (night) prayer. The Messenger ﷺ then sent instructions to Abu Bakr to lead the people in prayer. Abu Bakr, who was a man of very tender feelings, asked 'Umar to lead the prayer. 'Umar said: 'You are more entitled than I.' Abu Bakr then led the prayer during those days. Afterwards the Messenger ﷺ felt a little better and he went out, supported by two men, one of whom was al-Abbas, to the noon prayer. Abu Bakr was leading the people in prayer. When Abu Bakr saw him, he began to withdraw, but the Messenger ﷺ told him not to withdraw. He told his two companions to seat him down beside him, so they seated him by the side of Abu Bakr. Abu Bakr said the prayer standing while following the prayer of the Messenger ﷺ, and the people said the prayer (standing) while following the prayer of Abu Bakr. The Messenger ﷺ was seated.'

Ubaydallah said: 'I visited Abdallah ibn Abbas and told him what 'A'ishah had said concerning the illness of the Messenger ﷺ, He objected to none of it, only asking whether she had told him the name of the man who accompanied al-Abbas. I said: 'No.' He said: 'It was 'Ali.' (Muslim 832, Bukhari 11.51.655)

Some traditionists therefore hold that these earlier traditions were thereby abrogated, but this is disputed. Some scholars maintain that since Abu Bakr was really leading the prayer, the argument does not apply. They point out that nobody ever stood while the Messenger ﷺ sat at any time during his lifetime when he was *actually* leading the prayer. Others take the view that this last public prayer of the Prophet ﷺ changed the earlier ruling:

Humaidi said: 'The saying of the Prophet ﷺ 'pray sitting if the Imam prays sitting' was said in his former illness (during his early life), but the Prophet ﷺ prayed sitting afterwards (in the last illness) and the people were praying standing behind him and the Prophet ﷺ did not order them to sit down. We should follow the last actions of the Prophet ﷺ.' (Bukhari 11.51.657)

Imam Shafi'i and Imam Abu Hanifah are of the opinion that it is not advisable to say prayer behind an Imam who has been obliged to take up a sitting posture through illness, or some other reason, in any case. There are always others available who can be delegated to act as Imam. They therefore base their argument on the assumption that the people stood behind the sick and sitting Prophet ﷺ during his last illness only because the Prophet ﷺ had

delegated Abu Bakr as Imam. (Muslim 817 n. 632). The School
of Malik does not hold that anyone should lead the prayer from
a sitting position at all. (Abu Dawud 601 n. 266)

WHERE TO STAND, IF THERE ARE ONLY FEW

When an Imam leads just one man and a woman in prayer,
he should place the man by his right side, and the woman behind
him.

Anas recorded: 'The Messenger of Allah ﷺ led him and one
of their women in prayer. He put him on his right side, and the
woman behind him.' (Abu Dawud 609)

If there are three male persons, the Imam can either set the
two behind him, or he can stand in the same row between them.
If there are more than two males, the Imam should always stand
at the front. When there are women and children, the children
can form a row behind the men, and the women always pray from
the back.

Anas ibn Malik recorded that his grandmother Mulaikah
invited Allah's Messenger ﷺ for a meal which she had prepared
specially for him. He ate some of it and said: 'Get up, I shall lead
you in the prayer.' I brought a mat that had become black from
excessive use, and I sprinkled water on it. Allah's Messenger ﷺ
stood on it and prayed two rak'ahs; and the orphan was with me
(in the first row) and the old lady stood behind us.' (Bukhari
12.79.819, see also Abu Dawud 612)

ONE SHOULD FOLLOW THE LEAD OF THE IMAM

It is always polite and correct to follow the motion and speed
of the Imam, and not try to go more quickly or more slowly, and
in either case draw attention to oneself.

Abu Hurayrah recorded: 'Does he who raises his head while

the Imam is prostrating not fear that Allah might change his head into that of a donkey?' (Abu Dawud 623)

AN IMAM'S MISTAKE DOES NOT INVALIDATE YOUR PRAYER

If an Imam makes a mistake during the prayer, it is a matter for his concern—it does not invalidate *your* prayer.

Abu Hurayrah recorded: 'If the Imam leads the prayer correctly then he and you will receive the rewards, but if he makes a mistake then you will receive the reward for the prayer and the mistake is only his.' (Bukhari 11.55.663)

Al-Hasan recorded that you could pray behind a man who was a victim of afflictions, or even a heretic—'You can pray behind that Imam and the sin of heresy will be against him (alone). (Bukhari 11.56)

Ubaydallah ibn Adi ibn Khiyar recorded that he said to 'Uthman ibn Affan while he was beseiged: 'You are the chief of all Muslims, and you see what has befallen you. We are led in prayer by a leader of afflictions and we are afraid of being sinful in following him.' 'Uthman said: 'Prayer is the best of all deeds, so when people do good deeds, do the same as they do, but when they do bad deeds, avoid those bad deeds.' Az-Zuhri said: 'In our opinion, one should not pray behind an effeminate person unless there is no alternative.' (Bukhari 11.56)

Anas ibn Malik recorded that the Prophet ﷺ said to Abu Dharr: 'Listen and obey (your Imam), even if he is an Ethiopian with a head like a raisin!' (Bukhari 11.56.664) The Prophet ﷺ was not being racist; it was Abu Dharr who had a problem regarding black people as servants and not equal Muslims.

WOMEN IMAMS

The Blessed Prophet even allowed women to act as Imam when the occasion arose. For example, Umm Waraqah bint Nawfal was a scholar of the Qur'an who asked to go with the Prophet ﷺ to the Battle of Badr to act as a nurse, but who was advised to remain at home—although she was still allowed to be called 'martyr'. She had the Prophet's permission to have a muadhdhin in her house (Abu Dawud 591). Umm Waraqah bint Abdallah ibn al-Harith also recorded a version of the same tradition:

'The Messenger of Allah ﷺ appointed a muadhdhin to call *adhan* for her, and he commanded her to lead those who lived in her house in prayer.' Abdal Rahman said: 'I saw her muadhdhin, who was an old man.' (Abu Dawud 592)

On the basis of this tradition many scholars maintain that it is permissible for a woman to act as Imam for those of her household, even if they include males. ('A'ishah and Umm Salamah both led women in prayer).

This poor lady, incidentally, met a sad end. She had promised her slave and slave-woman that they would be freed after her death, and one night they strangled her with a sheet of cloth. When 'Umar caught the guilty pair, he had them crucified.

Sunnah Prayers

.... ❦ ....

SUNNAH PRAYERS

Anyone observing the public prayers of devout Muslims will notice that most of them offer more *rak'ahs* than the set number laid down as being obligatory. They may wonder why this is so These extra *rak'ahs* are known as *nafl* or voluntary prayers, and a certain number of them are regarded as *sunnah* prayers, or extra *rak'ahs* offered by the devout following the *sunnah* of the Blessed Prophet ﷺ. Tradition indicates that to perform twelve *sunnah* *rak'ahs* during each twenty-four hours is particularly blessed. His wife Umm Habibah recorded: 'If anyone prays in a day and a night twelve *rak'ahs* voluntarily, a house will be built for him (or her) in Paradise.' (Abu Dawud 1245)

The details of these *sunnah* prayers were recorded by 'A'ishah:

'Before the noon prayer, he would pray four *rak'ahs* in my house, then go out and lead the people in prayer, then return to my house and offer two *rak'ahs*. He would lead the people in the sunset prayer, and then return to my house and pray two *rak'ahs*. Then he would lead the people in the night prayer, and enter my house and pray two *rak'ahs*. He would pray nine *rak'ahs* during the night, including witr. At night he would pray for a long time standing and for a long time sitting. When he recited the Qur'an while standing, he would bow and prostrate himself from the standing position; and when he recited while sitting, he would bow and prostrate himself from the sitting position; and when dawn came he prayed two *rak'ahs*, then he would come out and lead the people in the dawn prayer.' (Abu Dawud 1246—on the authority of Abd Allah ibn Shaqiq).

Although many Muslims pray *nafl* and *sunnah* prayers in the mosque, the Blessed Prophet ﷺ actually stressed the importance of praying them in one's own home, in private and not 'overlooked' by anyone but Allah, as a means of developing a true sense of piety and sincerity.

Ka'b ibn Ujrah recorded: The Prophet ﷺ came to the mosque of Banu Abd al-Ashhal. He prayed the sunset prayer there. When they finished, he saw them praying voluntary prayers after it, and he said: 'This is the prayer to be offered in your house!' (Abu Dawud 1295)

Sunnah prayers are of two types—*Ratiba Muwakkada* ('stressed' ones), and *ghayr muwakkada* or *ghayr rawatib* (not 'stressed' ones). One of the benefits of regularly offering these prayers is that it gives a way of compensating for any omission in the *fard rak'ahs*. The Messenger ﷺ stressed their importance, even though they were not compulsory:

Abu Hurayrah recorded: 'Do not omit them even if you are driven away by horses.' (Abu Dawud 1253)

In order, the most important are considered to be two *rak'ahs* before the *fard* dawn prayer, then two *rak'ahs* of the evening prayer, noon prayer and *isha'* prayer, all of them after the observance of the *fard* prayer, and lastly four *rak'ahs* of the noon prayer before the *fard rak'ahs*. (Mirqat Vol 111, p. 111, Muslim 1579 n. 986)

'A'ishah recorded that: 'The Messenger of Allah ﷺ was more particular about observing the extra voluntary prayers before the dawn prayer than about any of the others.' (Abu Dawud 1249)

However, these prayers are a private matter between the

believers and Allah. One's *niyyah* is all-important, as usual. They should never be used in the wrong spirit, as a way of showing off, or trying to indicate that one is more pious than other people. In fact, it is not considered polite if one's private prayer makes a disturbance of others or embarrasses them, or makes them feel guilty or uncomfortable. This is especially commented on for the pre-dawn prayer, where other people have the right to rest in sleep, and might not wish to be disturbed.

'A'ishah recorded the Prophet's ﷺ ironic comments on one noisy neighbour who got up at night and recited in a loud voice:

'May Allah have mercy on so-and-so, who reminded me of many verses I had nearly forgotten!' (Abu Dawud 1326)

'A'ishah also commented: 'The Prophet ﷺ would pray (his) two *rak'ahs* before the dawn prayer so lightly that I would say: 'Did he recite *surah al-Fatihah* in them?' (Abu Dawud 1250)

THE NIGHT PRAYERS OF THE BLESSED PROPHET ﷺ

In the stillness of the last watches of the night, when the rest of the world sleeps, the individual soul is elevated and brought very close to Allah. Various ayahs in the Qur'an make this clear:

'O you folded (in your sheet)! Rise and pray in the night, but not all night—half of it, or a little less, or a little more; and recite the Qur'an in slow, measured tones. Soon We shall send down to you a weighty message. Truly the rising in the night is the most potent way to govern (the soul) and most suitable for (framing) the Word.' (*Surah* 73:1-6)

'And during a part of the night, forsake sleep to offer prayer, besides that which is incumbent on you; maybe your Lord will raise you to a position of glory.' (*Surah* 17:79)

Prayers during the night are called Salat-ul-Layl, *Tahajjud* and *Qiyam*-ul-Layl. These are frequently taken to be one and the same thing, but there is a slight distinction between them. *Tahajjud* is that optional prayer which is observed after one has slept—after midnight, in the small watches of the morning, whereas Salat-ul-Layl or Qiyam-ul-Layl includes the prayer before sleeping which is recommended as a substitute for *Tahajjud* prayer for one who knows he or she is not going to be able to wake up at the early time for *Tahajjud*.

Tahajjud prayer is voluntary, but it is considered the most effective prayer for developing true religious devotion and love of God, and therefore it is highly recommended.

There are no fixed *rak'ahs* in the *tahajjud* prayer, but it varies from five to thirteen, and sometimes the two *sunnah rak'ahs* of the dawn prayer are also included in it. The final part of the prayer is known as witr which means 'One'. The Blessed Prophet ﷺ used to say: 'Allah is One, so He likes the number one.' Praying witr at the end of the night prayer makes the number of *rak'ahs* into an odd number.

In the witr prayer, one should only sit for *tashahhud* in the last but one *rak'ah*, and then get up for the last single *rak'ah* and complete it. The prayer is called witr bil fasal if one says the last *rak'ah* after the salutation is given.

Witr can be offered at any time after the *isha'* prayer up to the break of dawn. Those who think they will not be able to get up and pray it before dawn can pray it immediately after *isha'*, but those who do pray *nafl* at night end their prayers with it.

Jabir recorded: 'Any of you who cannot get up in the end part of the night should pray witr in the first part of the night; but any of you who think they can get up in the end part should pray witr then, because the angels are present for the prayer at the end of the night.' (Ahmad, Tirmidhi, Ibn Majah, Muslim 1651)

The school of al-Shafi'i regards witr as part of Salat-ul-Layl, but the Hanafites regard witr and *tahajjud* as two distinct prayers. The Hanafites regard the witr as three *rak'ahs* only, but the Shafi'ites, Malikites, Hanbalites and Ahl-i-*Hadith* say say it can be anything from one to eleven *rak'ahs*. Practically speaking, one can say that the night prayer plus witr is generally just called witr for the sake of brevity. (Muslim 1604 n. 1000)

'A'ishah recorded one touching private moment when her husband ﷺ was at prayer in their house:

'The Messenger of Allah ﷺ never offered the night (*isha'*) prayer and thereafter came to me but he offered four or six *rak'ahs* of prayer. One night the rain fell, so we spread a piece of leather (for his prayer), and now I see it as if there is a hole in it from which the water is flowing. I never saw him protecting his clothes from the earth (as he did on that occasion). (Abu Dawud 1298)

The Blessed Prophet ﷺ did not expect his wives to pray the same long hours that he did, but he liked 'A'ishah to say witr with him:

'A'ishah recorded that the Messenger of Allah ﷺ used to offer prayer at night while she lay in front of him, and when the witr prayer was yet to be observed he would awaken her, and she prayed with him. (Muslim 1619)

'A'ishah recorded her beloved husband's ﷺ gentleness towards her.

'When the Messenger of Allah ﷺ finished his prayer late in the night, he would (look and) see. If I was awake, he would talk to me. If I was sleeping, he would waken me, and pray two *rak'ahs*, then he would lie down until the mu'adhdhin called him for the dawn prayer. Then he would pray two *rak'ahs* softly, and come out for prayer.' (Abu Dawud 1257)

'When he prayed the two *rak'ahs* of the dawn prayer, he would lie down (again) if I was asleep, but when I was awake he would talk to me.' (Abu Dawud 1258)

If a person missed the two early *rak'ahs*, the Blessed Prophet ﷺ did not prevent him or her from saying them after the *fajr* prayer.

Qays ibn 'Amr recorded: 'The Messenger of Allah ﷺ saw a person praying after the congregational prayer at dawn was over. He said: 'There are (only) two *rak'ahs* of the dawn prayer.' The man replied: 'I did not pray the two *rak'ahs* before the dawn prayer, hence I offered them now.' The Messenger of Allah ﷺ kept silent.' (Abu Dawud 1262—an example of an occasion when the silence of the Prophet ﷺ was taken as a sign that he did not object). Different scholars have recommended different times for these extra prayers—after the dawn prayer, after sunrise, when the sun has risen higher, but always before the meridian.

'A'ishah was asked at what time the Prophet got up to make his early prayer. In fact, he made use of a very natural and accurate 'alarm clock'. She said:

'When he heard the cock crow, then he got up and prayed.' (Abu Dawud 1312, Bukhari 21.6.2232, Muslim 1614)

Anyone who has kept cockerels will verify that the moment there is the slightest change in the light at the approach of dawn, he will begin to raise his voice!

This time was regarded as the most blessed time in particular for seeking the forgiveness and blessings of Allah:

Abu Hurayrah reported the Messenger of Allah ﷺ as saying: 'Our Lord Who is blessed and exalted descends every night to the lowest heaven when the last third of the night remains, and says: Who is making supplication to Me that I may answer him? Who is asking of Me that I may give to him? Who asks My forgiveness so that I may forgive him?' (Abu Dawud 1310, Muslim 1656)

'Amr ibn Anbasat al-Sulami once asked the Blessed Prophet

which was the best part of the night for one's prayer to be accepted. He replied:

'In the last part. Pray as much as you like, for the prayer is attended by the angels and it is recorded till you offer the dawn prayer.' (After this he offered further advice about the times of prayer throughout the day). 'Then stop praying when the sun is rising till it is the height of one or two lances, for it rises between the two horns of the devil, and the infidels offer prayer at that time. Then pray as much as you like, because the prayer is witnessed and recorded until the shadow of a lance becomes equal to it; then cease prayer, for at that time the Hell-fire is heated up and the doors of Hell are opened. When the sun declines pray as much as you like, for the prayer is witnessed till you pray the afternoon prayer; then cease prayer until the sun sets, for it sets between the horns of the devil and at that time the infidels offer prayer.' (Abu Dawud 1272)

The Blessed Prophet ﷺ recommended that husband and wife should look after each other during the night if they both wished to pray. Whichever one woke up first had the duty to wake the other. Abu Hurayrah recorded:

'May Allah have mercy on a man who gets up at night and prays, and awakens his wife; if she is hard to waken, he should sprinkle water on her face. And may Allah have mercy on a woman who gets up at night and prays, and awakens her husband; if he is hard to waken, she should sprinkle water on his face.' (Abu Dawud 1303 and 1445)

Both Abu Sa'id and Abu Hurayrah recorded:

'If a man wakens his wife at night and then both offer two *rak'ahs* together, the man and the woman will be recorded among those who mention the name of Allah.' (Abu Dawud 1304, 1446)

This did not mean that a husband was obliged to force his wife to pray, or vice versa; since the prayers are voluntary it only suggests the loving practice of a devout couple who have both agreed in advance on this procedure. Neither husband nor wife has the right to try to make the other partner feel shame if they do not pray, nor the right to feel themselves superior.

The Blessed Prophet ﷺ used to offer sometimes fifteen, sometimes thirteen and sometimes eleven *rak'ahs* during the night. 'A'ishah recorded that:

'The Messenger of Allah ﷺ used to pray thirteen *rak'ahs* during the night, observing a witr out of that with five; he did not sit during the five except during the last, and then gave the salutation.' (Abu Dawud 1336, Muslim 1604). She also said: 'He used to pray thirteen *rak'ahs* during the night, he then offered two light *rak'ahs* of prayer when he heard the call to the dawn prayer.'

(Abu Dawud 1334)

Abu Salamah ibn Abd al-Rahman asked 'A'ishah how he prayed during Ramadan. She said: 'The Messenger of Allah ﷺ did not pray more than eleven *rak'ahs* during Ramadan and other than Ramadan. He would pray four *rak'ahs*... then four *rak'ahs*... then three *rak'ahs*.' 'A'ishah said: 'I asked: Messenger of Allah, do you sleep before observing witr?' He replied: "A'ishah, my eyes sleep, but my heart does not sleep.' (Abu Dawud 1336, Muslim 1607)

A very interesting *hadith* recorded by Sa'd ibn Hisham threw light on the authority of 'A'ishah, and also the sad conflict between herself and Ibn Abbas (on account of his siding with 'Ali in the battle of the Camel). Sa'd recorded that he came to Ibn Abbas and asked him about the witr observed by the Prophet ﷺ. He said: 'I point you to the person who is most familiar with the witr observed by the Messenger of Allah ﷺ. Go to 'A'ishah.' On the way, he asked Hakim ibn Aflah to accompany him, who at first refused, but then agreed to go. They sought her permission to enter.

She said: 'Who is this?' He said: 'Hakim ibn Aflah.' She asked: 'Who is with you?' He replied: 'Sa'd ibn Hisham.' She said: 'Hisham son of Amir who was killed in the battle of Uhud?' I said: 'Yes.' She said: 'What a good man Amir was!' I said: 'Mother of the Faithful, tell me about the character of the Messenger of Allah ﷺ.' She asked: 'Do you not recite the Qur'an? The character of the Messenger of Allah ﷺ *was* the Qur'an.' I asked: 'Tell me about his vigil and prayer at night.' She replied: 'Do you not recite 'O thou folded in garments?' I said: 'Why not?' When the opening verses of this *surah* were revealed, the Companions stood praying until their feet swelled; and the concluding verses were not revealed from the heavens for twelve months. At last the concluding verses were revealed, and so the night prayer became voluntary after it was obligatory.' I said: 'Tell me abut the witr of the Prophet ﷺ.' She replied: 'He used to pray eight *rak'ahs*, sitting only during the eighth of them. Then he would stand up and pray another *rak'ah*. He would sit only after the eighth and ninth *rak'ahs*. He would utter the salutation only after the ninth *rak'ah*. He would then pray two *rak'ahs* sitting, and that made eleven *rak'ahs*, my son. But when he grew old and became fleshy he observed a witr of seven, sitting only in the sixth and seventh *rak'ahs*, and would utter the salutation after the seventh *rak'ah*. He would then pray two *rak'ahs* sitting, and that made nine *rak'ahs*, my son. The Messenger of Allah ﷺ would not pray through a whole night, or recite the whole Qur'an in a night, or fast a complete month except in Ramadan. When he offered a prayer, he made it a regular habit. When he was overtaken by sleep at night, he would pray twelve *rak'ahs*.'

The narrator said: 'I came to Ibn Abbas and told all this to him. (He aid:) 'By Allah, this is really a tradition. Had I been on speaking terms with her, I would have come to her and heard it from her mouth.' I said: 'If I had know that you were not on speaking terms with her, I would never have narrated it to you!' (Abu Dawud 1337, Muslim 1623)

Ibn Abbas was the nephew of the Blessed Prophet's ﷺ wife Maymunah bint al-Harith. Sometimes he used to spend the night in his aunt's room, and occasionally he observed the Blessed prophet ﷺ at his prayer with his own eyes. A client of Ibn Abbas recorded:

'I spent a night with him when he was with Maymunah. He slept, and awoke when half the night or one third of it had passed. He stood up and went to a leather bag containing water. He performed ablution, and I also performed ablution with him. He

then stood up and I also stood at his left side. He made me stand
at his right side. He then put his hand upon my head, and he
tugged my ear to awaken me. He then prayed two light *rak'ahs*
and recited *sūrah al-Fatihah* in each of them, and uttered the
salutation. He then prayed eleven *rak'ahs* observing the witr, and
slept. Then Bilal came to me and said: 'Prayer, Messenger of
Allah.' He got up and prayed two *rak'ahs*, then came and led the
people in prayer.' (Abu Dawud 1359, see also Muslim 1671, 1691
for the contents of his prayer).

Ibn Abbas himself recorded: 'I spent a night in the house of
my maternal aunt Maymunah, daughter of al-Harith. The Prophet
ﷺ offered the night prayer. He then came and prayed four *rak'ahs*
and slept. He then stood up and prayed. I stood at his left side. He
made me go round and made me stand at his right side. He then
prayed five *rak'ahs* and slept, and I heard his snoring. He then got
up and prayed two *rak'ahs*. Afterwards he came out and offered
the dawn prayer.' (Abu Dawud 1352, see also Bukhari 3.42.117,
4.37.183, 4.5.140, 21.1.289, etc.)

A variant version recorded: 'I lay towards the width of the
pillow and the Messenger of Allah ﷺ and his wife slept along its
length. The Messenger of Allah slept. When half the night passed,
or a little before it or a little after it, the Messenger of Allah ﷺ
awoke and began to rub his face (eyes) to remove the sleep. He
then recited ten verses from the last part of *sūrah* al-Imran. He then
came to the bag of water that was hanging. He performed ablution
from it, and performed his ablution thoroughly. He then stood up
and prayed. I also got up and did as he did. I then went and stood
at his side. The Messenger of Allah ﷺ placed his right hand upon
my head and took me by my ear, twisting it. He then prayed two
rak'ahs, then two *rak'ahs*, then two *rak'ahs*, then two *rak'ahs*, then
two *rak'ahs*, then two *rak'ahs*. He observed the witr prayer, and

then slept until the mu'adhdhin came. He got up and prayed two light *rak'ahs*; and then he came out and offered the dawn prayer.' (Abu Dawud 1362)

Zurarah ibn Awfa recorded another interesting version of the Prophet's nocturnal devotions:

'A'ishah said: 'He used to offer his night prayer in congregation and then return to his family and pray four *rak'ahs*. Then he would go to bed and sleep, but the water for his ablution was placed covered near his head, and his tooth-stick was also kept there until Allah awakened him at night. He then used the tooth-stick and performed ablution perfectly and came to the place of prayer and would pray eight *rak'ahs*, in which he would recite *sūrah al-Fatihah* and a *sūrah* from the Qur'an as Allah willed. He would not sit during any of them but sit after the eighth *rak'ah*, and would not utter the salutation, but recite the Qur'an during the ninth *rak'ah* and then would sit and supplicate as long as Allah willed, and beg Him and devote his attention to Him; and he would utter the salutation once in a loud voice, so much so that the inmates of the house were almost awakened by his loud salutation. He would then recite *sūrah al-Fatihah* while sitting and bow while sitting, and then recite the Qur'an during the second *rak'ah*, and would bow and prostrate while sitting, and supplicate Allah as long as He willed, and then utter the salutation and turn away. This much prayer of the Messenger of Allah ﷺ continued until he became fleshy. During that period he reduced two *rak'ahs* from nine and began to pray six and seven *rak'ahs* sitting. This continued until he died.' (Abu Dawud 1341)

Several recorders reported that he began his supplications with the prayer:

'O Allah, place light in my heart, light in my tongue, light in my hearing, light in my eyesight, light on my right hand, light on my left hand, light in front of me, light behind me, light below me; O Allah, give me abundant light.' (Abu Dawud 1348, Muslim 1671, etc.)

Khalid al-Juhani recorded yet another tradition about his practice:

He said: 'I shall watch the prayer of the Messenger of Allah ﷺ at night. I slept at the threshold of the door of his tent. The Messenger of Allah ﷺ prayed two light rak'ahs, and then he prayed two long, long, long rak'ahs. He then prayed two rak'ahs that were not so long as the two before them; again he prayed two rak'ahs that were less in length than the preceding rak'ahs; he again prayed two rak'ahs that were less in length than the previous rak'ahs. This made altogether thirteen rak'ahs.' (Abu Dawud 1361)

In fact, the Blessed Prophet ﷺ took a dim view of a Muslim who could not manage to pray any prayers during the night.

Abdallah ibn Mas'ud reported that a mention was made of a man who slept the whole night till morning. The Prophet ﷺ remarked: 'That is a man in whose ears the devil urinated!' (Muslim 1700)

Apparently the Prophet's daughter Fatimah and her husband 'Ali did not always manage to pray tahajjud.

Husayn ibn 'Ali narrated on the authority of his father that the Messenger ﷺ came òne night to see him and Fatimah, and said: 'Don't you observe tahajjud?' 'Ali said: 'Messenger of Allah, truly our souls are in the hand of Allah, and when He wants to waken us, He wakens us.' The Messenger ﷺ walked off when said this, striking his hand upon his thigh (an Arabic way of expressing disapproval) and I heard him say: 'Truly this man disputes many things!' (Muslim 1701)

It is important to notice that although the Holy Prophet ﷺ

wanted them to pray this prayer, he did not attempt to force them, as it is voluntary. (See also Bukhari 11.79.696, for the Prophet showing by example when a prayer was not compulsory.)

DO NOT RECITE IN TOO LOUD A VOICE

The Blessed Prophet ﷺ taught that one should always recite the Qur'an in a moderate voice, based on the command in *sūrah* 17:110 'Neither speak your prayer aloud nor speak it in a low tone, but seek a middle course between.'

If people recite too loudly, what is their motivation for it? You may think you are being pious, or pleasing to God, or setting a good example; but if you are in the company of other people, then when they hear your raised voice it can easily result in their disturbed thoughts. No Muslim should try to impose his or her thoughts on another, unless requested to do so by being made leader. It is not necessary to speak in a loud voice to reach the attention of Allah—He can hear the unspoken murmurings of your heart!

The Blessed Prophet ﷺ did not approve of people attempting to 'show off' in their devotions. Even as regards the worship in the mosque, Abu Sa'id recorded the Prophet ﷺ as saying:

'The Messenger of Allah went to the mosque, and heard the people reciting the Qur'an in a loud voice. He removed the curtain and said: 'Lo! Every one of you should call his Lord quietly. One should not trouble the other, and one should not raise the voice in recitation or in prayer over the voice of the other!' (Abu Dawud 1327)

Uqbah ibn Amir al-Juhani recorded: 'One who recites the Qur'an in a loud voice is like one who gives alms openly; and one who recites the Qur'an quietly is one who gives alms secretly (i.e. without showing off).' (Abu Dawud 1328)

Abu Musa recorded: 'We were riding along with Allah's Messenger ﷺ on a journey when the people began to pronounce *takbir* in a loud voice. Thereupon Allah's Messenger ﷺ said: 'O people! Have mercy on yourselves, for you are not calling One Who is deaf or a long way off. Truly, you are calling One Who is All-Hearing and Near to you, and is with you.' (Muslim 6526) In another version, he added: 'He to Whom you are praying to is nearer to every one of you than the neck of your camel!' (Muslim 6531)

Abu Qatadah recorded: 'The Prophet ﷺ went out at night and found Abu Bakr praying in a low voice, and then he passed 'Umar ibn al-Khattab praying in a raised voice. When they both met the Prophet ﷺ together he said: 'I passed by you, Abu Bakr, when you were praying in a low voice.' He replied: 'I made Him hear with Whom I was holding intimate conversation, Messenger of Allah.' The Prophet said to 'Umar: 'I passed by you when you were praying in a loud voice.' He replied: 'Messenger of Allah, I was awakening the drowsy and driving away the devil.' (Abu Dawud 1324) Al-Hasan added in his version: 'The Prophet ﷺ said: 'Raise your voice a little Abu Bakr', and he said to 'Umar: 'Lower your voice a little.'

ON NOT MAKING VOLUNTARY PRAYERS COMPULSORY

Although highly recommended, *sunnah* prayers were always to be regarded as voluntary, and not ever intended to be made compulsory. Therefore a Muslim was not to be held at fault or looked down on if he or she did not do them.

Abd Allah al-Muzani recorded: The Messenger of Allah ﷺ said: 'Pray two *rak'ahs* before the sunset prayer.' Then he said again: 'Pray two *rak'ahs* before the sunset prayer—this applies (only) to those who wish to do so.' (He said) that because he feared

that the people might treat it as *sunnah*. (Abu Dawud 1276)

Anas ibn Malik commented that he used to offer the two *rak'ahs* before the sunset prayer, and the Messenger saw him; but he insisted that 'he neither commanded us nor forbade us to do so.' (Abu Dawud 1277)

'A'ishah once commented: 'The Messenger of Allah ﷺ never offered prayer in the forenoon, but I offer it. The Messenger of Allah ﷺ would give up an action, though he liked to do it, if he thought the people would continue it and (think it was) obligatory for them.' (Abu Dawud 1288)

'A'ishah once recorded the occasion when the Blessed Prophet ﷺ refused to come out for the night prayer for three nights, because he did wanted to show it was not compulsory to always pray it in congregation. (Bukhar 11.79.696)

PRAYERS IN RESPONSE TO NATURAL CONDITONS

Occasionally the Blessed Prophet ﷺ said special prayers in response to particular conditions of nature—for example when there was a time of drought and the people were suffering from lack of rain, or when they were being deluged by too much rain.

Jabir ibn Abdallah recorded that the people came to the Prophet ﷺ weeping (because of the drought). He said: 'O Allah! Give us rain which will replenish us, abundant, fertilising and profitable, not injurious; and grant it without delay.' Thereupon the sky became overcast.' (Abu Dawud 1165)

It is important to realise the knowledge of when it would rain was one of the things specifically listed by the Blessed Prophet ﷺ as being beyond the knowledge of human beings:

Ibn 'Umar recorded: 'Keys of the unseen knowledge are five, which nobody knows but Allah—nobody knows what will happen tomorrow; or what is in the womb; or what he will gain tomorrow; or what place he will die; or when it will rain.' (Bukhari 17.28.149)

When the Prophet prayed for rain, he used to raise his hands in supplication.

Anas recorded that the Prophet ﷺ was not in the habit of raising his hands in any supplication he made except when praying for rain. He would then raise them to such a height as that the white of his armpits became visible.' (Abu Dawud 1166)

A detailed and moving *hadith* was recorded on this subject by 'A'ishah:

'The people complained to the Messenger of Allah ﷺ of the lack of rain, so he gave orders for a pulpit. It was then set up for him in the place of prayer. He fixed a day for the people on which they should come out. When the rim of the sun appeared, the Messenger ﷺ sat down on the pulpit, and having pronounced the greatness of Allah and expressed His praise, he said: 'You have complained of drought in your dwellings, and of delay in receiving rain at the beginning of its season. Allah has ordered you to supplicate Him, and promised that He would answer your prayer.'

Then he said: 'Praise be to Allah, the Lord of the Universe, the Compassionate, the Merciful, the Master of the Day of Judgement, there is no God but Allah, Who does what He wishes. O Allah, You are Allah, there is no God but You, the Rich, while we are the poor. Send down rain upon us and made what You send down a strength and a satisfaction for a time.'

He then raised his hands to such a level as made the whiteness under his armpits visible. He then turned his back to the people and turned round his cloak while keeping his hands aloft. He then faced the people, descended and prayed two *rak'ahs*. Allah then produced a cloud, and a storm of thunder and lightning came on. Then the rain fell, by Allah's permission, and before he reached his mosque streams were flowing. When he saw the speed with which the people were seeking shelter, he laughed till his back teeth were visible. Then he said: 'I bear witness that Allah is Omnipotent, and that I am His servant and Messenger.' (Abu Dawud 1169)

Another version was recorded by Anas:

'The people of Madinah had drought during the time of the Prophet ﷺ. While he was preaching on a Friday, a man stood up and said: 'Messenger of Allah, the horses are dying, the goats are dying, pray Allah to give us water.' He spread his hands and prayed. The sky was like a mirror. Then the wind blasted, a cloud appeared (in the sky) and it spread over; the sky poured down water. We came out paddling through the water until we reached our homes. (But) the rain continued until the next Friday. The same or some other, person (then) stood up and said: 'Messenger of Allah, (now) the houses are being demolished, pray Allah to stop it.' The Messenger of Allah ﷺ smiled and said: '(O Allah,) let the rain fall around us and not upon us. Then, while I looked at it, the cloud encircled around Madinah just like a crown.' (Abu Dawud 1170, see also Bukhari 13.33.55, 17.6.127, 17.9.130, Muslim 1955)

Another natural event which stirred the people up was an eclipse.

Before the time of the Prophet ﷺ eclipses were largely seen as ominous portents of something about to happen, or superstitious signs. The Prophet ﷺ assured the people that they were just natural phenomena, and did not in any way indicate either bad or good fortune, or anything else 'supernatural'.

For example, one eclipse of the sun took place on the day that the Prophet's ﷺ infant son Ibrahim died, and many people instantly began to connect it with the death of the child.

Jabir ibn Abdallah recorded that there was an eclipse of the sun in the time of the Messenger of Allah ﷺ. This was the day when Ibrahim the son of the Messenger ﷺ died. The people began to say that the eclipse was on account of the death of Ibrahim. The Prophet ﷺ stood up and led the people in prayer, performing six bowing and four prostrations. He said: 'Allah is Most Great', and then recited from the Qur'an a long recitation. He then bowed for nearly as long as he had stood. He then raised his head and recited from the Qur'an, but less than the first time. He then bowed for nearly as long as he had stood. He then raised his head and recited again from the Qur'an, but it was less than the second time. He then bowed nearly as long as he had stood. Then he raised his head and went down for prostrations. He then stood and made three bowings before prostrating himself, the preceding bowing being more lengthy than the following, but he bowed nearly as long as he stood. He then stepped back during the prayer, and the rows (of people) stepped back along with him. Then he stepped forward and stood in his place, and the rows

stepped forward also. He then finished the prayer and the sun had become bright. He said: 'O people, the sun and the moon are two of Allah's signs. They are not eclipsed on account of a person's death. So when you see anything of that nature, offer prayer until the sun becomes bright.' (Abu Dawud 1174, Muslim 1975)

There are different traditions recommending the number of *rak'ahs* to offer during an eclipse. The schools of Malik, al-Shafi'i and Hanbal favour two *rak'ahs* with bowing and prostrating four times in each *rak'ah*. Sufyan al-Thawri and the Hanafis maintain that one should only bow once in each *rak'ah*. Other traditions suggest that the Prophet ﷺ bowed six times and prostrated four times in two *rak'ahs*; or that he bowed ten times and prostrated four times in two *rak'ahs*. Probably the Prophet ﷺ adjusted the length of his prayer according to how long the eclipse lasted.

The following *hadith* suggests that it was *sunnah* to offer two *rak'ahs* of prayer in congregation in the event of an eclipse, and to bow three times in each *rak'ah*.

'A'ishah recorded: 'There was an eclipse of the sun in the time of the Prophet ﷺ. He stood for a long time, accompanied by the people. He then bowed, raised his head, then he bowed and raised his head, and again he bowed and prayed two *rak'ahs* of prayer. In each *rak'ah* he bowed three times. After bowing for the third time he prostrated himself. He stood for such a long time that some people fainted away and buckets of water had to be poured on them. When he bowed, he said: 'Allah is Most Great'; and when raised his head he said: 'Allah listens to him who praises Him'; till the sun became bright. Then he said: 'The sun and the moon are not eclipsed on account of anyone's death or birth, but they are two of Allah's signs; He produces dread in His servants by means of them. When they are eclipsed, hasten to prayer.' (Abu Dawud 1173, see also Bukhari 18.2.154, Muslim 1968)

'A'ishah (also) recorded: 'The sun and the moon are not eclipsed on account of anyone's death or anyone's birth. So when you see one, supplicate Allah, declare His greatness, and give in charity.' (Abu Dawud 1187)

Asma ('A'ishah's sister) recorded: 'The Prophet ﷺ used to command us to free slaves on the occasion of an eclipse.' (Abu Dawud 1188, Bukhari 18.11.163)

Other natural phenomena that made people pray included sudden extraordinary darkness, and things like hurricanes, earthquakes and so forth.

Ubaydallah ibn al-Nadr recorded on the authority of his father that in the time of Anas ibn Malik it once went very dark. He came to Anas and said: 'Abu Hamzah, did anything like this happen to you in the time of the Messenger of Allah ﷺ? He replied: 'Take refuge in Allah! (Even) if the wind blew violently we would run quickly towards the mosque, for fear of coming of the Day of Judgement!' (Abu Dawud 1192)

It was widely believed that such natural phenomena would occur as signs that the End of Days was about to come:

Abu Hurayrah recorded the Prophet ﷺ as saying: 'The Hour will not be established until knowledge ceases due to the death of learned men of religion, earthquakes will be frequent, time will pass quickly, afflictions will appear, murders will increase and money will overflow amongst you.' (Bukhari 18.26.146)

It was reported that once during the time of the Prophet ﷺ on the occasion of a very strong wind a certain man began to abuse it by cursing and shouting violently against it. The Prophet ﷺ said: 'Do not abuse it. It has been ordained by Allah. But say— 'I ask You for the good of it, and what is good in it, and the good of what You commanded; and I take refuge in You from its evil, and what is evil in it, and the evil of what You have commanded.'

(Abu Dawud 1192 n. 615, Muslim 1962)

Muslims also prostrated themselves in prayer when they observed some accident.

Ikramah recorded that when Ibn Abbas was informed that a certain wife of the Prophet ﷺ had died, he fell down prostrating himself. He was asked why he did that, at that particular moment. He said: 'The Messenger of Allah ﷺ said—'Whenever you see a portent, prostrate yourselves. And what portent could be greater than the death of a wife of the Prophet ﷺ?' (Abu Dawud 1193)

PRAYERS FOR PARTICULAR OCCASIONS

It has become Muslim tradition to utter certain brief prayers when doing certain particular things, and a selection is listed here.

When waking up:

'Al-hamdu lillahi ahyana badama amatana wa'ilayhin nushur.'

'Praise be to Allah, Who gave us life after death, and to Him will be the return.'

When getting up in the morning:

'La ilaha Illallah.'

'There is no God but Allah.'

When going into the bathroom or toilet

'Allahumma inni a'uzu bika minal khubuthi wal-khaba'ith.'

'O our Lord! I seek refuge in You from male and female demons.'

When leaving the bathroom or toilet:

'Ghufranak.'

'I seek Your forgiveness (O Allah)!'

When you perform wudu':

'Allahummaghfirni thanbi, wawassili fi dari wabarikli fi rizqi.'

'O our Lord, forgive my sins and bless my home and my

livelihood.'

When you have finished *wudu'*:

'*Ashhadu alla ilaha illallah. Wahdaho la sharika lah. Wa 'ashhadu anna Muhammadan abduhu warasuluhu. Allahumma jalni minat tawwabin, wajalni minal mutatahhirin.*'

'I bear witness that there is no God but Allah. He is the Alone, and has no partner. And I bear witness that Muhammad is His servant and messenger. O our Lord! Make me one of those who repent and purify themselves.'

When you see your face in a mirror:

'*Allahumma anta hassanta khalqi fahassin khulqi waharrim wajhi alannar. Alhamdu lillahi ladhi sawwa khalqi fa 'adalah wakarrama soorata wajhi fa 'ahsanaha. Waja alani minal muslimeen.*'

'O our Lord! You made my physical personality good, so make my disposition good also, and keep my face safe from Hell-fire. Thanks be to Allah, Who designed me and made me of acceptable proportions, and honoured my face and made me (one) of the Muslims.'

When you leave the house:

'*Bismillahi tawakkaltu Alal-Lah. La hawla wala quwwata illa billah.*'

'In the name of Allah, I depend on Allah. There is no possibility nor power save in Allah.'

When you go into the mosque:

'*Bismillah. Allahumma salli ala Muhammad Allahumma ftahli anwaba rahmatik.*'

'In the name of Allah. O our Lord, bless Muhammad. O our Lord, open Your gates of mercy for me.'

When you have finished your prayer:

'*Subhanallah*'—three times—'Glory be to Allah'

'*Alhamdulillah*'—three times—'Praise be to Allah'

'*Allahu Akbar*'—three times—'God is the Most High'

'*La ilaha illallah. Wahdahu la sharika lah. Lahul mulk wa lahalhamd, wahowa alakulli shayin qadir.*'

'There is no God but Allah. He is the One Alone, and has no partner. His is the power and the glory, and He is Omnipotent.'

When you leave the mosque:

'*Allahumma inni assaluka min fadlik.*'

'O our Lord! I beg You (to grant me) of Your grace.'

When you meet a Muslim:

'*Assalaamu alaikum*

'Peace be upon you'

When you reply to a greeting:

'*Wa'alaikum as-salaam*'

'And peace be upon you also'

When you hope to be able to do something:

'*Insha Allah*'

'If Allah wills.'

When you wish to praise someone:

'*Subhanallah!*'

'Glory be to Allah!'

When you wish to express appreciation:

'*Ma'sha Allah*'

'As Allah likes'

When you wish to see someone off:

'*Fi amanillah*'

'(Go) in the protection of Allah'

When getting into a vehicle for travel:

'*Subhanal ladhi sakh-khara lana hatha. Wama kunna laho*

muqrineen. Wa inna ila rabbina lamunqaliboon.'

'Glory be to Him Who has provided these for our (use), for we could never have achieved these (things) (by ourselves). And to our Lord we must surely return.'

When you wish to thank someone:
'Jazakallahu khairan'
'May Allah give you the best reward'

When you wish to solve a problem:
'Tawakkaltu al-Allah'
'I rely on Allah'

When you sneeze:
'Alhamdulillah'
'Praise be to Allah'

When you hear someone else sneeze:
'Yarhamukallah!'
'May Allah bless you'

When in pain or distress:
'Ya Allah!'
'O Allah!'

When suffering, or facing a problem:
'Allahumma la sahla illa ma ja 'altahu sahla wa' anta taj 'alul hazna idha shi'ta sahla.'

'O our Lord! There is nothing easy except what You make easy, and You make the difficult easy, if it is Your will.'

When you wish to say sorry for a bad thought or action:
'Astaghfirullah'
'O Allah, forgive me'

When you wish to show dislike:
'Na 'udhubillah.'

'We seek refuge in Allah'

When you hear about the death of someone:

'Inna lillah'

'We are for Allah!'

When you go into your house:

'Allahumma inni as'aluka khayral maolij. Wakhayral makhraj. Bismillahi walajna wabismillahi kharajna wa'alal lahi Rabbina tawwakalna'

'O our Lord! I ask You the best entering in and the best existence. In the name of Allah, we entered in, and in the name of Allah we went out, and upon Allah our Lord we depend.'

When starting a meal:

'Allahumma bariklana fima razaqtana waqina adhabannar. Bismillah.'

'O our Lord! Bless (what) You have provided for us, and save us from the punishment of Hell-fire. In the name of Allah.'

When the meal is ended:

'Alhamdu lillahilladhi at'amana wasaqana waja'alana Muslimin.'

'Praise be to Allah Who has given us food and drink and made us Muslims.'

When going to sleep:

'Bismika Rabbi wadato janbi wahiba arfaoh. Fa'in amsakta nafsi faghfirlaha. Wa inarsaltaha fahfazha bima tahfazobihi ibadakas salihin.'

'In Your name, O Allah, I lie down to sleep, and by Your leave I (will) rise up again. If You take away my soul, forgive it, and if You send it back, protect it—even as You protect (all) Your pious servants.'

When you wake up after a nightmare:

'Aiuzu bikalimatil lahit tammati min ghadabihi wa iqabihi wa sharri ibadihi wamin hamazat ish-shayateen wa'an yahdoroon.'

'I seek refuge in the perfect words of Allah, from His displeasure and punishment and from evil persons, and from the (evil) promptings of devils and from their presence.'

When visiting a sick person:

'Allahumma ath-hibil bas Rabban nas. Oshfi wa 'antash shafi la shifa 'a illa shifa 'ok. Shifa 'al layoghadiro saqama.'

'O our Lord! Remove the hardship, O Lord of Humanity. Give the cure, for You are the Healer. There is no cure but from You, a cure which leaves no illness behind.'

When consoling a bereaved person:

'Innalillahi ma akhatha walaho ma 'a ta. Wakkolo shayin indaho bi'ajalim musamma faltasbir waltahtasib.'

'Allah takes away that which is due to Him, and whatever was given belongs to Him. Everything has a fixed time span with Him; so have patience and seek His reward.'

When visiting someone's grave:

'Assalamu alaikum ahlad diyari minal Mu'mineena walmuslimeen. Wayarhamol lahol mustaqdimeena minkum walmusta'khireen. Wa 'inna inshaallaho bikum lahiqoon. As 'alollaha lana walakumul afiyah. Antom lana faraton. Wanahno lakum taba 'on. Allahumma la tahrimna ajrahom wa la tudillana badahom.'

'Peace be upon you, O dwellers in these abodes, believers and Muslims. May Allah have mercy on those of you who (died) before, and those who (have died) recently. When Allah wills, we shall be joining you. I beg of Allah salvation for us and for you. You went before us, and we will follow you. O our Lord, do not take away our reward, and lead us not astray after they are gone.'

Healing Prayer

THE BLESSED PROPHET ﷺ ORDERED PRAYERS FOR HEALING

The Blessed Prophet ﷺ spent much of his time caring for people in many different ways. One of the most important of his activities was visiting the sick, and praying for a solution to their problems.

Umm Salamah recorded the Blessed Prophet ﷺ as saying: 'Whenever you visit the sick or the deceased, pray for good, because the angels say 'Amen' to whatever you say.' (Muslim 2002)

Visiting the sick was one of the seven obligations the Blessed Prophet ﷺ laid upon his followers as things which a believer should definitely seek to do:

Al-Bara ibn Azib recorded that Allah's Messenger ﷺ ordered us to do seven things: to follow the funeral procession, to visit the sick, to accept invitations, to help the oppressed, to fulfil oaths, to return greetings and to bless the person who sneezes.' (Bukhari 23.2.331)

Abu Musa al-Ashari recorded: 'Feed the hungry, visit the sick, and free the captive.' (Abu Dawud 3099, Bukhari 70.4.552)

Those who do pray for the sick are frequently aware of the presence of God's angels, joining in with the prayer and bringing serenity and peace of mind, and inner strength.

Abu Darda recorded that the Prophet ﷺ said: 'There is no believer who prays for his brother (or sister) behind his back that the angels do not say: 'The same be for you, too.' (Muslim 6588)

Agharr abi Muslim recorded that he also said: 'The people do not sit (to pray) but they are surrounded by angels and covered by Mercy, and there descends upon them tranquillity as they remember Allah...' (Muslim 6520)

People who take the trouble to be kind towards those who are suffering will find that Allah welcomes and appreciates their compassion.

Abu Hurayrah recorded: 'Those who alleviate the suffering of a brother (or sister) from the sufferings of this world, Allah will alleviate their suffering from the sufferings of the Day of Resurrection; and those who find relief for one who is hard pressed, Allah will make things easy for them in the Hereafter...' (Muslim 6518)

THE IMPORTANCE OF VISITING THE SICK

'Ali recorded: 'If a person visits a patient in the evening, seventy thousand angels come along with that one seeking forgiveness from Allah for him (or her) until the morning, and he (or she) will have a garden in Paradise.' (Abu Dawud 3092)

Sometimes the Blessed Prophet ﷺ took steps to keep the hurt or sick person near at hand, so that he could visit frequently.

'A'ishah recorded: 'When Sa'd ibn Mu'adh had an arrow shot into his arm on the Day of the (Battle of the) Trench, the Messenger of Allah ﷺ had a tent pitched for him in the mosque so that he might visit him from close at hand.' (Abu Dawud 3095)

The Blessed Prophet ﷺ visited many people who were not Muslims—it did not make any difference to his kindness; he never discriminated.

Anas recorded that a young Jew became ill. The Prophet ﷺ went to visit him. He sat down by his head and said to him: '(Why do you not) accept Islam?' He looked at his father, who was sitting near his head and he said: 'Obey Abu al-Qasim (i.e. the Prophet).' So he accepted Islam, and the Prophet ﷺ stood up saying: 'Praise be to Allah Who has saved him from Hell through me.' (Abu Dawud 2089, Bukhari 23.78.438, see also Bukhari 70.11.561)

THE IMPORTANCE OF *SABR*, OR PATIENCE

It is very important that a Muslim suffering affliction should not begin to lack faith, or start to attack God or complain about Him. People who have been involved with serious illness know only too well the natural temptation to try to demand 'why has this happened to me, or my family?'—as if they really believe that of all the people of the world, they alone, or their family alone, should prove to be immune from suffering and sickness and calamity.

However, it is the Muslim duty to be aware that misfortunes and illnesses affect every person from time to time, no matter how saintly they might happen to be. They have to practice *sabr* or patience, and to accept the eventuality with as good grace and as much faith as possible.

Abu Hurayrah recorded the Messenger of Allah ﷺ as saying: 'If Allah wants to do good to somebody, He afflicts them with trials.' (Bukhari 70.1.548)

As Allah warned in the Qur'an:

'Do you think that you will enter the Garden without such (trials) as those that happened to those who passed away before you? They encountered sufferings and adversity, and were so shaken in spirit that even the Messenger and those believers who were with them cried: 'When will the help of God come?' Ah, in truth, the help of God is (always) near!' (*Sūrah* 2:214)

No human being knows the full picture of why it is that

certain people are given pains and torments and anxieties to suffer—only God Alone has that knowledge. It is important to realise that a person who has faith in God is in a far better position to withstand and accept illness, disappointment, distress and death than a person with no faith, no belief in Divine Justice, and no hope for a Hereafter. God does not always take away the 'storm', but He is always with us 'in the middle of it'; He is ever close, to give us strength and courage.

Faith is therefore the key to strength and inner calm—but this does not mean that a person is obliged to remain unaffected by the calamity in an inhuman and unfeeling manner.

Abu 'Uthman recorded that Usamah bin Zayd said that while he, Sa'd and Ubayy bin Ka'b were with the Prophet ﷺ, one of his daughters sent a message to him saying: 'My daughter is dying, please come to us.' The Prophet ﷺ sent her his best wishes and added: 'It is for Allah what He takes and what He gives; and everything before His sight has a limited time-span. So, let her hope for Allah's reward, and (accept) with patience.' She again sent a message, begging him, by Allah, to come. So the Prophet ﷺ and the couple got up and (went where the child was). The child was placed on his lap, and he was breathing only with difficulty. Tears flowed from the eyes of the Prophet ﷺ. Sa'd said to him: 'What is this, O Allah's Messenger?' He said: 'This is pity, which Allah has embedded in the hearts of whoever He wished of His slaves. And Allah does not bestow His compassion except on those of His slaves who are compassionate.' (Bukhari 70.9.559)

PRAYERS FOR HEALING

The Blessed Prophet ﷺ frequently used verses from the Qur'an while making healing prayers, in particular the two verses known as Mu'awwidhatan, *surahs* 103 and 104—the last *surahs* in the Qur'an.

'I seek refuge with the Lord of the Dawn, from the mischief of created things, from the mischief of the spreading darkness, from the mischief of those who practice secret arts, and from the mischief of the envious one as he practises envy.' (*Sūrah* 103)

'I seek refuge with the Lord and Guardian of humanity, the King of humanity, the Judge of humanity, from the mischief of the whisperer (the devil) who withdraws (saps strength and energy), who whispers into the hearts of humanity, among jinns and among humans.' (*Sūrah* 104)

Both *sūrahs* make very clear that illness is not just a physical thing, but involves the battle against spiritual forces for evil, and the whole realm of creation including the jinn, the spirit forces, and those who tamper with them or try to manipulate them.

Abu al-Darda recorded the Prophet 鸞 as saying: 'If any of you is suffering from anything, or his brother is suffering, he should say: Our Lord is Allah Who is in the heaven, Holy is Your Name, Your Kingdom reigns in heaven and on earth; as is Your mercy in the heaven (so) make Your mercy in the earth; forgive us our sins and our errors; You are the Lord of good people, send down Your mercy from Your Mercy, and healing from Your healing on this pain, so that it is healed up.' (Abu Dawud 3883— any Christian readers will note immediately how similar this prayer is to the 'pattern prayer' taught by the Blessed Jesus in St. Matthew's Gospel chapter 6, verses 9-14.)

Many different prayers that the Blessed Prophet 鸞 said for healing have been recorded in the *hadith*. Here are two famous examples:

'Lord of the people, remove this trouble, for in Your Hand alone is the cure; there is none who can relieve him (or her), but only You.' (Muslim 5437, Bukhari 71.438.640)

'A'ishah recorded: 'O Lord of the people! Remove the difficulty and bring about healing, as You are the Healer. There is no healing but Your healing, a healing that will leave no ill remaining.' (Bukhari 71.40.646)

DO NOT PRAY FOR DEATH

No matter how ill a person may be, or how distressed, it is wrong to beg Allah to be allowed to die. Many times human nature cries out because of suffering; it may be that all one's friends or loved ones have already gone, and there seems to be nothing left. However, the person does not know in what ways Allah is using their suffering in order to teach them something, or to make good their sins, or as example to aid others; and death will always come when Allah wishes it. It is better to pray for strength and courage, and to try to develop inner peace, and accept that Allah will grant death to an individual when it is 'better' for him or her.

Anas recorded: 'None of you should wish for death for any calamity that befalls you, but should say: 'O Allah! Cause me to live so long as life is better for me; and cause me to die when death is better for me.' (Abu Dawud 3102, Bukhari 70.19.575)

A POSITIVE ATTITUDE

The Blessed Prophet ﷺ took a very positive attitude when visiting sick people. He *expected* Allah to hear his petition, and heal the sick one. He also expected other people's prayers to be heard too.

Ibn Abbas recorded the Prophet ﷺ as saying: 'If anyone visits a sick person whose time (of death) has not yet come, and says with that one seven times: 'I ask Allah, the Almighty, the Lord of the Mighty Throne, to cure you!' then Allah will cure him (or her) from that disease.' (Abu Dawud 3100)

Ibn 'Amr recorded: 'When a person comes to visit a sick person, he (or she) should say: 'O Allah! Cure Your servant, who may then wreak havoc on an enemy in Your cause, or walk at a funeral for Your sake.' (Abu Dawud 3101)

Some people wonder how one can reconcile making prayers for a sick person to be cured with the belief that everything that happens is God's will anyway. They wonder whether it is actually a lack of faith to pray for health. If it is God's will, for some reason known only to Him, for that person to be ill, or to die, then what is the point of anyone praying that they may be made better?

We have to think about two things. Firstly, a very great number of people pray desperately for healing for themselves or their loved ones, and it is not granted. There is no miraculous cure—the person remains ill, or perhaps dies. Does this mean that God does not care about that person, or enjoys the spectacle of watching them suffer and waste away? By no means—God is with us in every bit of our suffering.

Secondly, we have the example of many of the famous prophets who prayed for healing, and some who even prayed and the dead person was raised to life. Three such raisings are recorded of the Blessed Jesus ﷺ, for example, and many, many healings. The Blessed Prophet Muhammad ﷺ was in complete accord with healing prayer and practised it regularly for his family and friends, and anyone who requested his help.

We can only assume from this, therefore, that no matter how illogical it might seem to a theological brain, it *was* quite in keeping with the will of Allah for such prayers to be made; and there *must* have been enough positive results to these prayers for them to be have been considered worthwhile.

Therefore, it is correct practice for a Muslim to exercise his or her compassion in praying for the healing of another, and to do their utmost to bring about that other person's restoration to health and happiness.

DO NOT RELY ON PRAYER ALONE, BUT USE MEDICINE AND OTHER AIDS TO HEALING

Having faith in Allah is not regarded as being in any way contrary to the desire to seek medical help and make use of medical expertise as well. The two—faith and medicine—go hand-in-hand. There is no virtue whatsoever in refusing to accept medical treatment out of a desire not to be thought lacking in faith!

Usamah ibn Sharik said: 'I came to the Prophet 鷺 and his companions were sitting (as still as) if they had birds on their heads. I saluted and sat down. Desert Arabs were coming from here and there, and asking: 'Messenger of Allah, should we make use of medical treatment?' He replied, '(Yes), make use of medical treatment, for Allah has not created a disease without also creating a remedy for it, with the exception of one disease (only)—namely, old age!' (Abu Dawud 3846)

Obviously, as Creator, Allah is ultimately responsible for the existence of sickness and disease on this planet—it was He who created the microbes and bacteria that surround us continually in the air we breathe and in the substances we eat and drink. However, the Blessed Prophet 鷺 was quite clear that Allah had provided everything necessary on this planet to deal with sickness or poison caused by other natural substances.

'Abu al-Darda recorded: 'Allah has sent down both the disease and the cure, and He has appointed a cure for every disease; so treat yourselves medically, but use nothing unlawful.' (Abu Dawud 3865, see also Bukhari 71.1.582)

The only times the Prophet 鷺 did not approve of using

medicine was when the
remedy contained *haram*
substances—for example,
pork or alcohol. (He also
mentioned medicine pre-
pared from frogs (Abu
Dawud 3862)—but this is
an unlikely prescription
these days!)

Abu Hurayrah re-
corded: 'The Messenger of
Allah ﷺ forbade unclean
medicine.' (Abu Dawud
3861)

Wail recorded that
Tariq ibn Suwaid asked the
Prophet ﷺ about wine
(used in medicine), and he
forbade it. He asked him again, and he (again) forbade him. He
said to him: 'Prophet of Allah, it is a medicine!' The Prophet ﷺ
said: 'No, it is a disease!' (Abu Dawud 3864)

It is important to bear this in mind when having prescriptions
made up by modern doctors or chemists, for many medicines
have alcohol bases, or may include animal fats or use gelatine from
animals killed in a *haram* manner. However, the rule of necessity
applies here—if the malady is a serious matter and there is nothing
else available, then the medicine may be taken—but it is highly
commendable to seek for alternatives and use them if they are
available, and press the medical authorities for more research into
medicine with non-alcohol bases, for there *are* substitutes that
could be used.

FOLK MEDICINE—HONEY

The Blessed Prophet ﷺ frequently advised taking honey as a medicine:

Ibn Abbas recorded: 'Healing is in three things, cupping, a drink of honey, or cauterisation (branding with fire), but I forbid my followers to cauterise.' (Bukhari 71.3.585, 597)

On another occasion, the Blessed Prophet ﷺ recommended honey for loose motions:

Abu Sa'id al-Khudri recorded that a man came to the Prophet and said: 'My brother has some abdominal trouble.' The Prophet ﷺ said: 'Let him drink honey.' (Bukhari 71.4.588, 71.24.614)

Other simple remedies included black cumin seed, a porridge made of milk, honey and flour ('it rests the heart of the patient and makes it active, and relieves some of the sorrow and grief.' (Bukhari 71.8.593)

The Prophet ﷺ was very concerned that people should use good knowledge, and not damage themselves by ignorant and perhaps dangerous folk medicine. Sometimes the Prophet ﷺ had to correct ignorant practices.

Umm Qays bint Mihsan recorded that she brought her son to the Messenger ﷺ, and that she had been squeezing his uvula because it was swollen (tonsilitis?). He said: 'Why do you make your children suffer by squeezing for a swelling of the uvula? Apply this Indian aloeswood, for it contains seven types of remedies, among them being a remedy for pleurisy. It is applied through the nose for a swelling of the uvula and poured into the side of the mouth for pleurisy.' (Abu Dawud 3868, Bukhari 71.13.599, 71.21.611)

The principle here is not that we should seek out Indian

aloeswood, but that we should avail ourselves of good knowledge and not cause more harm than good by acting in ignorance.

ADVICE AGAINST IGNORANCE & SUPERSTITION

As well as medicine, the Blessed Prophet ﷺ also made use of the current medical practises to relieve painful symptoms—in his case 'cupping' or drawing blood.

Salmah, the maidservant of the Messenger of Allah ﷺ said: 'No-one complained to the Messenger of Allah ﷺ of a headache, but he told him to get himself cupped, or dye painful legs with henna.' (Abu Dawud 3849)

On the other hand, the Prophet ﷺ took pains to teach people that ignorant and superstitious medicine and practices were wrong and should be abandoned. There are several *hadith* about cauterisation, for example, because the Arabs had a superstitious belief that cauterisation was a sure healer of any ill, and that those who did not apply it were bound to die. The Prophet ﷺ did cauterise Sa'd ibn Muadh's arrow wound, to staunch the flow of blood from his vein, but in other cases he taught that cauterisation was worse than useless—it might even prove harmful.

Imran ibn Husayn recorded: The Prophet ﷺ forbade us to cauterise; we did cauterise, but these (attempts) did not benefit us, nor prove useful for us.' (Abu Dawud 3856, Bukhari 71.15.603, 71.17.605)

THE PROPHET'S ﷺ METHOD OF HEALING

The Blessed Prophet ﷺ did not consider it right to spend long hours at a person's bedside merely *praying* for healing when there were practical things to do.

Sa'd recorded: 'I suffered from an illness. The Messenger of Allah ﷺ came to visit me. He put his hand on my breast and I felt its coolness at my heart. He said: 'You are suffering from heart sickness. Go to al-Harith ibn Kaladah, brother of Thaqif. He is a man who gives medical treatment. He should take seven good quality dates of Madinah and grind them with their kernels, and put them into your mouth.' (Abu Dawud 3866)

This does not mean that today's heart cases should rely on eating seven dates to cure them, but that they, too, should seek out those best qualified to help them today—the medical experts.

The Blessed Prophet ﷺ was a great believer in gently touching or stroking his 'patients'.

'A'ishah bint Sa'd recorded that her father said: 'I became ill in Makkah. The Messenger of Allah ﷺ came to pay a sick-visit to me. He put his hand on my forehead, massaged my chest and belly, and then said: 'O Allah! Heal Sa'd, and complete his immigration.' (Abu Dawud 3098)

Another interesting case with a different method was recorded by 'Uthman ibn Abi al-As.

'I had a pain which was about to destroy me. So the Prophet ﷺ said: 'Stroke it with your right hand seven times and say: 'I seek refuge in the dominance of Allah and His might, from the evil of what I find.' Then I did this, and Allah removed the pain which I had, and I thereafter recommended this to my family and others.' (Abu Dawud 3881)

The Blessed Prophet ﷺ sometimes used earth and water as a healing aid.

Muhammad ibn Yusuf quoted his father on the authority of his grandfather as describing the cure by the Prophet ﷺ or Thabit ibn Qais. He said: 'Remove the harm, O Lord of Humanity, from Thabit ibn Qais ibn Shammas.' He then took some earth of Bathan (Valley), and put it in a bowl, then mixed it with water, blew in it, and poured it on him.' (Abu Dawud 3876)

His usual method, however, seems to have been the laying on of hands, with recitation of the last two *surahs*, and gentle stroking.

'A'ishah recorded: 'When the Messenger of Allah ﷺ suffered pain, he recited mu'awwadhat in his heart and blew. When the pain became severe, I recited (them) over him and stroked him with his (own) hand in the hope of its blessing.' (Abu Dawud 3893)

'A'ishah recorded that when any members of the household fell ill, Allah's Messenger ﷺ used to blow over them and recite Mu'awwidhatan; and when he suffered from his own final illness 'I used to blow over him and stroke his body with his own hand, for his hand had greater healing power than my hand.' (Muslim 5439, see also Bukhari 71.32.631)

'A'ishah was stroking and loving her sick husband in this manner when he finally passed away:

'A'ishah recorded: 'When any of us became ill, Allah's Messenger ﷺ used to stroke him with his right hand and say: 'O Lord of the people, grant him health, heal him, for You are the Great Healer. There is no healer, but with Your healing Power one is healed and illness is removed.' She further added: 'When Allah's Messenger ﷺ fell ill, and his illness took a serious turn, I took hold of his hand so that I should do with it what he used to do with it. But he withdrew his hand from my hand, and said: 'O Allah, pardon me and let me join the companionship on high.' She said: 'I never took my eyes away from him, until he had passed away.' (Muslim 5432)

SUFFERERS ARE FORGIVEN THEIR SINS, AND RECEIVE OTHER BLESSINGS

If a Muslim is stricken with illness, there is at least the consolation that Allah may, as a result of it, forgive us some of our sins. The Blessed prophet ﷺ revealed that suffring due to illness moved Allah's compassion, so that sins were forgiven.

Umm al-Ala recorded that the Messenger ﷺ visited her when she was sick. He said: 'Be glad, Umm al-Ala, for Allah removes the sins of a Muslim for his (or her) illness, as fire removes the dross from gold and silver.' (Abu Dawud 3086)

'A'ishah recorded that she told the Messenger of Allah that the most severe verse in the Qur'an was: 'If anyone does evil, he will be requited for it.' He said: 'Do you know, 'A'ishah, that when a believer is afflicted with a calamity or a thorn, it serves as an atonement for his evil deed.' (Abu Dawud 3087, Bukhari 70.1.544)

Abu Sa'id al-Khudri and Abu Hurayrah recorded: 'No fatigue, nor disease, nor sorrow, nor sadness, nor hurt, nor distress befalls a Muslim, even if it were (as small as) the prick of a thorn, but Allah expiates some of his (or her) sins for it.' (Bukhari 70.1.545)

Sometimes, even though an illness or death seems such a terrible tragedy, other good things arise out of it, or blessings are given to make up for the suffering.

Umm Salamah recorded that the Messenger of Allah ﷺ said: 'If any Muslim who suffers some calamity says what Allah has commanded him,—'We belong to Allah and to Allah we shall return; O Allah, reward me for my affliction and give me something better than it in exchange for it', then Allah *will* give something better in exchange.' (Muslim 1999)

In the case of Umm Salamah, who lost her dearly beloved husband, one of the Blessed Prophet's ﷺ consins, she gained a second husband—the Blessed Prophet himself!

She added: 'When Abu Salamah died, I went to the Messenger of Allah ﷺ and told him he had died. He told me to recite:

'O Allah! Forgive me and him, and give me a substitute for him better than he was,' and Allah gave me in exchange Muhammad ﷺ.' (Muslim 2002)

CHARMS (OR *RUQYA*) AND THE 'EVIL EYE'

The use of charms and incantation for healing was in general disapproved of by the Prophet ﷺ although he did not altogether forbid it. Anything that was mere superstition, or involved the calling up of spirits, angels or other entities, was completely forbidden.

Also forbidden was the superstitious use of even genuinely pious practices, if they did not include the awareness that it was *not* the charm, or the act, or the water, or the blowing that healed—it was the grace and mercy of Allah. That mercy was freely available, as He willed, without any 'magical practices'.

In other words, concentration on trying to perform an incantation or ritual method of healing 'in a correct way' is a pointless practice. The concentration should be on drawing close to Allah, asking His help, listening for His reply, and putting into practice whatever practical aid we feel would best carry out His will.

That some words have healing power is a matter that can be vouched for by many people who have used charms or *ruqya* as aids to healing. Various forms of incantation are almost universal. The mere fact that the process is beyond the realm of our senses does not prove it to be mere superstition. Islam purged the practice of incantation from evil things.

Abdal-Rahman ibn al-Aswad recorded on the authority of his father: 'I asked 'A'ishah about incantation. She said: 'Allah's Messenger ﷺ granted its sanction to the members of an Ansari family in order to cure poisoning (especially that of a scorpion).' (Muslim 5442)

'A'ishah recorded that when any person fell ill with a disease or had any ailment or any injury, the Messenger of Allah ﷺ placed his forefinger on the ground then lifted it while reciting the name of Allah, (and said): 'The dust of our earth with the saliva of any of us would serve as a means whereby our illness will be cured, if Allah wills.' (Muslim 5444, Abu Dawud 3886)

'A'ishah also recorded the use of incantation for curing the influence of the evil eye. (Muslim 5446)

Many modern-day people do not believe in the truth of a person being ill-wished by somebody else, the practice referred to as afflicting someone with the 'evil eye'. The Blessed Prophet ﷺ like the famous Prophet-Healer Jesus ﷺ before him certainly believed in psychic attack, and not only did not ridicule the idea, but took steps to counter it.

Abu Hurayrah recorded the Messenger of Allah ﷺ as saying: 'The evil eye is genuine.' (Abu Dawud 3870)

'A'ishah recorded that the Prophet ﷺ ordered the person causing the evil eye to perform ablution, and then the affected person was washed with that water.' (Abu Dawud 3871)

Although the Prophet ﷺ disapproved strongly of superstitious magic, yet nevertheless he occasionally sanctioned the use of charms as an aid to healing.

Jabir ibn Abdallah recorded: 'I had a maternal uncle who used to treat the sting of the scorpion with the help of incantation. Allah's Messenger ﷺ forbade incantation. He came to him and said: 'Allah's Messenger, you forbade to practise incantation, but I use it for curing scorpion stings.' He said: 'He who amongst you is capable to employing it as a means to do good, should do that.' (Muslim 5454)

Imran ibn Husayn recorded: 'No spell is to be used except for the evil eye or a scorpion sting.' (Abu Dawud 3875)

Awf ibn Malik Ashjai recorded: 'We practised incantation before the coming of Islam, and we asked Allah's Messenger ﷺ his opinion about it. He said: 'Let me hear your incantation', and then said: 'There is no harm in the incantation that does not smack of worship of other gods.' (Muslim 5457)

Maqil ibn Yasar recorded the Prophet ﷺ as saying: 'Recite *surah* Yasin (36) over your dying.' (Abu Dawud 3115)

Kharijah ibn al-Salt quoted his paternal uncle as saying that he passed a clan of Arabs who (brought to him) a lunatic in chains. He recited *surah al-Fatihah* over him three days, morning and evening. When he finished, he collected his saliva and then spat it out; (he felt relief) as if he were set free from bonds. They gave him some payment. Then he came to the Prophet ﷺ and told him. The Messenger ﷺ said: 'Accept it, for by my life, some accept it for a worthless charm, but you have done so far a genuine one.' (Abu Dawud 3413; there is a longer version in Abu Dawud 3412; see also Abu Dawud 3887f)

However, the Blessed Prophet ﷺ always countered mere superstition, and showed how it was the grace and mercy of Allah that lay behind all healing.

Zaynab, the wife of Abdallah ibn Mas'ud recorded that Abdallah heard the Messenger ﷺ saying: 'Spells, charms and love-spells are worship of false gods.' I (Zaynab) asked: 'Why do you say this? I swear by Allah, my eye was discharging and I used to go to such man, the Jew, who applied a spell to me. When he applied the spell, it calmed down.' Abdallah said: 'That was just the work of the devil who was picking it with his hand, and when he uttered the spell, he stopped doing it. All you need to do is to say as the Messenger of Allah ﷺ used to say—'Remove the harm, O Lord of humanity and heal. You are the Healer. There is no remedy but Yours, which leaves no disease behind.' (Abu Dawud 3874, see also Bukhari 70.20.579)

QUARANTINE, AND CLOSE CONTACT

The Blessed Prophet ﷺ knew about quarantine. He advised that people in a region stricken by plague should not flee away from that place, but should stay there and try to contain the disease in that one place.

Sa'd recorded that the Prophet ﷺ said: 'If you hear of an outbreak of plague in a certain place, do not go there; but if the plague breaks out while you are there, do not leave that place.' (Bukhari 21.30.624, see also 71.27.618)

However, the Blessed Prophet ﷺ always trusted in Allah's

will for him, and therefore did not turn away from or despise people afflicted with incurable and catching diseases. There is a moving *hadith* of how he proved this point by touching and eating from the same dish as a leper.

Jabir recorded: The Messenger of Allah ﷺ took by the hand a man who was suffering from tubercular leprosy; he then put (his hand) along with his own hand in the dish, and said: 'Eat with confidence in Allah, and trust in Him.' (Abu Dawud 3914)

Prayers For The Dead

............❦............

DUTIES WHEN A LOVED ONE IS DYING

In Muslim families new babies are welcomed into the world at birth by the purification of their bodies and by joyful exclamations of 'There is no God but Allah!' They are bidden farewell at death by the washing and shrouding of the body by loved ones and by prayer said over them.

When Muslims are at the point of death, they should if possible be turned so that they are facing in the direction of Makkah. This can be done in several ways; the best is to place them on their right side, with their faces turned towards the Ka'bah. The second way is to lie them in their backs, with their feet in the direction of the Ka'bah, and their heads raised slightly so that their faces are turned towards the *qiblah*. If the dying person is in a movable bed, it is often quite a simple matter to turn the bed to the correct position without disturbing the occupant overmuch.

The dying one should then be encouraged to think about Allah by somebody saying aloud so that they can hear—'There is no God but Allah, and Muhammad ﷺ is the Prophet of God.'

Abu Sa'id al-Khudri recorded: 'Encourage the recitation of 'There is no God but Allah' to those of you who are dying.' (Muslim 1996, Abu Dawud 3111)

Mu'adh ibn Jabal recorded the Messenger of Allah ﷺ as saying: 'If anyone's last words are 'There is no God but Allah', he will enter Paradise.' (Abu Dawud 3110) Even if someone has denied belief in Allah during their lifetime—if they die in belief, Allah will show mercy.

It is the *ideal* in Islam if the dying words of a person can be the life-long affirmation of their faith, but this is not a matter for fanaticism. God is not disappointed if these are *not* their last words; He knows best. He understands very well the state of dying person's heart and beliefs. It is far more important that the dying person dies in the state of *belief* of those words, than that they actually are made to mutter them. Any well-meaning Muslims who made their piety a matter of distress to a dying person would be going against the spirit of Islam, and would be being very tactless.

Many prayers for the dying and for those who will be bereaved by their parting should be offered up, and passages from the Qur'an, especially *surah* Yasin (*Sūrah* 36—'Surely We shall give life to the dead' etc.) should be recited—though the reciter must recite inaudibly so as not to disturb the dying person. Once again, it is unkind and unnecessary to make a dying person feel as if they are being hurried into the next world, and perhaps even being made to feel they are being a nuisance if they linger on.

As soon as the person has died, all recitation in their presence should stop. It is not obligatory—it is not even *Sunnah*, and the early Muslims did not continue to recite. If a relative or loved one feels that they wish to go on reciting, that is a matter for them—but it is not *sunnah*.

The moving death of the Blessed Prophet's friend Abu Salamah is recorded in the *hadith*, with a good example of a farewell prayer:

Umm Salamah (who later married the Blessed Prophet) recorded: The Messenger of Allah ﷺ came to Abu Salamah. (He died with) his eyes fixed open. He (the Prophet) closed them, and then said: 'When the soul is taken away, the sight follows it.' Some of the people of Abu Salamah's family wept and wailed, so he said: 'Do not entreat for yourselves anything other than good, for the angels will say 'Amen' to what you say.' He then said: 'O Allah, forgive Abu Salamah, raise him to high rank among those who are rightly guided; make him as a guardian of his descendants who survive him. Forgive us and him, O Lord of the Universe, and make his grave spacious and grant him light in it.' (Muslim 2003)

WEEPING BUT NOT WAILING

It is commendable to inform people so that they may attend the funeral, but this should be done without raising the voices in lament—as that was the way people used to announce deaths in the days of jahiliyyah (before Islam).

Usayd ibn Abu Usayd recorded on the authority of a woman who had taken oath of allegiance to the Prophet ﷺ: 'One of the oaths which the Messenger of Allah received from us about the virtue was that we would not disobey him in it; that we would not scratch the face, nor wail, nor tear the front of the garments nor dishevel the hair.' (Abu Dawud 3125)

Abdallah recorded: 'He who slaps his cheeks, tears his clothes and follows the ways and traditions of the days of jahiliyyah is not one of us.' (Bukhari 23.34.382)

Islam does not approve of raising the voice in lament, shrieking, wailing, beating the cheeks, tearing the garments and so forth, or any kind of histrionics. No matter what the grief of the deceased's loved ones who are left behind, a Muslim should trust in Allah that their dead loved one will go on to a better place, and that they themselves will be able to survive afterwards and pick up the threads of their lives, thanks to their faith. Hence, shrieking and wailing is a sign of lack of faith, and not recommended.

Umm Salamah recorded: When Abu Salamah died, I said: 'I am a stranger in a strange land; I shall weep for him in a manner that will be talked of.' I made preparation for weeping for him, and a woman from the upper side of the city came there who intended to help me (in weeping). She happened to come across the Messenger ﷺ and he said: 'Do you intend to bring the devil back into a house from which Allah has twice driven him out?' I therefore refrained from weeping, and I did not weep.' (Muslim 2007)

Obviously, there is no objection to grief—the Blessed Prophet ﷺ did not object to normal weeping, and indeed, he wept himself on many occasions.

There are moving *hadith* that record the reaction of the Blessed Prophet to the death of his little son Ibrahim:

Anas ibn Malik recorded: We went with Allah's Messenger to the blacksmith Abu Saif, and he was the husband of the wet-nurse of Ibrahim. Allah's Messenger ﷺ picked Ibrahim up and kissed him, and smelled him; later we went back to Abu Saif's house and this time Ibrahim was drawing his last breaths. The eyes of the Messenger of Allah ﷺ started shedding tears. Abdur Rahman ibn Auf said: 'O Allah's Messenger, even you are weeping!' He replied: 'O Ibn Auf, this is compassion.' Then he wept more and said: 'The eyes are shedding tears and the heart is grieved, and we will not speak except what pleases our Lord. O Ibrahim! Indeed we are grieved by your being separated (from us).' (Bukhari 23.42.390, Abu Dawud 3120)

When his friend Sa'd ibn Ubadah died, the Blessed Prophet ﷺ was very overcome with emotion:

Abdallah ibn 'Umar recorded that Sa'd ibn Ubadah complained of illness. The Messenger of Allah ﷺ came to visit him, accompanied by Abdur Rahman ibn Auf, Sa'd ibn Abi Waqqas, and Abdallah ibn Mas'ud. As he entered (his room) he found he had fainted away. He said: 'Has he died?' They said: 'Messenger of Allah, it is not so.' The Messenger of Allah ﷺ wept. When the people saw Allah's Messenger weeping, they also began to weep. He said: 'Listen, Allah does not punish (anyone) for the tears that the eye sheds or the grief the heart feels; but He punishes for this (pointing to his tongue), or He shows mercy.' (Muslim 2010)

Mourners should bear themselves patiently, in faith and hope, believing that their loved one will be pardoned by Allah for any sins and shortcomings, and will be received by the angels into the next world with love and welcome.

Jabir ibn Abdallah recorded: 'When my father was martyred, I lifted the sheet from his face and wept; and the people forbade me to do so, but the Prophet ﷺ did not forbid me. Then my aunt Fatimah began weeping, and the Prophet ﷺ said: 'It makes no difference (to him) whether you weep or not. The angels were shading him all the time with their wings until you carried him from the field.' (Bukhari 23.3.336)

FUNERAL PRAYER—SALAT UL-JANAZA

This is a religious duty, and a collective obligation; it has to be performed by at least one Muslim. The fittest person to pray over the deceased is whoever the deceased himself or herself chose prior to their death, provided only that this person is not immoral or a non-believer. After that, in order of preference, the one to give the prayer should be the Imam or his deputy, the deceased's father, grandfather or great-grandfather, then the deceased's son, grandson or great-grandson; then the closest male relative.

First the resolve (or *niyyah*) of saying the funeral prayer is expressed from the heart. Then the formula 'God is Most Great' is repeated four times. The first is upon beginning the prayer, and after one recites the *Surah al-Fatihah* alone, without a following recitation from the Qur'an as is normal. Then the hands are raised while the second *takbir* is said ('God is Most Great'), and after this the prayer of Ibrahim is recited, as follows:

'O Allah, bless Muhammad and his family, as you blessed Ibrahim and his family. You are the Most Gracious, the Exalted One. Grant Your blessings to Muhammad and to his family as You granted it to Ibrahim and his family. You are the Most Gracious, the Exalted One.'

Then the hands are raised and the third *takbir* is said, ('Allah is the Most Great'), after which one prays for the deceased, using the traditional prayer as follows:

'O Allah, grant forgiveness to us all, the living and the dead, those present here with us and those absent from us, our young and our old, our men and our women. O Allah, keep those of us who remain here always true to Your will; keep those of us who are experiencing death steadfast in strong faith. O Allah, deprive us not of the recompense for our departed one, and do not subject us to trial as a result of his (or her) death.' (From Abu Dawud 3195, recorded by Abu Hurayrah)

It is quite permissible to use prayers other than those quoted here. It is not compulsory to learn these by heart, although many Muslims do. One's own prayers in one's own words are perfectly in order.

Another of the Blessed Prophet's ﷺ beautiful prayers over a dead body was:

'O Allah, You are its Lord, You created it, You did guide it into Islam, You have taken its spirit, and You know best its inner nature and outer aspect. We have gathered as intercessors, so

forgive him (or her).' (Abu Dawud 3194—recorded by Abu Hurayrah)

The following prayer could be made here, or at the graveside:

'O Allah, forgive him, have mercy on him, give him peace and absolve him. Receive him with honour, and make his grave spacious; wash him with water, snow and hail. Cleanse him from faults as You would cleanse a white garment from impurity. Requite him with an abode more excellent than his abode (was here), with a family better than his family, a mate better than his mate. Admit him to the Garden and protect him from the torment of the grave and the torment of the Fire.' (Muslim 2106, recorded by Auf ibn Malik, who said at the end: 'I earnestly desired that I had been that dead body,' because of the prayer.) (Incidentally, it is perhaps worth pointing out here that this does not mean the deceased man will be granted a super new woman and family in Paradise; the Prophet of Allah made it clear that one's own spouse and family would be created afresh and young and without their faults.)

Then one raises the hands in the fourth *takbir*, and here a short silence is kept; or else one may repeat phrases from the above prayer. Then the closing prayer of the *salah* is said once, and with this the funeral prayer is ended.

Notice that the whole prayer is made standing. There is no prostration or sujud, as in the normal prayer, with Muslims bowing and kneeling with their foreheads on the earth.

The practice laid down in the *sunnah* is that the funeral prayer should be performed in a group if a number of Muslims are present, with the Imam or prayer leader standing in front, and those present praying in three rows behind him. If someone comes late, they should join the prayer and when the Imam finishes with the words 'Peace be upon you', they can then complete their prayer by reciting any sections they missed.

The prayer for a child is the same as for an adult, except that after the third *takbir*, instead of the request for God's forgiveness the following prayer is said: 'O Allah, make him (or her) a runner going on ahead, to lead the way for his (or her) parents, and make him (or her) a recompense and a treasure laid up for them.'

CARRYING THE BIER

The funeral procession should then proceed without delay, for the Blessed Prophet ﷺ said:

'Convey the deceased swiftly, for if he was a good man then you are taking him to good things, and if he was not, then you should lower the evil from your shoulders as quickly as possible.' (Muslim 2061, Bukhari 23.50.401)

People should always stand in respect when a funeral procession passes, even if they do not know who is being buried.

Amir ibn Rabia recorded: 'Should anyone of you come across a funeral procession, even if he does not intend to accompany it, he must stand up until it passes by him or is lowered on the ground.' (Muslim 2091)

The Prophet left an example of standing when funerals passed by, even when the deceased was not a member of his own faith.

Jabir ibn Abdallah recorded: 'A bier passed by and the Holy Prophet ﷺ stood up for it, and we also stood up along with him. We said (when we found out): 'Messenger of Allah! That was the bier of a Jewess!' Upon this, he remarked: 'Truly, death is a matter to be concerned about, so whenever you come across a (i.e. any) bier, stand up.' (Muslim 2095; see also Muslim 2098 where the Blessed Prophet ﷺ stood for a Jewish man, and when questioned said: 'Was he not a human being, and does he not have a soul?'

The Blessed Prophet ﷺ, who lived in a time before the invention of the motor vehicle, always preferred mourners to walk in procession rather than ride.

Thawban recorded: An animal was brought to the Messenger of Allah ﷺ while he was walking with a funeral. He refused to ride on it. When the funeral was over, the animal was brought (again) to him and (this time) he rode it. He was asked about it, and said: 'The angels were on their feet. I was not going to ride while they were walking. When they went away, I rode.' (Abu Dawud 3171)

When people are accompanying a funeral procession on foot, they should keep as close to the bier as possible. It does not particularly matter whether they walk in front, behind of, or at the side of the bier.

Al-Mughirah ibn Shubah recorded: 'A rider should go behind the bier and those on foot should walk behind it, in front of it, on its right and on its left, keeping near it.' (Abu Dawud 3174)

Walking to the grave is considered more respectful than riding, but using vehicles is virtually the universal practice for funerals in the west, especially in crowded cities, or places where the cemetery is a long distance from the place where the deceased is. The principle is to be respectful, without being ostentatious. It is normal these days to hire such things as a black car, or even make use of a funeral company to organise the proceedings. These always behave with respect and dignity, and can be a great consolation to a grieving relative. The vehicle should not speed along at the normal pace, but should proceed gently and slowly.

If there are walkers and vehicles, the walkers should be precede the vehicles.

Women were allowed to accompany the procession of

mourners, but it was not recommended:

Umm Atiyya recorded: 'We were forbidden to follow the bier, but it was not made absolute on us.' (Muslim 2039)

The way to complete farewells to the deceased was to pray and then depart. This can be done in one of three ways:

praying over the deceased, and then leaving;

following the bier to the grave, then waiting until the deceased has been buried, and then depart;

or, those present may wait until after the burial, and then pray for God's forgiveness for the deceased and request Him to strengthen him (or her) in faith, and pray for mercy on his (or her) soul. This is that the way most rewarded by Allah.

AT THE GRAVE

Funerals should be simple and inexpensive. Extravagance is forbidden in Islam, and since there is no class system for the dead, there should be no special cemeteries for the celebrities. Mourners should be humble and not ostentatious; they should pay heed to their own end in due course, and take warning from the fact of death and from the fate of the dead.

Mourners at the graveside should not be made to suffer the distractions of people speaking of worldly things or indulging in laughter or idle talk. One would not have thought this appropriate anyway, but sometimes the coming together of friends and relatives, and the atmosphere of release from strain (particularly if the deceased passed away after a long illness, for example) leads to 'small talk' and even high spirits. People at the graveside should remember the sorrow of the bereaved and not behave in a manner that is not appropriate, or that would cause further hurt.

It is recommended that people who are at the graveside should remain standing, and not sit until the deceased has been buried, even if it takes quite a long time; but there is no objection to any who arrived early at the graveside before the funeral procession sitting while they wait for it to arrive.

Abu Sa'id al-Khudri recorded: 'Whenever you come across a bier you should stand up, and he who follows it should not sit down until it is placed in the ground.' (Muslim 2094)

The grave should reach the depth of a man's chest, and should be well made and large. The sunnah is that a qiblah niche should made in the side wall of the grave, as was done in the grave of the Blessed Prophet ﷺ. This niche is a hollow which is dug out at the bottom of the grave in the side wall which faces the Ka'bah, and the deceased is placed in it.

'Amir ibn Sa'd ibn Abu Waqqas recorded that Sa'd, during his final illness, said: 'Make a niche for me in the side of the grave, and set up bricks over me, as was done in the case of Allah's Messenger ﷺ.' (Muslim 2112)

The Blessed Prophet ﷺ preferred what was called lahd, a niche in the side of the grave, and then covering it with unbaked bricks. But if the soil was not conducive to this type of lahd, then shiqq, in which the lahd is not prepared in the niche but in the middle of the grave, is also permissible.

If a niche cannot be made, then a trench is dug in the ground for the deceased in the floor of the grave, and after the deceased has been laid in it, it is roofed over so that no earth falls upon the body.

It is preferable if the deceased can be buried in a Muslim cemetery, or a part of a cemetry made over to Muslims, except for martyrs slain in battle, who should be buried where they fall.

It is commendable to put the deceased into the grave from the direction where his feet will be, if that is possible, and it is commendable to cover a woman's grave with a sheet.

A woman should be lowered into her grave by a male relative within the forbidden degrees of marriage. All bodies should be placed in the grave legs first.

Abu Ishaq said that al-Harith left in his will that Abdallah ibn Yazid should offer his funeral prayer, so he prayed over him. He then put him in the grave from the side of his legs, and said: 'This is a *sunnah* (of the Prophet 鬯).' (Abu Dawud 3205)

The deceased is placed on the right side with the face in the direction of the Ka'bah. He or she should be placed close to the wall, so that they do not fall on their faces, and be supported by a pile of earth behind them so that they do not roll over on to their backs.

Whoever places them in the grave should say:

'In the name of Allah, we commit you to the earth, according to the way of the Prophet of God.'

The fastenings of the shroud at the head and feet are undone. Once the deceased is in place, a wall of bricks is erected next to the body, stopped with mud, to prevent any earth from falling on to it. If there are no bricks, canes or large leaves can be used.

Then it is commendable to sprinkle a little dust over the grave three times, saying:

'We created you from it, and return you into it, and from it We will raise you a second time.' (*Sūrah* 20:55)

After this the earth is heaped over the grave, while people make their own private prayers, or use the beautiful prayers of the Prophet.

The surface of the grave should be raised a hand's breadth from the ground, so that it will be recognised as a grave and passers-by will take care not to tread upon it, and will pray for God's mercy on the person who is in the grave. It should not be more than that, but the place should be levelled.

Abdul-Hayyaj al-Asadi recorded that 'Ali had said to him: 'Should I not send you on the same mission that Allah's Messenger ﷺ sent me? Do not leave an image without obliterating it, or a high grave without levelling it.' (Muslim 2115, Abu Dawud 3212)

It may be marked with a stone, or something to show that it is a grave, but money should not be spent on tombstones or memorials. Instead donations can be given to the poor. The only writing on the grave should be the person's name.

Al-Muttalib recorded that when 'Uthman ibn Mazun died, he was brought out on his bier and buried. The Prophet ﷺ ordered a man to bring him a stone, but he was unable to carry it; so the Messenger of Allah ﷺ got up and went over to it and rolled up his sleeves. The one who told al-Muttalib remarked: 'I still see the whiteness of the forearms of the Messenger of Allah ﷺ as he rolled up his sleeves.' He then carried it and placed it at his head, saying: 'I am marking my brother's grave with it, and I shall bury beside him those of my family who die.' (Abu Dawud 3200)

Al-Qasim said that he asked 'A'ishah to show him the grave of the Messenger of Allah ﷺ and his two companions. She showed him three graves which were neither high nor low, but were spread with soft red pebbles in an open space. (Abu Dawud 3214)

It is forbidden to make any building or shrine over the grave, this was pre-Islamic practice. It is also considered wrong and disrespectful to sit or lean against a grave, and seeking sanctuary among the graves is forbidden.

Jabir recorded that Allah's Messenger ﷺ forbade that the graves should be plastered, or that they be used as sitting places, or that a building should be made over them.' (Muslim 2116, Abu

Dawud 3219)

Abu Hurayrah recorded: 'It is better that one of you should sit on live coals which burn his clothing and come in contact with his skin, rather than he should sit on a grave.' (Abu Dawud 3222)

MAKING GRAVES INTO SHRINES

It is not correct Islam to erect mosques over the graves or light lamps over them. The Blessed Prophet ﷺ would have disapproved strongly of the practice carried on in various places where pious zealots have turned the resting places of the faithful into shrines. Thinking about these exalted grave-shrines, he said:

'May God curse women who visit the graves (for the wrong purposes), and those who erect mosques and light lamps over them.' (Abu Dawud 3230)

It was (and is) the culture of many places to go to the graves of saintly persons for superstitious motives, to pray to the holy soul to help them become fertile, or make other requests. This is forbidden in Islam.

'May God curse the Jews, who used the graves of their prophets as places of worship.' (Bukhari 23.60.414)

It is absolutely forbidden to ask the dead to answer one's prayers, or to seek to involve their aid, or to solicit their intercession. Stroking the grave with the hand, circumambulating it, and similar superstitious practices are also forbidden—these are acts which only lead to idolatry and giving 'partners' to God. The many venerated shrines to the relatives of the Blessed Prophet ﷺ and other faithful dead to be found in various places in the Islamic world are actually against the spirit of Islam.

The Blessed Prophet's ﷺ own grave was not originally inside the mosque of Madinah, but in the room of his wife 'A'ishah, adjacent to it. Only later was the mosque building extended to include it—and many Islamic purists feel that this is wrong practice and should be rectified.

As regards the visitors to an ordinary family grave, the commendable prayer for a visitor is:

'Peace be upon you, O believers and Muslims who dwell here; we shall, God willing, be joining you. We ask God to grant well-being to us and to you.' (Muslim 2126)

It is also recommended to pray for forgiveness and mercy for the dead.

Abu Hurayrah recorded that a negress (or young negro youth) who used to sweep the mosque had died. The Prophet ﷺ missed him, and when he asked about him the people told him that he had died. He said: 'Why didn't you inform me?' Then he said: 'Lead me to his grave.' So they led him, and he prayed over him. (Abu Dawud 3197)

Abu Hurayrah recorded that the Messenger of Allah ﷺ visited his mother's grave and wept, and caused those around him to weep. The Messenger ﷺ then said: 'I asked my Lord's permission to pray for forgiveness for her, but I was not allowed. I then asked His permission to visit her grave, and I was allowed. So visit graves, for they make you mindful of death.' (Abu Dawud 3228)

CONDOLENCES

Because Muslims should all have a strong faith in life after death, and the continued existence of their departed loved one, it is not considered appropriate to grieve too much. This would show a lack of obedience to the will of Allah, who took back that soul when it was His will. However, grief is inevitable for a loved one, and condolences may be offered to the bereaved for up to three days and nights after a death. The traditional formula is:

'May God make your reward abundant and your solace great, and grant forgiveness to the departed.'

to which the reply is:

'May God hear your prayer, and have mercy upon us and you.'

Muhammad ibn Sirin recorded that when one of the sons of Umm Atiyya died, and when it was the third day, she asked for yellow perfume and put it over her body, and said: 'We were forbidden to mourn for more than three days, except for our husbands.' (Bukhari 23.30.369)

Muslims are expected to mourn a husband (or wife) for four months and ten days. (Bukhari 23.30.370)

It is a kind practice if visitors to the bereaved remember their sad state and do not make themselves a burden to them by expecting food and meals to be prepared for them. Kind visitors bring provisions with them.

Abdallah ibn Jafar recorded the Messenger ﷺ as saying: 'Prepare food for the family of Jafar, for an incident has come upon them and occupied them.' (Abu Dawud 3126)

The common custom of holding gatherings during which the Qur'an is recited for three nights following the death, and of arranging a mourning celebration and special gatherings or rawdahs on the day of the death, or on the third day after it or on the fortieth day, or on the anniversary of the death, have no basis in the Qur'an, the *sunnah* of the Blessed Prophet ﷺ or in the practice of the early Muslims, may God have mercy on them all.

'To Allah we belong, and to Allah we return.' (*Sūrah* 96:8; 2:156; 28:70)

'Do humans think that We shall not assemble their bones? Yes, surely, yes—We are able to restore even their fingerprints.' (75:3-4)

Thanks be to God. Amen.

THE LAST PUBLIC APPEARANCE OF THE BLESSED MESSENGER OF ALLAH ?

The Blessed Prophet ﷺ continued to lead the people in prayer although he became very ill, for as long as he was able to do so. When he realised that he was not going to recover, he began asking which of his wives he would be with that night. Realising that he wished to be with 'A'ishah, the other wives gave permission, and he was placed in her chamber for his final days.

Eventually he became too ill to come out to lead the prayer, and the people missed seeing him for three days.

He entrusted the leading of the prayer to his old friend Abu Bakr, 'A'ishah's father. 'A'ishah was concerned about this, for she realised that her father was an emotional man, and could scarcely hold himself back from his tears at his beloved friend's illness; but the Prophet ﷺ chided her gently, and insisted on having his way.

Abu Musa recorded: 'When the Messenger of Allah ﷺ became seriously ill he ordered Abu Bakr to lead the people in prayer. At this, 'A'ishah said: 'Messenger of Allah, Abu Bakr is a man of tender feelings; when he stands in your place (he will be so overwhelmed by grief that) he will not be able to lead the people in prayer.' The Holy Prophet ﷺ said: 'You order Abu Bakr to lead the people in prayer!' and he added: 'You are like the female companions of Joseph!' (those who tried to tempt Joseph to go astray. The Prophet ﷺ frequently used this expression to his beloved when she tried to make him do something he did not wish to do. It was a gentle and humourous rebuke.) So Abu Bakr led the prayer in the life of the Messenger of Allah ﷺ.' (Muslim 844)

Then, one day, while the people were at night prayer, the

curtain of the apartment was moved, and the Blessed Prophet ﷺ stood in the doorway, smiling at them.

Anas ibn Malik recorded: 'Abu Bakr led them in prayer due to the illness of the Messenger of Allah ﷺ from which he died. (The Prophet ﷺ had not come out of 'A'ishah's apartment for three days). It was a Monday when they stood in rows for prayer. The Messenger of Allah ﷺ drew aside the curtain of ('A'ishah's) apartment and stood there gazing at us, and his face was as pale as the paper of the Holy Book. The Messenger ﷺ felt happy, and smiled. And we were overcome with joy while in prayer, due to the appearance of the Messenger ﷺ. (A variant version says: 'No sight was more endearing to us than the face of the Messenger of Allah ﷺ as he appeared to us.'—Muslim 843) Abu Bakr stepped back upon his heels to say prayer in a row, (to let the Blessed Prophet ﷺ lead the prayer) perceiving that the Messenger ﷺ signed with his hand for them to complete their prayer. He (then) went back into his apartment and drew the curtain. The Messenger of Allah ﷺ breathed his last on that very day.' (Muslim 840)

The Compassion of Allah

THOUGHTS ON FAITH

The Blessed Prophet ﷺ was always conscious of the presence of God, wherever he was and whatever he was doing. Allah was his constant Companion and Guide, and the Prophet ﷺ lived totally aware that Allah was his most beloved and most constant Friend.

Sometimes people get the feeling that Allah is afar off, and that somehow He needs to be summoned and beseeched and 'shouted at' in such a way that implies He is *not* present and cannot hear us. The Blessed Prophet ﷺ taught, in his gentle and humourous way, that with real faith we should have more confidence.

Abu Musa al-Ashari recorded that once he was with the Blessed Prophet ﷺ on a journey. When they neared Madinah, the people began to shout aloud: 'Allahu Akbar! God is Most Great!' and they raised their voices. The Messenger of Allah ﷺ commented: 'O people! You are not calling upon One who is deaf and afar off, but One Who is nearer to you than the neck of your riding beast!' (Abu Dawud 1521, Muslim 6526)

Abu Hurayrah recorded the Blessed Prophet's ﷺ beautiful teaching about the consolation of Allah the Compassionate One, showing how even when people felt utterly alone and in despair during the long hours of the night, Allah was there in the darkness listening, and waiting in advance for those who needed to call upon Him.

'Allah descends every night to the lowest heaven, when a third of the night is over, and says: 'I am the Lord! I am the Lord! Who is there who beseeches from Me, that I may answer him? Who is there begging (something) of Me, that I may grant him? Who is there seeking forgiveness from Me, so that I may forgive him?' He continues in this way until the break of day.' (Muslim 1657)

It is a fundamental part of the awareness of a Muslim known as *taqwa* or 'god-consciousness', that God can see everything and know everything, even our deepest and most secret inner thoughts—even if we sometimes forget this. A famous *hadith* recorded by Abu Hurayrah described an occasion when the Blessed Prophet ﷺ was visited by the angel Gabriel. In the middle of this passage, the Blessed Prophet ﷺ made clear the Muslim way to *ihsan* or realisation about God's presence.

One day the Prophet ﷺ was sitting in the company of some people. (The angel) Gabriel came and asked: 'What is faith?' Allah's Messenger ﷺ replied: 'Faith is to believe in Allah, His angels, (the) meeting with Him, His Messengers, and to believe in the Resurrection.' Then he further asked: 'What is Islam?' The Messenger replied: 'To worship Allah alone and none else, to offer prayers perfectly, to pay the compulsory charity, and to observe fasts during the month of Ramadan.' Then he further asked: 'What is *ihsan* (realisation)?' Allah's Messenger ﷺ replied: *'To worship Allah as if you see Him, and if you cannot achieve this state of devotion, then to be aware that He is looking at you.'* Then he further asked: 'When will the Hour come?' He replied; 'This person answering has no better knowledge than the one asking the question—but I will tell you what will be the signs of it; when a female slave gives birth to her master, and when the shepherds of black camels start boasting and competing with others in the construction of higher buildings. The Hour is one of five things which nobody knows except Allah.' The Prophet 🕮 then recited: 'Truly, the knowledge of the Hour is with Allah Alone' (*Sūrah* 31:34). Then Gabriel left and the Prophet 🕮 asked his companions to call him back, but they could not see him. Then the Prophet 🕮 said: 'That was Gabriel, who came to teach the people about their religion.' (Bukhari 2.38.47)

Faith is the key to everything in Islam. Many, many times believers would love to *know* the truth about something, but it is not granted to them. They might long to know whether what they were doing was right or wrong, whether their course of action was going to lead to success or disaster—but there is no way of knowing this kind of thing for sure. It is like when a person buys a house—it is an enormous amount of money to spend, and there is no way of knowing whether or not that house will still be standing in thirty years' time; it might get swallowed by an earthquake the very next day, or destroyed by a bomb. Buying the house is an act of faith that there will be a future, and even if there will not be, it is better to live in the belief that there will be. If nobody was prepared to take a chance, nobody would live in their own homes, nothing would ever get done. If we did not post our letter until we could be *certain* that it would reach its destination, then we would never post the letter.

It is the same with belief in Allah. People make a commitment to live according to what they understand to be the will of God, and try hard to pass a successful, peaceful and caring life on earth; they do it with every hope that God really does exist, and that there will be an Afterlife in His nearer presence, even if they have no idea of what the years on earth will bring.

With faith, a person can form a firm judgement of whether or not in their opinion what they are doing, or proposing to do, is in accordance with the will of God, so far as they understand it—and if it is, then they can go ahead and do it with the comfort of believing that they are doing whatever it is for the best, in the best possible way. If anything then befalls them, or some accident or unpleasant thing occurs, they can reassure themselves that they acted as they thought was the best way, and the eventualities of life are all in the hands of Allah, nobody knows them or their reason but Him.

Faith and realisation (*iman* and *ihsan*) bring sincerity, and a calm and serenity in the depth of the Muslim's soul that nothing can shake.

Abu Hurayrah recorded that Allah's Messenger ﷺ said: 'Whoever establishes prayer during the nights of Ramadan faithfully, out of sincere faith, hoping to attain Allah's blessings, all their past sins will be forgiven.' (Bukhari 2.28.36)

The *niyyah* or intention is what counts. It does not matter how many prayers are said, or of what length they are; what matters is what is there, in the heart.

'Umar ibn al-Khattab recorded that Allah's Messenger ﷺ said: 'The reward of deeds depends upon the intention; every person will get the reward according to what he (or she) has intended.' (Bukhari 2.42.51, 52)

This does not only apply to prayer, but to every action during the day or night, no matter how small or seemingly insignificant, which is done out of love for Allah.

Sa'd ibn Abu Waqqas recorded: 'You will be rewarded for whatever you spend for Allah's sake, even if it were for a sweet which you popped into your wife's mouth.' (Bukhari 2.42.53)

The Blessed Prophet ﷺ taught that the true way to serve Allah was to love.

Abu Hurayrah recorded the Messenger of Allah ﷺ as saying:

THE COMPASSION OF ALLAH

'By Him in Whose hand is my soul, you will not enter Paradise until you believe, and you will never believe until you love one another.' (Abu Dawud 5174)

Faith, to a Muslim, is not just a matter of ritual devotions but of *living*.

Abu Hurayrah recorded: 'Faith has over seventy branches, the most excellent of which is the declaration that there is no God but Allah, and the humblest of which is the removal of a bone from the road.' (He added) 'and modesty is one branch of faith.' (Abu Dawud 4659, Muslim 55, 56)

Being the sort of character that *can* bend and remove a piece of rubbish from the road is a sign of both love and modesty. It is love of Allah and our neighbour and environment, and it is being humble enough to do a servile deed oneself—out of love. This modesty is the quality known in Arabic as al-Haya. It does not simply mean 'shyness', but it reflects a state of mental piety. It means not being too proud to be held back from doing kind acts of love and goodness, plus also the restraint from doing anything displeasing to Allah because of constant awareness of Him. The calm and serene mind brings a calm and serene way of life, always devoted to Allah in every aspect. It should not engender weakness, fear or misplaced courtesy which would prevent a person from speaking out in defence of the will of Allah.

Qatadah recorded that he was sitting with Imran ibn Husayn in a company that also included Bushayr ibn Ka'b. Imran narrated that on a certain occasion the Messenger of Allah ﷺ had said: 'Modesty brings forth nothing but goodness.' Upon this, Bushayr ibn Ka'b said: 'Truly, it is recorded in certain books of wisdom that it is God-inspired peace of mind or sobriety for the sake of Allah, but that there is also a weakness in it.' Imran was so enraged that his face became red, and he said: 'I am narrating to you the saying of the Messenger of Allah ﷺ and you are contradicting it.' (Muslim 60)

It is not true modesty to be so quiet and unwilling to cause trouble that one would not speak up to protect the weak from tyranny, or help a person in need who was being persecuted or done down by another.

It is important to remember this when coming across the type of person who is outwardly extremely religious, praying and fasting long enough to put others to shame, but who is perhaps inwardly arrogant and lacking in love.

'A'ishah recorded: 'I heard the Messenger of Allah ﷺ say: 'By his good character a believer will attain the same degree as one who prays all night and fasts all day.' (Abu Dawud 4780)

Abdallah ibn Mughaffal recorded: 'Allah is gentle, likes gentleness, and gives for gentleness what He does not give for harshness.' (Abu Dawud 4789)

Prayer is an important part of a person's faith. Allah Himself revealed in the Qur'an:

Allah will never allow your prayers to be lost. (Sūrah 2:143)

It is a person's faith that will bring him or her to Paradise, and not the amount of good deeds done or the hundreds of prayers recited.

Anas recorded: 'Whoever says—'None has the right to be worshipped but Allah', and has in his (or her) heart good (faith) equal to the weight of a grain of barley, will be taken out of Hell... And whoever says (it) and has (faith) equal to the weight of an atom will be taken out of Hell.' (Bukhari 2.34.42)

Abdallah ibn Mas'ud recorded: 'None shall enter the fire of Hell who have in their heart the weight of a mustardseed of faith, and none shall enter Paradise who have in their heart the weight of a mustardseed of pride.' (Muslim 165; see also 367 and 376)

Abu Dharr recorded that the angel Gabriel came to the Messenger of Allah ﷺ and gave him the information: 'Truly, the one among the *Ummah* who dies without associating anything with Allah will enter Paradise.' I said: 'Even if that one committed adultery and theft?' He (the Holy Prophet) said: 'Even if he (or she) committed adultery and theft.'

Abu Hurayrah recorded the beautiful statement of Allah passed through His Messenger ﷺ to give us confidence and hope: 'I live the thought of My servants as they think about Me, and I am with them as they remember Me; if they remember Me in their heart, I also remember them in My heart; and if they remember me in congregation, I also remember them in congregation—better than they do; and if they draw near to me by the span of a palm, I draw near by the cubit; and if they draw near by the length of a cubit I draw near by the stretch of the arm; and if they come towards me walking, I come at the run towards them.' (Muslim 6498)

Abu Hurayrah also recorded a long *hadith* describing the presence of angels during the prayers of the faithful.

Allah's Messenger ﷺ said: Allah has whole (legions) of angels who have no other work but to (look out for) those who gather in prayer; and when they find such assemblies they sit in their midst, and some of them enfold everything with their wings, until the space between them and the sky of the world is fully covered; and when they leave after the prayer they go up to the heaven and Allah, the Exalted and Glorious One, asks them—although He has full knowledge of them—'Where have you come from?' They say: 'We come from Your servants upon the earth who have been glorifying You, uttering Your Greatness and Oneness, and praising You and asking of You.' He would say: 'What do they ask of Me?' They say: 'They ask Paradise of you.' He would say:

'Have they seen My Paradise?' They say: 'No, our Lord (but they have faith).' He would say: '(Very well), they (will) see My Paradise.' They would say: 'They seek Your protection.' He would say: 'Against what do they seek it?' They said: 'Our Lord, from the Hellfire.' He would say: 'Have they seen My fire?' They said: 'No (but they believe in it).' He would say: 'What it would be if they were to see My fire.' They (also) said: 'They beg forgiveness of You.' He would say: 'I grant pardon to them, and confer on them what they ask for, and grant them protection against which they seek protection.' The angels said: 'Our Lord, there is (also) one amongst them, such-and-such a simple servant, who happened to pass by (those praying), and he (merely) sat there along with them.' (He (the Lord) would say: 'I grant him pardon as well, for anyone who sits with them shares their good fortune.' (Muslim 6505)

THOUGHTS ON FORGIVENESS

Abu Hurayrah recorded that Allah's Messenger ﷺ said: 'When Allah created the creation as He was upon the Throne, He put down in His Book—Truly, My mercy is greater than My anger.' (Muslim 6626)

Every person who has ever committed a sin, or failed in some way, or done that of which they were ashamed and later regretted it, has deep awareness of one of the most gracious aspects of Allah the Almighty—He is the Most Merciful, the Most Compassionate.

His whole message breathes out forgiveness and love, and reconciliation. For a start, the moment a person comes to accept Islam in his or her heart, the whole of their past record of sins and shortcomings is wiped away and they are given chance to start anew. For many, this is a huge burden just rolling away!

Abu Sa'id al-Khudri recorded: 'If a person embraces Islam in sincerity, then Allah shall forgive all past sins and the settlement of account shall begin after that moment.' (Bukhari 2.32)

Secondly, the Compassionate Lord always rewards us for things that we do right out of all proportion to the punishment for the things we do wrong. It is a very positive and rewarding faith.

Abu Hurayrah recorded: 'If any of you follows Islam, then the good deeds will be rewarded ten to seven hundred times for each good deed done, but a bad deed will only be recorded as it is.' (Bukhari 2.32.40, see also the end of the previous *hadith*.)

There are three words used in the Qur'an to express Allah's forgiveness; 'afa—which means to forget and obliterate from one's mind; safaha—which means to turn away from, to ignore, to treat the matter as if it did not affect you; and ghafara, which means to cover up something as Allah does to our sins with His grace. This latter word is particularly appropriate in God's attribute of al-Ghaffar, the One Who forgives again and again.

The Qur'an tells us:

'Quite a number of the people of the Book wish they could turn you back to infidelity (even) after you have believed, out of selfish envy, (even) after the Truth has been made manifest to them; but forgive and overlook, until God accomplishes His purpose; for God has power over all things.' (*Sūrah* 2:109)

Allah states:

'If any do evil or wrong their own soul, but afterwards seek God's forgiveness, they will find God Oft-Forgiving and Most Merciful.' (*Sūrah* 4:110)

'O My servants, who have transgressed against your own souls! Do not despair of the mercy of Allah; for Allah forgives all sins; He is the Oft-Forgiving, the Most Merciful. Turn to your

Lord and bow to His will before the Penalty comes upon you; after that you shall not be helped.' (*Sūrah* 39:53-54)

'Tell those who believe to forgive those who do not look forward to the Days of God; it is for Him to recompense each person according to what they have earned (and not for you to be unforgiving!)' (*Sūrah* 45:14)

The *hadith* abound with beautiful sayings that illustrate Allah's love and mercy, and also the gentle good humour of His Blessed Messenger ﷺ. For example:

Ibn Mas'ud narrated that a man kissed a woman (when he should not have done so!) and then went to the Prophet and admitted (his fault). (It was at this very incident that) Allah revealed: 'And offer prayers perfectly at the two ends of the day day and in some hours of the night (i.e. the compulsory prayers). Truly, good deeds annul the evil deeds. (*Sūrah* 11:114).' The man then asked Allah's Messenger ﷺ: 'Is this (revelation just) for me?' He replied: 'It is for all my followers.' (Bukhari 10.4.504)

What a wonderful promise and assurance. It is difficult indeed to pass a lifetime without committing sins and falling short—yet nobody need despair. Such is the love of Allah that repentance brings with it the blessing of His divine forgiveness, a forgiveness way beyond that which a human heart can imagine, and one way in which a person can acquire this forgiveness is by the practice of daily prayers!

Abu Hurayrah recorded: 'If there was a river flowing at the door of any of you, and he took a bath in it five times a day, would you notice any dirt (left) on him?' They said: 'Not a trace would be left.' The Prophet ﷺ added: 'That is the example of the five prayers with which Allah blots out evil deeds.' (Bukhari 10.6.506)

Abu Bakr reported that he once asked the Blessed Prophet ﷺ for a supplication that he could repeat in his prayer. The

Prophet 	 said:

'Recite—'O Allah, I have done great wrong to myself, and there is none to forgive the sins but You Alone.' Say—'Grant me Your pardon, have mercy upon me; for You are the Oft-Forgiving, the Compassionate.' (Muslim 6533)

'A'ishah recorded the Blessed Prophet's 	 own prayer: 'O Allah, I seek refuge in You from the trial of Hell-fire and from the torment of Hell-fire; from the trial and torment of the grave; from the evil of the trial of wealth and the evil of the trial of poverty; and I seek refuge in You from the evil of the turmoil of the Dajjal. O Allah, wash away my sins with snow and hail and water, purify my heart from sins as a white garment is purified from dirt, and keep my sins as far away as the distance yawning between the East and the West; O Allah, I seek refuge in You from sloth, from senility, from sin and from debt.' (Muslim 6534)

The key to the forgiveness of Allah is awareness of Him, and of the need for repentance. Sometimes a person might be committed to Hell for what might seem to be a very trivial offence:

Abu Hurayrah recorded Allah's Messenger 	 saying that a woman would be thrown into Hell-fire because of a cat which she had tied up and did not provide with food, nor did she set it free to eat insects of the earth, until it died inch by inch.' (Muslim 6638)

On the other hand, a person could be a tremendous sinner, and yet not be sent to Hell-fire, so long as they *did* have awareness of Allah and the need for repentance:

Abu Hurayrah recorded that Allah's Messenger 	 told of a person who had never done a good deed in his life asking the members of his family to burn his dead body when he died, and to cast his ashes to the wind and to the ocean. (He said): 'By Allah, if my Lord takes hold of me, He will torment me as He has not tormented anybody else!' They did as he asked them to do. (But) the Lord said to the earth: 'Return what you have taken' (and also said this to the ocean), and he was thus restored to his (original form). Allah said to him: 'What made you order that?' He said: 'My Lord, it was fear and awe of You.' And Allah pardoned him, because of this (awareness).' (Muslim 6637-6638)

The forgiveness of Allah is far beyond what any human being has a right to expect, and far beyond what they deserve.

Abu Hurayrah recorded that Allah's Messenger ﷺ said that the Lord said: 'A servant committed a sin and he said: 'O Allah, forgive me my sin', and Allah said: 'My servant who sinned came to realise that he had a Lord Who forgives the sins and takes account for the sin.' (But) the man committed a sin again and again said: 'O Lord, forgive me my sin', (and Allah replied in the same way once again). He again committed a sin (and asked for forgiveness), and Allah the Exalted said... 'O servant, do what you like, I have granted you forgiveness.' (Muslim 6642)

'If Allah were to punish people according to what they deserve, He would not leave on the earth a single living being; but He gives them a chance for a certain length of time.' (Sūrah 36:45; 16:61)

So long as the attitude of the believer is one of humility and not defiance, and the person is truly anxious to repent and is not just re-committing the sins in the false illusion that God does not care what he does but will always forgive anyway, Allah grants forgiveness no matter what the person has done.

Abu Musa recorded: 'Allah, the Exalted the Glorious, stretches out His hand during the night so that people may repent of the fault committed between dawn and dusk; and He stretches out His hand during the day so that people may repent for the fault committed from dusk to dawn.' (Muslim 6644)

Abu Hurayrah recorded: 'The Messenger of Allah ﷺ got up for the prayer, and we also stood along with him. A Bedouin said during the prayer: 'O Allah, show mercy to me and to Muhammad, and do not show mercy to anyone along with us.' When the Messenger ﷺ uttered the salutation, he said to the Bedouin: 'You narrowed down a vast (thing)', meaning the mercy of Allah.' (Abu Dawud 881)

The example of the Blessed Prophet ﷺ was shown when he was wounded by his enemies at the Battle of Uhud.

Anas recorded that the Messenger of Allah ﷺ had his front teeth damaged on the Day of Uhud, and got a wound on his head. He was wiping the blood from his face and was saying: 'How will these people attain salvation who have wounded their Prophet and broken his tooth (even) while he was calling them towards God?' It was as this time that God the Exalted and Glorious revealed the verse: 'You have no authority over the decision whether He turn to them in mercy or punish them, even if they are indeed wrongdoers (Sūrah 3:128).' (Muslim 4417)

Abdallah ibn 'Umar added: 'It appeared to me as if I saw the Messenger of Allah ﷺ and heard him relate the story of a Prophet who had been beaten by his people, and was wiping the blood from his face and was saying: 'My Lord, forgive my people, for they do not know (what they are doing).' (Muslim 4418—compare the words of the Blessed Jesus in St. Luke's Gospel 23:34)

What a wonderful example, putting into practice the appeal of Allah Himself, who praised 'those who avoid the greater crimes and shameful deeds, and, even when they are angry, even then forgive.' (Sūrah 42:37)

That is the true Muslim, who is of those 'who hearken to their Lord... and who, when an oppressive wrong is inflicted on them (are not cowed but) help and defend themselves. The recompense of the injury is an injury equal to it; but if a person forgives and makes reconciliation, his reward is due from Allah... Indeed, if any show patience and forgive, that is truly an exercise of courageous will and resolution in the conduct of affairs.' (*Sūrah* 42: 38-40, 43)

The person who seeks forgiveness has to truly repent, however, and not forget that God sees into the secrets of the heart. It is no good imagining that God will forgive every sin if it is not earnestly repented.

Abu Hurayrah recorded: 'The fornicator who fornicates is not a believer so long as he keeps on doing it, and no thief who steals is a believer so long as he goes on committing theft, and no drunkard who drinks alcohol is a believer so long as he goes on drinking.' (Muslim 104)

A true Muslim is always aware that God knows everything. He or she therefore has no need to go out searching for the faults of others, or rejoicing in pointing out anyone else's shortcomings. Allah requests that a Muslim should 'cover the faults' of another, in graciousness and mercy, and not triumphantly point them out with an 'I am better than you' attitude aimed at making the sinner feel small.

'It is part of the mercy of Allah that you deal gently with them. If you are severe or harsh-hearted, they will break away from about you; so pass over (their faults), and ask for God's forgiveness for them; and consult them in affairs (that matter) then, when you have taken a decision, put your trust in God.' (*Sūrah* 3:159)

Abu Barzat al-Aslami recorded: 'O community of people who believe by their tongue, but belief has not entered their hearts! Do not backbite Muslims, and do not search for their faults; for if anyone searches for their faults Allah will search for his fault, and if Allah searches for the fault of anyone, He disgraces him in his house.' (Abu Dawud 4862)

In other words, if people search for the faults of others, Allah will reveal their faults, even if they do not disclose them, and that will be their disgrace. As the Blessed Prophet ﷺ put it another way:

'If anyone eats at the cost of a Muslim's honour, Allah will give him a like amount of Hell to eat; and if anyone clothes himself with a garment at the cost of a Muslim's honour, Allah will clothe him with a like amount of Hell; and if anyone puts himself in a position of reputation and show, Allah will disgrace him with a place of reputation and show on the Day of Resurrection!' (Abu Dawud 4863—recorded by al-Mustawrid)

Another *hadith* was even more forthright:

Mu'adh ibn Anas recorded: 'If anyone guards a believer from a hypocrite, Allah will send an angel who will guard his flesh on the Day of Resurrection from the fire of Hell; but if anyone attacks a Muslim saying something by which he wishes to disgrace him, he will be held back by Allah when he reaches the bridge over Hellfire until he is acquitted of what he said.' (Abu Dawud 4865)

Mu'awiyah recorded that he heard the Messenger ﷺ say: 'If you search for the faults of the people you will corrupt them.' (Abu Dawud 4870)

Zayd ibn Wahb said: A man was brought to Ibn Mas'ud, who was told who he was and that wine was dripping from his beard. At this, Abdallah (b. Mas'ud) said: 'We have been prohibited to seek out faults. If anything becomes obvious to us, we shall seize it.' (Abu Dawud 4872)

Uqbar ibn Amir recorded: 'He who sees something which

should be kept hidden and conceals it will be like one who has brought back to life a girl who was buried alive.' (Abu Dawud 4873)

Abdallah ibn 'Umar recorded: 'A Muslim is another Muslim's brother; he does not wrong him nor abandon him. If anyone cares for his brother's need, Allah will care for his need; if anyone removes a Muslim's anxiety, Allah will remove from him, on account of it, one of the anxieties on the Day of Resurrection; and if anyone conceals a Muslim's fault, Allah will conceal his fault on the Day of Resurrection.' (Abu Dawud 4875)

A man once went to the Blessed Prophet 鑾 and asked him how often he ought to forgive his servant. The Messenger made no reply, so the man repeated what he had said—yet still the Prophet kept silence. When he asked the third time, the Blessed Prophet 鑾 replied: 'Forgive him seventy times daily.' (Abu Dawud 5145—a saying very similar to that of the Blessed Jesus recorded in St. Matthew's Gospel chapter 18 verse 22.)

THOUGHTS ON EXTREMISM

The Blessed Prophet 鑾 warned against the kind of attitude towards religious practices that was of an extremist and servile nature, and tried to teach that although disciples of this type might well be exceedingly devout, their devotion was misplaced, and caused more harm than good.

Abu Hurayrah recorded the Blessed Prophet 鑾 as saying: 'Religion is very easy, and whoever overburdens himself in his religion will not be able to continue in that way. So you should not be extremists, but try to be near to perfection, and accept (in your hearts and minds) the good news that you *will* be rewarded; and gain strength by worshipping in the mornings, afternoons, and during the last hours of the nights.' (Bukhari 2.30.38)

The Blessed Prophet really took a strong view against extremists:

Abdallah ibn Mas'ud reported the Prophet ﷺ as saying: 'Beware! The extremists will perish,' and saying it three times. (Abu Dawud 4591)

It is vitally important that all good and devout Muslims stop and consider these *hadiths*, and think out for themselves what is meant by them. What *is* an extremist? An extremist (in the Islamic sense) is not an unbeliever, or an evil and wicked person. It is someone who is entirely devoted to Allah, who maybe tries very hard to spend every waking moment thinking about Allah and serving Allah by various deeds, practices and prayers—but who has unfortunately developed a perverse, ignorant and limiting view about God that causes them to feel superior to others while at the same time living in constant anxiety that they are not doing enough, or getting each little detail right.

There are countless thousands of these in the 'Brotherhood' of Islam, and they have the unfortunate result that the more fervent and outspoken they are, the more they drive people *away* from Allah and cause misunderstandings and resentments.

Take, as a simple example of pious extremism or zealotry, the case of a woman friend of the Prophet's wife 'A'ishah, who became a legend in her own lifetime and was widely admired for her sessions of all-night prayer.

'A'ishah recorded that once the Prophet ﷺ came while a woman was sitting with her. He asked: 'Who is she?' I ('A'ishah) replied: 'She is so-and-so,' and told him about her (extremes of) praying.' He (actually) spoke with disapproval (about it): 'Do deeds which are within your capacity—as Allah never tires, but (certainly) you will get tired (and then give up). The best practice in the sight of Allah is (a routine) which can be done regularly.'

(Bukhari 2.33.41)

That woman, with the best will in the world, was actually serving Allah in the wrong way.

Allah does not place unbearable burdens upon people, or gross inconveniences, taxing their devotion to the limits and making people feel guilty or inferior if they cannot keep up the extreme practice of these masochistic believers.

Another example was that of Abdallah ibn 'Amr ibn al-As. He narrated that Allah's Messenger ﷺ said to him: 'O Abdallah! I have been informed that you fast during the day and offer prayers all the night.' Abdallah replied: 'Yes, O Allah's Messenger.' The Prophet ﷺ said: 'Do not do that; fast for a few days, and then give it up for a few days; offer prayers and also sleep at night; because your body has a right on you, and your wife has a right on you. And it is quite sufficient that you fast three days in a month, as the reward of this good deed is multiplied ten times, so it will be the same as fasting throughout the year.' (Bukhari 31.56.196)

This pious man had forgotten to take care of his own body, and he had forgotten the rights of his poor wife, who was forced by his long abstinences to abstain herself—whether she wished it or not. There is a point here, that all believers must stop and consider whether or not their pious practices are in fact selfish, or might perhaps be hurting or depriving others.

When a person goes to such extremes in religion that they are cruel to their own God-given bodies, and make themselves a burden to others, they should pause and try to work out for themselves what are their motives for this?

Psychological studies have made it quite clear that the extremist attitude in religion comes from self-conceit and pride in one's piety—whereas the true Islam teaches humility and modesty, and love.

An extremist is someone who will cling on to the bitter end, suffering themselves and making other people suffer too—not the least by being aware of their rigours!

An extremist will not comprehend the truth of the *hadith* recorded by 'A'ishah:

'A believer can attain the degree (of sanctity) of one who prays all night and fasts all day—by his (or her) good character.' (Muslim 4780)

Extremists are always on the lookout for other people's faults—but this is not the correct Islamic attitude.

Abu Barzat al-Aslami recorded. 'O community of people which believes with the tongue but belief has not entered their hearts—do not back-bite (other) Muslims, and do not search for their faults; for if anyone searches for their faults, Allah will search for his fault, and if Allah searches for the fault of anyone, He disgraces him in his house.' (Abu Dawud 4862)

All sins end up in punishment, but many are punished during life in this world, before one arrives in the Hereafter. Extremists tend to forget that oppression, arrogance, pride, hypocrisy, self-conceit and severing ties of relationship are very serious sins in the eyes of Allah, much more so than the petty sins of human weakness.

The most important thing for a Muslim should be to follow the teachings of the Qur'an, and the *sunnah* of the Blessed Prophet ﷺ. If people deviate from the path and follow innovations (beliefs and practices which are not part of the Qur'an or *sunnah*) they are in the wrong; and if they become extremists they are also in the wrong—for these people really do nothing but drive others away from Allah, or make them feel small or uncomfortable about their own Islam.

Conclusion

Let us conclude by imagining in our mind's eye several scenes—all different, but all linked by the love our Dear Lord.

Let us imagine an immaculate young man, dressed in white, his bare feet gliding over cold marble in the dark moments before dawn, entering under a huge ornate portal to find his way to the *qiblah* in some vast and echoing hall. We could be in Rabat, or Islamabad, or Brunei or Makkah itself. It doesn't matter where. The young man has come, with those of like mind, to a place created with enormous care and skill to be one of the most beauteous and lavish centres of the worship of God on earth.

At the same time, in countless humbler buildings, village mosques, converted barns, churches, empty and disused amenity buildings, and people's houses, the same scene is taking place, with the same love and devotion.

Similarly, on mountain tops, in the desert, by the side of lakes, and in millions of private bedrooms, the faithful are stirring, and coming to their meeting with their Lord, in response to His call.

The world is hushed and still, and a vast wave of love and happiness encompasses it. Gliding down, unseen but maybe deeply felt, is the joyful companionship of angels, who care for each one of us, and convey to us the blessings and compassionate love of the Creator of all. They look out for each one of us, and note our yawns and aches and pains as we stumble to perform the motions that bind us all together in the fellowship of Islam.

And over all, the outstretched and everlasting 'arms' of the One to Whom we turn and to Whom we will return, when He wills.

O our dear Lord, here we are, at your service. Forgive us all our shortcomings and failings and help us to grow strong and every day closer on our path to You. Bless all who love You, all who have committed themselves to Your service; bless our families and loved ones, our friends and neighbours—keep them strong in hope and compassion for others, trying every day to live as You would have them live. Bless all who are suffering, or in distress of any kind; give them the strength and patience to cope with the times of testing, and the insight to see what it is You would have them do. Bless all those who are outside the fellowship of believers, or who are struggling to cope with personal beliefs that have led them astray. May their eyes and the eyes of their minds be opened, that they may realize Your great love and Your glory and turn to You in humble hopes of new life. Bless us all, dear Lord, and keep us close to you, always. Even when our eyes are clouded and we do not think clearly, keep us close in Your sight and protected by Your grace. O our dear Lord, we are bold to ask all these things, confident in Your love for us. Amen, Amen.

Glossary

.........❦.........

adhan—the words of the call to prayer

anza—spear-headed stick

'asr—the compulsory prayer in mid-afternoon

ayah—a verse of the Qur'an

Bait ul-Maqdis—the mosque at Jerusalem on the site of the Jewish
    temple

bid'a—an innovation

chador—a sheet used by women to cover themselves or pray in

darud—blessing on the Prophet Muhammad

du'a—personal supplication and prayer requests

du'al-istiftah—prayer before starting the *rak'ah*

Eid—the Muslim word for 'Feast'

Eid-ul-Adha—the Feast of sacrifice at the end of *Hajj*

Eid-ul-Fitr—the Feast to break the fast at the end of Ramadan

Fard—compulsory

ghayr muwakkada (or *ghayr rawatib*)—voluntary prayer not stressed by
    the Prophet

ghusl—a full bath

al-Fatihah—the first *surah* of the Qur'an

hafiz—someone who knows the entire Qur'an by heart

hajj—the pilgrimage to Makkah

halal—allowed

haqiqi—combining two prayers at the one time

haram—forbidden

haya—modesty, humility

hullah—a shroud made in one piece

ihsan—realisation (that God exists)

Imam—the one who leads the prayer

iman—faith

iqamah—the second call to prayer, when the Imam is ready in the mosque

isha'—the compulsory prayer during the hours of darkness

istanja—washing after toilet

i'tikaf—seclusion for prayer alone, usually during the last ten days of Ramadan, but it could be for any 24 hours

jalsa—the sitting position during and after prayer

jam'ah—congregation

jahri—the three prayers—evening, night and pre-dawn

jahiliyyah—the 'time of ignorance' before coming of Islam

jumah—Friday prayer

junub—the state of impurity after sexual intercourse, before taking a bath

Ka'bah—the holy shrine at Makkah

khalq—a scent made from saffron, disliked by the Prophet

khutbah—the sermon (usually given at Friday prayer)

lahd—qiblah-niche made in the side of a grave

Laylat ul-Qadr—the Night of Power, when Muhammad first received revelation—one of the last odd days in Ramadan

Madinah—the city to which the Prophet migrated

maghrib—the compulsory prayer just after sunset

Makkah—the Holy City, home of the Ka'bah shrine

masjid—a place of prayer, lit. place of prostration

mihrab—an alcove in the wall, showing the direction of Makkah

minbar—pulpit

mosque—communal meeting-place, place of prostration

mu'takif—a person in *i'tikaf*

mu'adhdhin—the person who calls to prayer

muawwidhaan—the last two *surahs* in the Qur'an—Nos. 103, 104

nafl—voluntary prayers

niyyah—intention

ﷺ—'peace be upon him'

qiblah—the direction of the Ka'bah

qiyam—standing upright half-way through the *rak'ah*

qiyam ul-Layl—voluntary night prayers

qunut—special supplications in prayer

Qur'an—the revelations given by Allah to the Blessed Prophet

rahila—fast camel

rak'ah—one complete unit of prayer-movements

Ramadan—the month of fasting

ratiba muwakkada—voluntary prayers stressed as important by the Blessed Prophet

rawdah—gathering to read Qur'an and mourn for dead person—often held the fortieth day after the death

ruku'—the bowing position during *salah*

ruqya—a charm

sabr—patience, acceptance

sajdah sahev—prayers to make up for something done incorrectly

salah—the compulsory prayers

salat-ul-Layl—voluntary night prayers

salat al-an-nabi—another name of *Darud*, blessing on the Prophet

sawm—fasting during the hours of daylight

shahadah—bearing witness that there is no God but Allah, and that Muhammad is the Prophet of Allah

shiqq—*qiblah* niche made in the centre of a grave

sirri—the 'daylight' prayers—noon and afternoon

subhah—thanksgiving, usually done with a bead necklace of 99 beads

suhur—light breakfast before dawn in Ramadan

sujud or *sajdah*—prostration in prayer with the forehead to earth

sumud—taking up position in straight rows for prayer

sunnah—the practice or example of the Blessed Prophet

sūrah—a chapter in the Qur'an

sutrah—a screen or barrier placed in front of a person at prayer

suwari—praying one prayer so late and the next one so early that they come together

taawwudh—seeking refuge in God from evil

tahajjud—voluntary night prayers

tahayyat al-masjid—two *rak'ahs* prayed on entering the mosque

tahmid—'To You, O Lord, be all thanks'

takbir tahrim—pronouncing 'Allah is the Most High'

tamin—the Amin said at the end of recitation of *sūrah al-Fatihah*

taqwa—being aware or conscious of God

tarawih—special night prayers during Ramadan

tarji—repeating the call to prayer oneself in a low voice

tasbih—thanksgiving, usually using a necklace of 99 beads

tashahhud—prayer for blessing on the Holy Prophet

taslim—the saying of 'Peace be with you' at the end of the prayer

tasmee—'Allah always hears those who praise Him'

tasmiyah—the Recommendation—'In the name of Allah, the Compassionate, the Merciful—Bismillah ar-Rahman ir-Rahim'

tawarruh—the sitting position for *tashahhud*, with the right foot upright with the toes on the grounding pointing to *qiblah*

tayammum—ritual 'washing' using sand, dust or earth when no water is available

ummah—the 'family' of Islam

wisal—continuous fasting without a daily 'break'

witr—a final single *rak'ah* to make prayers an odd number of *rak'ahs*

witr bil fasal—when the final witr *rak'ah* is said after the salutation

wudu'—ritual ablution before prayer

zakah—the religious tax, generally a fortieth of surplus income

zuhr—the compulsory prayer just after noon

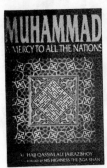

MUHAMMAD
MERCY TO ALL THE NATIONS

AL HAJJ QASSIM ALI JAIRAZIBHOY
FOREWORD BY HIS HIGHNESS THE AGA KHAN

Heart of the Koran

Lex Hixon

The Soul of the Qur'an

INSPIRING PRAYERS TO KINDLE HEART AND MIND

SANIYASNAIN KHAN

Steps to Leadership
from the Qur'an and Words of the Prophet Muhammad

compiled by Abdur Chan Hamid Baria

The Muslim Marriage Guide

Ruqaiyyah Waris Maqsood

Living Islam
TREADING THE PATH OF THE IDEAL

RUQAIYYAH WARIS MAQSOOD

BASIC DICTIONARY OF ISLAM

RUQAIYYAH WARIS MAQSOOD

THE MUSLIM PRAYER ENCYCLOPAEDIA
A COMPLETE GUIDE TO PRAYERS AS TAUGHT BY THE PROPHET MUHAMMAD

Ruqaiyyah Waris Maqsood

HISTORY of the Prophet MUHAMMAD

PHILIP K. HITTI

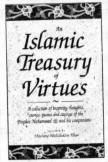

An Islamic Treasury of Virtues

A collection of inspiring thoughts, stories, quotes and sayings of the Prophet Muhammad and his companions

compiled by Maulana Wahiduddin Khan

Islam AND MODERN CHALLENGES

Maulana Wahiduddin Khan

ISLAM AND THE MODERN MAN

Maulana Wahiduddin Khan

The Essential Arabic
A Learner's Practical Guide
ما يلزم من العربية

Rafi'el-Imad Faynan

THE HOLY QUR'AN
TRANSLATION AND COMMENTARY BY ABDULLAH YUSUF ALI

The Qur'an
The Noble Reading

TRANSLATION AND COMMENTARY BY T.B. IRVING
(AL-HAJJ TA'LIM ALI)

The Qur'an
TRANSLATION
القرآن الحكيم

MUHAMMAD
A PROPHET FOR ALL HUMANITY

MAULANA WAHIDUDDIN KHAN

The Wonderful
Universe of
ALLAH
INSPIRING THOUGHTS FROM
THE QUR'AN ON NATURE

Compiled by SANIYASNAIN KHAN

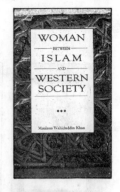

WOMAN
BETWEEN
ISLAM
AND
WESTERN
SOCIETY

• • •

Maulana Wahiduddin Khan

QUR'ANIC WISDOM FOR MODERN LIVING

PRESENTING
THE QUR'AN
A BRIEF INTRODUCTION TO ALL THE
114 CHAPTERS OF THE QUR'AN
SANIYASNAIN KHAN

RELIGION
and
SCIENCE

Maulana Wahiduddin Khan

The
Beautiful
Promises of
Allah

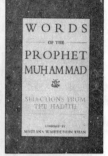

WORDS
OF THE
PROPHET
MUHAMMAD

SELECTIONS FROM
THE HADITH

COMPILED BY
MAULANA WAHIDUDDIN KHAN

THE LIFE OF THE PROPHET
MUHAMMAD

MUHAMMAD MARMADUKE PICKTHALL

HIJAB
IN ISLAM

Maulana Wahiduddin Khan

The Beautiful
Commands of
ALLAH

Compiled by Rashteeda Wazir Maqsood

WOMAN
IN ISLAMIC SHARI'AH

Maulana Wahiduddin Khan

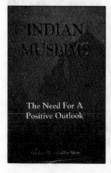

INDIAN
MUSLIMS

The Need For A
Positive Outlook

Maulana Wahiduddin Khan

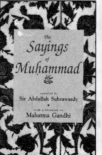

The
Sayings
of
Muhammad

compiled by
Sir Abdullah Suhrawardy

with a foreword by
Mahatma Gandhi

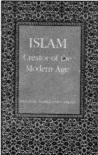

ISLAM
Creator of the
Modern Age

MAULANA WAHIDUDDIN KHAN

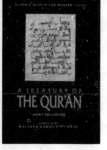

QUR'ANIC WISDOM FOR MODERN LIVING

A TREASURY OF
THE QUR'AN

ISBN 1-781-0-000-151

COMPILED BY
MAULANA WAHIDUDDIN KHAN